THE ECONOMY OF
BRITISH CENTRAL AFRICA

A CASE STUDY
OF ECONOMIC DEVELOPMENT
IN A DUALISTIC SOCIETY

WILLIAM J. BARBER

STANFORD UNIVERSITY PRESS
STANFORD, CALIFORNIA

Stanford University Press
Stanford, California

Printed in Great Britain

THE ECONOMY OF
BRITISH CENTRAL AFRICA

CONTENTS

PREFACE

THIS study deals with the dualism of the British Central African economic system and its implications for economic development. If it can contribute to the present dialogue about the theoretical tools appropriate for studying the economics of developing areas and if it identifies problems which urgently require further research, it will have served its major purpose. I hope also that this study may be useful in providing a background to the economic issues at stake in the determination of the political future of Rhodesia and Nyasaland. The latest economic materials available at the time this book goes to press seldom referred to events beyond the late 1950s. No one can write about problems of contemporary Africa at this moment in its history without being acutely aware that some of his words will be outdated before the ink is dry. Nevertheless, the analysis of the factors which have shaped Central African economic history may still yield insights into matters of current concern.

My debts for assistance in the preparation of this study are many. I wish to mention particularly Professor S. H. Frankel, who supervised an earlier version of the manuscript which was written as a D.Phil. thesis at the University of Oxford; and Colin Leys, Professor Kenneth Kirkwood, and Dr. Bruce M. Johnston, each of whom gave generously of his time in criticizing various drafts. I am also indebted to the Ford Foundation for a grant which made my studies in Central Africa possible; to the Warden and Fellows of Nuffield College, Oxford, for providing a stimulating environment in which to draft the manuscript; and to the Trustees of Wesleyan University for a faculty research grant which enabled me to use the excellent secretarial skills of Mrs. Marian Haagen and Miss Catherine E. Cooney. I should emphasize that the persons and institutions mentioned above are in no way responsible for the views expressed in this work or for errors which may remain in it.

One of my deepest debts is to the people of Rhodesia and Nyasaland for the kindness they have extended to my wife and to myself. In particular, I wish to acknowledge the helpfulness of the staff of the Central African Statistical Office and the Central African Archives.

I am grateful to the editors of *Economic Development and Cultural Change* and *Oxford Economic Papers* for their permission to use portions of materials published in those journals. Part of the discussion in chapter IV appeared in *Economic Development and Cultural Change*, April 1960, and, in modified form, portions of the argument in chapter VIII appeared in *Oxford Economic Papers*, February 1961.

Throughout the preparation of this study my labours have been eased immeasurably by the encouragement and patience of my wife. Her support has been invaluable.

March 1961   W. J. B.

INTRODUCTION

By global standards, the territories now linked into the Federation of Rhodesia and Nyasaland are small. Their total population is less than 8,500,000 people and the land mass of roughly 488,000 square miles which they inhabit is only a small fraction of the world's total.

But British Central Africa now has a significance which far transcends its size. Since 1953 when the Federal Government was established, these territories have been embarked on a challenging experiment in social relations. The preamble to the constitution which brought federation into being commits its government to pursue policies which will 'foster inter-racial partnership' among the area's 308,000 Europeans, 7,980,000 Africans, and 39,000 persons of Asian or mixed race. This approach to the vexed questions of race relations was heralded as a new departure in the multi-racial communities of Africa and its success or failure may have a profound influence on the future course of events throughout the continent. Officially, the Federal Government has yet to spell out an unambiguous definition of partnership or to state specifically the steps to be followed in reaching the goal. One point, however, was clear to the British Government which authorized the Federal undertaking. The social structure originally envisaged under inter-racial partnership was to be sharply differentiated from the white-controlled *apartheid* practised in the Union of South Africa and from the black nationalism of the new West African states. Instead, a middle ground between these extremes was to be sought — a ground on which members of all races could stand and live in harmony.

For students of economic analysis, the interest which this portion of the African interior holds is initially quite different. By the conventional measures of economic growth, the Rhodesias can rightly claim one of the highest rates of economic expansion among those territories now classified as 'underdeveloped'. This phenomenon, in itself, deserves close inspection. It is true that the Rhodesias have possessed an attractive endowment of physical resources — an advantage which many underdeveloped territories can not claim. Southern Rhodesia's geological structure contains valuable deposits of gold, chrome, manganese, coal, and a host of lesser minerals. But these are far surpassed by the wealth of Northern Rhodesia's Copperbelt which contains one of the free world's most important copper ore reserves.

The generosity of nature has clearly permitted economic expansion at a pace which otherwise would have been impossible. But the task of harnessing this potential and transforming it to economic advantage has confronted formidable obstacles. The Rhodesian part of the African interior has been aptly described as a 'landlocked island'. The areas richest in natural wealth are situated at least four hundred miles, and often more, from the sea. But distance is only part of the difficulty. Nature, in its provision of terrain, has been less than kind. The relief of the area as a whole has been likened to an 'inverted saucer'. Plateau land begins not far from the coasts, thus ruling out long-distance river transport to the sea. Moreover, the interior is broken by rugged escarpments which obstruct surface transportation. These barriers, which for so long preserved the isolation of Central Africa, stood equally as obstacles to the expansion of the money economy. That the rudiments of a transport link with the outside world were, in fact, provided from an early date is a tribute to the engineering and administrative skills which European settlement supplied. But the cost was heavy — and has continued to be. Even so, Central Africa is still far from being served with a transport system adequate to meet the demands of an expanding money economy.

The impressive record of economic expansion which the Rhodesias have compiled has been accomplished in face of other handicaps as well. As is the case in much of the underdeveloped world, most of the prerequisite facilities for highly organized production and exchange were lacking. The African interior which European settlers found in the 1890s was raw and remote. The land and its peoples had scarcely been touched by the dynamic changes in which Western Europe and North America had been swept up. No dramatic technological advance had occurred there and its peoples had not developed the skills which could readily fit them into Westernized modes of economic organization. In all forms — technical, managerial, and entrepreneurial — the skills prerequisite for rapid economic advance have always been in short supply in Central Africa. The Rhodesian system has overcome this deficiency by importing trained manpower from abroad. This solution to the problem has undoubtedly accelerated the rate of economic expansion. One of the costs of the gain achieved in this fashion, however, is a set of delicate and complex social problems.

The success of the Central African economic system in overcoming serious handicaps to achieve a remarkable economic advance provides only a small part of its interest as a subject for a case study. Another facet of its experience deserves even more careful attention. The central fact about the economic system is the co-existence of two distinct forms of economic and social organization within the same geographical area. The performance which strikes the eye of outside observers in such measurements as national income aggregates refers to only one component of the system — the money economy. Much of the economic life of Central Africa's population cannot be subjected to the measuring rod of money and is not, therefore, taken into account in such statistical compilations. To the African peoples, non-marketed agricultural production is still an important source of real income. The conventional measures, in other words, fail to embrace the economic system as a whole, but describe only one part of it.

The dualistic economic system of Central Africa is, in fact, composed of two distinct economies. Of the two forms of economic organization, the money economy is the more readily observable and, to those familiar with Western economic life, the simpler to comprehend. The traditional economy of the indigenous peoples — although less amenable to analysis in the familiar categories of economic theory — still is an important component of the total economic structure. The overall functioning of the economic system cannot be understood in isolation from it. The interaction between these two economies and its implications for the process of economic development presents the central problem to be investigated in this study.

This task demands departures from the analytical procedures conventionally employed in advanced and Westernized economic systems. Many of the analytical tools which are useful for understanding the processes of industrialized economies have little relevance to a dualistic underdeveloped economy. A. C. Pigou once described the economist's job as one of 'looking beyond the veil of money'. In the analysis of underdeveloped economies, this directive might well be rephrased to enjoin economists to look beyond the veil of the money economy.

In some form, a dualistic economic structure is not uncommon throughout the poor countries of the world. Central Africa, however, has a special recommendation as a laboratory specimen for the study of the economic consequences of dualism. The contrasts there stand out in bold relief. The accidents of geology have brought to this area an advanced type of money economy. And the accidents of geography, which for so long isolated this part of Africa from the influences of the wider world, have preserved the identity of its indigenous economies to a degree remarkable in the twentieth century. Many aspects of the form of dualism which has evolved in British Central Africa are, of course, unique to that area. But an examination of the process of interaction between the two economies within its dualistic structure may illuminate general problems which might usefully be investigated in detail in other parts of the underdeveloped world.

Within the context of Rhodesia and Nyasaland, analysis of the interaction between the economic components of the dualistic system has yet another justification. As has been noted, no precise formulation of 'partnership' has yet been made by the Federal Government. The interpretation most widely accepted by the European population of the Rhodesias is that the economic and social advancement of the indigenous peoples should precede their political advancement. Improvement in the standard of living for Africans thus has political as well as economic implications. By clarifying the conditions under which economic change can bring higher real incomes to the indigenous peoples, economic studies may thus provide an insight into the issues at stake in this novel social experiment. This is not to suggest that economic factors are the sole, or even the most important, determinants of social and political change. A complexity of factors — many of which lie beyond the bounds of economic analysis — will ultimately determine whether or not 'partnership' can be translated into a practicable formula of government.

CHAPTER I

DUALISM AND ECONOMIC DEVELOPMENT: A PROBLEM IN DEFINITION

ECONOMICS is not an exact science. Indeed it may be illusory to entertain the expectation that it can ever become one. As long as human beings retain an attractive element of unpredictability in their behaviour, economic studies can never match the degree of precision achieved by the natural sciences. While it may never be that the tools of economic analysis can be used to make infallible forecasts, they still have a valuable and important function to perform. With their aid, our understanding of social change can be sharpened and refined. But this task, in turn, requires systematic and precise formulation and use of intellectual categories. Only in such fashion can economists attempt to penetrate into the interconnexions between the parts of a complex system.

In setting out his basic concepts with technical precision, the economist labours under a serious handicap. Many of the terms he employs are not the exclusive property of economic analysis. Often they are also a part of everyday speech. But the economist's and the layman's understandings of the same vocabulary are usually quite different. Confusions stem from this fact in all branches of economic study. They are forcefully apparent in the 'economics of underdeveloped areas'.

A moment's reflection on the notion of 'underdeveloped areas' will illustrate the point. Economics has assimilated this term from popular usage. But can it be given precise technical meaning? On first inspection, one might expect that it would be applied only to countries possessing resources which, as yet, had not been fully developed. In practice, however, this is not the case. Those countries now categorized as 'underdeveloped' usually have only one characteristic in common: they are poor. And, in many cases, their poverty is not accompanied by any known store of untapped resources. Strictly speaking, the economist would be on surer ground if he were to drop the term 'underdeveloped' and to use 'low income' countries as a substitute. This amendment would eliminate much ambiguity. But the notion of 'underdeveloped economies' has now acquired such popularity that it probably has sufficient survival power to transcend its lack of technical precision. If the term can not be eliminated, caution in its use can still be recommended. At least it should be recognized that the application of the simple label 'underdeveloped' to much of the world obscures the heterogeneity of countries whose economic problems and circumstances are vastly different.

Of greater importance is the lack of precision which pervades the term 'economic development'. In a general sense, everyone has some understanding of what the expression means. But when specific criteria of development are under discussion, a variety of divergent views spring forth. Many different approaches have emerged in the recent efforts of economists to define the development process. One group, for example, focuses primarily on quantitative indicators of development. Thus, development is defined by some writers as a growth in aggregate output. Others concentrate on improvement in real income *per capita*. Still others associate development with increased rates of capital formation. In another view, development is identified with expansion in the scope of monetary exchange transactions. All of these criteria are related and each is relevant. But they are not identical, despite their similarity. Policies designed to satisfy any one of these criteria would not always be consistent with those framed to maximize other quantitative criteria offered for development.

Another strand of interpretation views development more in qualitative than in quantitative terms. Hirschman, for example, defines development as a process of cumulative disequilibrium which impels and sustains change within the economic system.[1] By the same token, Bauer and Yamey regard the essential property of economic development as the creation and expansion of alternatives.[2] These interpretations, of course, are not completely at odds with the quantitative definitions of

[1] See A. O. Hirschman, *The Strategy of Economic Development* (Yale University Press, New Haven, 1958), esp. pp. 65–70.
[2] P. T. Bauer and B. S. Yamey, *The Economics of Under-developed Countries* (London: James Nisbet, and Cambridge: Cambridge University Press, 1957).

development. But the qualitative approach is distinguished by the emphasis it places on intangibles in the economic climate as opposed to magnitudes which are readily measurable.

A similar lack of unanimity can be observed in the notions of 'dualism' which economists have employed in the literature on low income countries. That significant cleavages in the economic structure form one of the dominant characteristics of most of these territories is apparent even to casual observers. The contrasts are reflected in extremes in income distribution, in productivity, in standards of technology, in education and cultural attainment, and often in conditions of health and sanitation. Some commentators on this familiar pattern have treated dualism by drawing lines of demarcation according to race. For others, the distinguishing feature has been political; i.e. whether the persons in question are members of the governed or the governing group. Others have defined dualism geographically, viewing it as arising from regional divisions within a country. Nor do the concepts of dualism end there. Another school concentrates on the dualism which distinguishes the foreign trade sector of the economy from a sector which produces for domestic consumption. A variation on the same theme is the literature which divides the economy into 'capitalist' and 'subsistence' sectors.[1]

As with the various interpretations of 'development', the differing concepts of 'dualism' tend to overlap. Each points to relevant aspects of the problem. But the emphasis, in each case, is different. For the purpose of formulating definitions of these concepts which are workable in a specific economy, two considerations are important. First, the definitions chosen must come to grips with realities of the economic system in question.

[1] J. H. Boeke's work gives major emphasis to cultural contrasts in defining dualism; see, for example, his *Economics and Economic Policy of Dual Societies as Exemplified by Indonesia* (Institute of Pacific Relations, New York, 1953). For an illustration of dualism viewed largely in regional terms, see A. O. Hirschman 'Investment Policies and Dualism in Under-developed Countries', *American Economic Review*, September 1957, pp. 550–70. H. W. Singer has given major attention to the distinction between the domestic and foreign trade sectors in underdeveloped countries; e.g. 'The Distribution of Gains between Investing and Borrowing Countries', *American Economic Association Papers and Proceedings*, May 1950, pp. 473–85. Much of W. A. Lewis's analysis rests on the distinction between 'subsistence' and 'capitalist' sectors; see, for example, 'Economic Development with Unlimited Supplies of Labour', *The Manchester School of Economic and Social Studies*, May 1954, pp. 139–91.

But it is equally important that they meet a second and more exacting standard — analytical usefulness in illuminating the significant interrelationships within the economic structure. Attention must now be turned to the definitions of 'dualism' and of 'economic development' which will meet these tests in the study of Rhodesia and Nyasaland.

The Concept of Dualism Appropriate to the Economy of Central Africa

The dualism of society in Rhodesia and Nyasaland is an all-pervasive phenomenon. It is expressed in all facets of social, political, and economic life. But its economic aspects can best be viewed through the contrasting forms of economic organization which coexist there. At one pole is the money economy organized, financed, and administered largely by Europeans, and heavily dependent on external trade and investment. It functions with money as a medium of exchange and its superficial properties resemble those of more advanced economies. At the opposite end of the spectrum is the traditional economy of the indigenous peoples. Within it, techniques of production are still primitive, productivity is low, and standards of real income often fail to rise much above the minimum required for subsistence.

It would be tempting to use familiar categories and classify these components of the dualistic economic structure as a 'money' (or 'capitalist') sector and a 'subsistence' sector. But these categories are not completely adequate. The usage of 'sectors' implies that the components of the economic system are interdependent and vital to one another. In Central Africa, this is not entirely the case. The traditional agricultural economy has an independent and autonomous status which such terminology obscures. Traditional agriculture is an economy in its own right, not just a segment of a larger whole. It functions according to its own peculiar sets of rules — rules which differentiate its economic processes from the remainder of the economic system. Moreover, the unique properties of the traditional economic organization are likely to have a crucial influence on the course of economic change. As a reminder of this point, it will be convenient to regard this component of the economic system, not as a sector, but as an economy with its own integrity.

Consideration of a term to identify the traditional economy creates further perplexities. A respectable tradition supports 'subsistence' as a descriptive label. But, for present purposes, this usage is not completely satisfactory. One deficiency lies in an ambiguity over the level of subsistence. The term can be interpreted in at least two senses — the physiological (or Malthusian) and the psychological — and failure to distinguish them can lead to misunderstanding. Nor does it follow that the traditional economy need always remain at the subsistence level (in either sense of the term). Under certain conditions, it may be possible for this economy to produce marketable surpluses while retaining its integrity as an autonomous economic unit. The appropriateness of 'subsistence' as a term to describe it would thus be called into question. To avoid some of these ambiguities, it is proposed to refer to the traditional economies of the Central African territories as simply 'the indigenous economies'.

It is now possible to set down the manner in which dualism within the Central African economic structure may be more profitably treated. The economic system has two distinct components: the indigenous economy (as defined above) and the money economy. In the latter, production and exchange are well organized and economic activity has been initiated with an orientation towards export markets. Within this dualistic structure, members of the indigenous population may, of course, derive part of their livelihood from both economies simultaneously or they may move between them at different times. Participation in the money economy, however, need not require them to sever their ties with the indigenous economy altogether.

Definitions of Economic Development Appropriate in the Analysis of Central Africa

The formulation of satisfactory criteria of economic development raises intriguing and complex problems. In large measure, these stem from the fact that the study of development calls upon economists to execute a methodological manœuvre which they have generally been reluctant to perform.

According to its conventional canons, economic analysis attempts to be scientific, positive, and value neutral. It divorces itself from the consideration of the goals of economic activity

B

and maintains instead that its function is merely the examination of the means for achieving them. The legitimacy of these claims may be challenged. It has been argued that theoretical economic analysis, even in most positive form, cannot escape a value element completely.[1] The presuppositions hidden in the economist's vocabulary may reflect a value bias — for example, the institution of private property or the 'principle' of consumer sovereignty in Western economic thought. To expect economic analysis to operate under totally *wertfrei* conditions may thus be unrealistic. While recognizing the inevitability of a value element in the selection of analytical categories, the strict code of professional behaviour calls for the economist to maintain neutrality in his use of value premises. He can accept the premises of the society under examination as a datum and proceed with his task on this basis. Alternatively, he may argue from value premises of his own; in this event, it is incumbent upon him to state them explicitly. In a professional capacity, he can claim no competence to judge what is good or desirable, or to determine what ought to be done. Of necessity, those operations involve value judgments which the economist has no special qualification to form.

In the discussion of development, detachment from value premises is impossible. It would be extreme to suggest, paraphrasing Sir Keith Hancock's verdict on 'imperialism', that 'development' is 'no word for scholars'.[2] But in using it, value overtones are inescapable. The term itself implies dissatisfaction with the *status quo* and that something 'ought' to be done. Consideration of alternative policy objectives and social goals and of the differing value premises supporting them lie at the core of the development problem. By the same token, differences in value emphases account, in large measure, for the failure of professional economists to reach agreement on a single definition of development. Each contributor, whether explicitly or implicitly, assigns his own scale of values to magnitudes which should be maximized or to 'ideal' conditions which should be created.

[1] For an admirable discussion of these points, see Gunnar Myrdal, *The Political Element in the Development of Economic Theory*, translated from the German by Paul Streeten (Routledge & Kegan Paul, London, 1953).

[2] W. K. Hancock, 'Agenda for the Study of British Imperial Economy, 1850–1950', *Journal of Economic History*, vol. xiii (1953), p. 257.

Professional economists concerned with the theory and policy of economic growth in the industrialized countries confront similar difficulties in separating the descriptive 'is' from the prescriptive 'ought'. But the problem there is much less acute than in the poor societies. By and large, the goals of economic activity are widely shared and often explicitly set out within the advanced economies. The analyst of economic growth in the United States, for example, can safely assume full employment with stable prices as among the goals desired by the bulk of American society. This simplifies his task enormously. With these value premises implicit in his argument, he can construct analytical models which indicate the conditions of growth which are compatible with these objectives.

The economist concerned with economic expansion in the low income countries, however, is in a less comfortable position. The objectives sought by the development process are central to his problem. But he can not expect to find widespread agreement on specific goals among his professional colleagues or, in most cases, among the populations of the countries under investigation.

It is now possible to proceed to the concepts of economic development which can be applied in a dualistic environment such as that of Central Africa. In this connexion, the value element implicit in 'development' must be recalled. Consideration of one type of quantitative criterion of development will illustrate its pertinence. It is often held, for example, that economic development has been accomplished when real income *per capita* has improved. This procedure, which requires the averaging of aggregate real income over the total population, neglects the question 'development for whom'? In many societies, particularly those with a multi-racial composition, this distinction is more than an academic quibble. With the above definition, it might be quite sufficient for development if real incomes expanded only in the money economy. Real income growth, however, could conceivably be accomplished either through the influx of immigrants or through favourable changes in terms of trade. Even with aggregate real income expanding steadily, the impact on the indigenous population might still be negligible. Should the results of this situation be regarded as economic development? Clearly, under the strict terms of the definition, the economy is developing. But this conclusion might not be shared by a sizeable segment of the population or, for that matter, by external observers holding a different value concept of development. With an important corollary (which will be examined in Chapter II), the governing group in Central Africa subscribes to this concept of development — i.e. that its conditions are satisfied when the money economy expands in real terms.

A more comprehensive concept of economic development should include the indigenous economy within its terms of reference. As an alternative formulation for the Central African case, it is proposed to treat the development condition as satisfied when two conditions have been met: (1) the money economy expands in real terms; (2) the *per capita* real income of the indigenous population also improves through time. This definition is also a value judgement and it is deliberately made explicit as such. Several comments on the second of these conditions are necessary. In the first place, it obviously requires that the aggregate real income available to the indigenous population must grow at a faster pace than its numbers increase. To this, a further consideration must be added: namely, that the indigenous population in this context will be defined as Africans permanently resident in the territory in which the money economy expands. The full significance of this definition will be more apparent at a later stage. But an example may be offered at this point to illustrate its force. This condition holds that if the money economy of Southern Rhodesia expands, for example, it is the impact upon the real income of the indigenous population in Southern Rhodesia which is relevant to an assessment of whether or not the second criterion of economic development has been fulfilled.

As the money economy expands, improvement in the real income of the indigenous population may be accomplished in either, or both, of two ways. Agricultural productivity of the indigenous economy may increase or members of the indigenous economy may obtain higher real incomes through the sale of their services. Formally, the latter may assume two forms. Labour may be employed for wages in the money economy and, conceivably, Africans may acquire a cash income as *entrepreneurs*. In practice, only the former has been quantitatively significant in the Central African territories; the empirical analysis will therefore concentrate attention on wage employment. Empirical measurement of productivity improvement in indigenous agriculture is much more difficult. Only scanty information on the volume of output is available. A rough approximation of productivity improvement may be gleaned from sales of indigenous agricultural output to the money economy. This treatment is not flawless, for it implicitly assumes that cash sales represent surpluses above the consumption requirements or the population. But, in the state of the indigenous economies of Central Africa, this assumption is reasonably realistic. Served with inadequate and unreliable communications, the indigenous economy, for strategic reasons, is well-advised to assign first priority to the maintenance of self-sufficiency and to offer only surpluses in exchange.

The second condition of development may now be restated in slightly modified form. The basic requirement is that the *per capita* real income of the indigenous population should improve. In view of the forms in which this improvement may be accomplished, it would appear that fulfilment of this condition turns on the degree to which the indigenous population acquires money income as the money economy expands. In other words, the second development condition may be reformulated to state that the entry of the indigenous population into the money economy should proceed progressively through time. This is not to suggest that use of money is desirable *per se*, but only that entry into the money economy provides a rough index of growth in real income for the indigenous population. But there is a qualification to this observation and an important one. The use of these measures is legitimate only when the relationship between population and the land resources of the indigenous economy is such that the *per capita* real income from agricultural production can rise or at least be maintained. Should population pressures reach the point that *per capita* output diminished, this index of development would no longer be applicable.

As reformulated, the second definition of development has the recommendation of bringing to the foreground the process of interaction between the money and the indigenous economies in the development process. This is the central issue for the understanding of the internal functioning of the system as a whole. External forces — changes in the terms of trade or in the rate of inflow of external capital, for example — have an obvious and influential bearing on the fortunes of the system. But the interaction between the components of the under-developed economic system may have an equally important, although less obvious, impact on its destiny. This aspect of the development process demands deeper probing and it requires experimentation with a method of analysis synthesizing the two divergent economies within the underdeveloped economy into a systematic pattern. In some form, similar problems of interaction between the money and indigenous economies arise in other underdeveloped areas. Through a case study in this form, a more thorough comprehension of the general issues may be gained. But no claim to universality is advanced for the results. For an analysis based on the economic properties of the indigenous economies must work within a specific setting. The characteristics of the indigenous economies differ widely in various parts of the underdeveloped world.

CHAPTER II

DUALISM IN CENTRAL AFRICA: ITS POLITICAL AND SOCIAL EXPRESSIONS

THE economic life of any society is fundamentally conditioned by the non-economic climate in which it is set. In underdeveloped economies, the influence of these factors on economic activity is often weightier than in more advanced communities. This is emphatically the case in Central Africa. The dualism which pervades the economic system is paralleled by a dualistic political and social structure. Indeed, these various expressions of dualism are not independent of one another. Throughout most of Rhodesia's modern economic history, the unique characteristics of the economic structure have been compatible with the established social and political framework. At the same time, Rhodesian political and social institutions have often bolstered the dualism in economic life.

The functioning of the Central African economic system cannot be fully understood apart from its non-economic context. The political and social framework has had a forceful impact on the allocation of economic energies and on the objectives set for economic policy. It is in this connexion that non-economic aspects of the Central African system deserve careful inspection in an economic study. The matter at issue is the extent to which the value premises reflected in the social organization which has emerged in Central Africa regulate artificially the contact between the money and the indigenous economies.

The discussion in this chapter will concentrate on the economic effects of policies pursued by the governing group. In all three territories, decisive political power has been held by Europeans. But distinctions must be drawn between the territories concerning the character of European rule. In the Rhodesias, European settlers have held effective control over policy. The dominant European voices in Nyasaland, on the other hand, have not been those of permanent residents but of colonial civil servants. Divergences between the patterns of policy pursued in Nyasaland and in the Rhodesias have been persistent throughout the history of British Central Africa. Important differences of view have also occurred within the settler community of the Rhodesias. But a broad area of agreement on the premises of social and political organization has traditionally characterized Rhodesia's European population. This set of shared assumptions has overshadowed in importance the differing views which have been expressed on specific issues. Consideration of the economic significance of these premises and of the policies based upon them can best proceed in two stages. First, the traditional approach will be surveyed. Subsequently, recent modifications in policy will be examined.

The Historical Roots of Central African Institutions and Policy

The unique coloration of the social system of Central Africa owes much to its historical origins. Initially, the prospect of economic advantage was but one of several factors in the extension of European authority to this part of the African interior. Reports of mineral wealth — some magnified in the re-telling — in the present Rhodesian territories offered an economic incentive for settlement. But one of the more influential factors leading up to the penetration of Central Africa was non-economic. The extension of the imperial dream and the competition between the rival metropolitan powers for territorial acquisitions in the late nineteenth century provided a compelling motivation. Rhodes, with his ambitions to 'paint the map red' and to annex 'my north', took the initiative. An imperial government, hesitant to assume more direct commitments itself but sympathetic with the objectives, authorized him to proceed. The instrument of the Chartered Company satisfied the aims of both parties. In 1889, a Royal Charter was granted to the British South Africa Company which authorized it to acquire powers of government over the territories lying immediately north of British Bechuanaland. The occupation of Southern Rhodesia was begun in the following year. But effective control was not complete until 1896 when the native population had been subdued by force of arms. Negotiations completed in 1894 gave the company powers of administration over the present area of Northern Rhodesia. Nyasaland, which had been proclaimed a British Protectorate in 1891, was excepted from company administration and was governed instead by imperial authorities. For some years, however, the British South Africa Company and the Consul General of Nyasaland exercised a condominium over a combined area in Nyasaland and North-Eastern Rhodesia until territorial demarcations along the present lines were negotiated in 1911. Thus was British control established over the territories of the present Central African Federation.

From the beginning, some divergence in the approach of government in the Rhodesian territories and in Nyasaland followed naturally from the differing character of their governmental authorities. Nyasaland had been brought into the imperial orbit on a wave of humanitarian sentiment. The imperial authorities saw their primary mission there as the abolition of the slave trade. But company government in the Rhodesias had other objectives. The term 'company government' itself implies a mixture of economics and politics. In practice, this was readily apparent.

In its governing role, the British South Africa Company was concerned with creating the facilities required for sound administration and with providing the minimum communications consistent with the exercise of its authority. As a joint-stock company, it was equally concerned with earning profits. Some of its governing powers could serve this purpose. It had the right to sell and dispose of land and held royalties to the mineral wealth of the area. In addition, it had the power to tax. But revenues from these sources depended upon the introduction of the money economy. To this end, the company extended its energies to the full by encouraging Europeans to settle in the territories under its jurisdiction.[1] Even so, the Chartered Company throughout its tenure of administration was never able

---

[1] The enthusiasm of the B.S.A. Company for the recruitment of permanent settlers waned, however, in the final phases of its rule in Northern Rhodesia. While settlers stimulated the money income stream and provided a tax base, they also demanded expensive public services. Such demands became increasingly insistent after the First World War. For its part, the company was relieved to pass on this administrative headache to the Colonial Office. The settler community in Northern Rhodesia also preferred Colonial to continued company rule. The Imperial Government, from their observation of its administration in Nyasaland, 'seemed to be favourably disposed towards European colonists'. See L. H. Gann, *The Birth of a Plural Society: the Development of Northern Rhodesia under the British South Africa Company, 1894–1914* (Manchester University Press for the Rhodes-Livingstone Institute, 1958), p. 173.

to pay a dividend.[1] In 1923 the company went out of business as a governing authority when its administrative responsibilities were transferred to the self-governing colony of Southern Rhodesia and, in the case of Northern Rhodesia, to the United Kingdom Government. Shortly after this transition, a director of the British South Africa Company summed up the financial record of its rule as follows:

The administrative work of the British South Africa Company has cost it dearly. Apart from the expenditure of the railway companies which it controls, and from the liabilities which it has assumed towards the debenture and note holders of those companies, the British South Africa Company itself has raised from the investing public for the creation, defence and development of Rhodesia no less than £13,000,000 and has borrowed £1,250,000 in debentures. As against these sums, the purely commercial assets of the company shown in its latest published balance sheet (31 March 1922) stood at under £8,000,000; and though the company has derived large revenues from its mineral rights and from other sources, the discharge of its public duties has called for them all, and it has never yet been able to distribute a dividend to shareholders.[2]

In compensation for its administrative work, the Chartered Company was awarded a sum of £3,750,000 by the Crown when it relinquished its control.

Measured solely in terms of profitability, the Chartered Company régime was unsuccessful as an economic enterprise. But as a political phenomenon, it had nevertheless achieved its major objectives. The heart of Central Africa had been opened to European settlement and stamped as a part of the larger network of empire. Moreover, the essential communications required both for administration and for modern economic activity had been provided, at least in a rudimentary form. But the lasting legacy of company government was more than that. The broad outlines of its policy towards the Rhodesias remained. Its character as a company had dictated the encouragement of an expanding money economy based on a community of per-

[1] Nevertheless, as L. H. Gann has noted, directors and senior officials of the company 'may have been able to profit from their inside knowledge of administrative and economic developments in the country' as shareholders and directors of other Rhodesian companies; Gann, op. cit., pp. 48–49.

[2] D. O. Malcolm, 'The British South Africa Company', *Quarterly Review*, January 1924, pp. 85–86.

manent European settlers. Although the forms of government changed, these major premises of policy were perpetuated.

These views were pressed most vigorously in Southern Rhodesia with the advent of self-government. The terms of the transfer of power in 1923 placed the government of the territory, including its 800,000 indigenous inhabitants, in the hands of roughly 34,000 Europeans. The governing minority was self-confident in its claims to a monopoly of political power. In the eyes of the settler community, its right to govern exclusively was supported by its higher degree of civilization. Moreover, it claimed supremacy by right of conquest, following the suppression of the African risings in the 1890s. The political status of the indigenous peoples could, therefore, be interpreted as that of inhabitants of an occupied country. Concerning its ability to enforce its rule with the weight of numbers heavily against it, however, the European community was less confident. Thus an expansion of the money economy based on permanent European settlement had more than economic betterment to recommend it. It was regarded as desirable, indeed urgent, in the interests of the security and political viability of the settler outposts.

With the transition to Colonial Office rule, the doctrine of settler supremacy underwent, in principle, some modifications in Northern Rhodesia. The United Kingdom Government there took on responsibility for protecting the interests of the indigenous peoples. But this had little effect on the thought or practice of the European community on the spot. Their numbers were small — only 3,634 Europeans were recorded in the 1921 census and the white population was still under 14,000 at the time of the 1931 census. Despite the trappings of Colonial Office authority, effective political power has been largely held by this local minority. It was not until 1938 that elected members achieved parity in the Legislative Council with colonial officials appointed by the governor, and the former did not acquire a majority of the Council until 1945.[1] But government policy was generally synchronized with the views of the settlers before these procedural changes were made. For a brief period — when Lord Passfield (Sidney Webb) was Colonial Secretary — official

---

[1] For an excellent discussion of constitutional evolution, see J. W. Davidson, *The Northern Rhodesian Legislative Council* (Faber & Faber, London, 1947).

Colonial Office policy challenged the settler view.[1] The publication in 1930 of a memorandum on native policy in East Africa, stating that the 'interests of the African natives must be paramount',[2] provoked an immediate protest from the elected members. As they put their position:

> To British settlers, the paramountcy of the Native appears to be incompatible with justice. To subordinate the interests of civilized Britons to the development of alien races, whose capability of substantial further advancement has not been demonstrated, appears to be contrary to natural law.[3]

Subsequently, the Colonial Government of Northern Rhodesia has generally avoided actions to which settler opinion was fundamentally opposed. The African had little direct voice in public affairs, although the nominated officials of the Colonial service were inclined to view his problems more sympathetically than did the settler community. The doors remained equally open to European immigration and the encouragement of permanent white settlement remained a high policy priority.

In Nyasaland, the aims of policy departed from those pursued in the Rhodesias. It had escaped a tradition of company rule with its inducements to European settlement. More significant was the fact that the physical resources of the Protectorate were less attractive to European immigration than in the other two territories. Plantation agriculture, the only form of economic activity into which European settlers were attracted, could not compete with the richer returns afforded by the mineral wealth of the Rhodesias. The forecast of Sir Charles Bowring in 1924 that the territory was not suited for a large-scale European colonization has largely been borne out.[4] Nevertheless the cleavage between the rights of the European and the African in the political arena was almost as marked in Nyasaland as in Northern Rhodesia.

These features of early European contact with the Central African territories have left their imprint on later events. They

[1] Lord Passfield (Sidney Webb) served as Colonial Secretary from 1929–31.
[2] *Memorandum on Native Policy in East Africa*, Cmd. 3573, 1930.
[3] *Correspondence with regard to Native Policy in Northern Rhodesia*, Cmd. 3731, 1930.
[4] Cited in Hailey, *Native Administration in the British African Territories* (H.M.S.O., 1950), Part II, p. 18.

have endowed Nyasaland and the Rhodesias with distinctly separate traditions and have contributed to the tensions which have emerged since the Federal form of government has linked these territories. The dominant preconceptions of the European minority in the Rhodesias have their roots in this early experience. 'Settler supremacy' has lately taken on unfavourable connotation.[1] But it should not be forgotten that it stands for a view of social organization which came naturally to the first generation of settlers. They confronted a mass of people whose way of life was completely alien to their own. Africans were different in complexion and in tongue. But this accounts for only part of the gulf which separated them from white men. The African's views on law, on property, on religion were far removed from those in the European tradition. Africans made little material provision for the future and appeared lacking in inventive energies. Moreover, before the coming of Europeans, they had neither developed a literature nor recorded their history. It is small wonder that men of the Edwardian age were bewildered by these people and looked on them as barbaric and inferior. Nor is it difficult to comprehend why they should have felt it prudent to erect defences around their own tradition and to insist that effective political power should be kept in European hands.[2] If this were to be accomplished, it was equally prudent to expand the European population.

The value premises around which the Rhodesian social structure was organized thus called for the preservation of a dual society and a dual economy. These divisions of the society have generally been drawn along racial lines, although the separation has not been complete. To some extent, the African can enter into the money economy. He is encouraged to do so when it is to the advantage of Europeans. But penetration of the money economy by Africans is subject to the terms set by the European governing minority.

[1] Rhodesians are often highly sensitive to this and similar expressions. It is interesting to note that the Speaker of the Federal Assembly ruled an African member out of order when speaking of 'white settlers'; this was ruled to be an 'un-Parliamentary expression', *Federation of Rhodesia and Nyasaland Newsletter*, London, 12 July 1958, p. 8.

[2] For an excellent discussion of these cultural contrasts, see Philip Mason, *The Birth of a Dilemma: the Conquest and Settlement of Rhodesia* (Oxford University Press under the auspices of the Institute of Race Relations, 1958).

The value premises of Rhodesian social organization also imply their own concept of the conditions of 'economic development'. Two criteria of economic development were set out in the preceding chapter. The definition most acceptable to those in a position to shape the economic policy of the Rhodesias has much in common with the first criterion — i.e. that the money economy should expand in real terms. To this criterion, settler supremacy adds a significant rider. The form of economic development which it pursues is one which would not only expand the money economy but would also expand the European population. Economic development in this sense has clearly been accomplished. The money economy has expanded and with it the European population, heavily fed by immigration, has swollen. Europeans are still but a small fraction of the total population. But the rate of expansion in their absolute numbers is impressive — particularly in the post-war years. By the time of the 1956 census, the European population of Southern Rhodesia was more than twice as large as it had been in 1946 and three and a half times greater than in 1931. Northern Rhodesia's European numbers have grown at an even faster pace. The European population recorded in the 1956 census was three times larger than in 1946 and nearly five times greater than it had been in 1931.

This approach to economic development is not entirely at odds with the monetization of the indigenous economy and growth in real income for its members. To the governing group, however, such an effect is a by-product of growth in the money economy, not a primary aim. This is not to suggest that Europeans are hostile to the economic advance of Africans. On the contrary, their attitude towards the indigenous population has generally been paternalistic and expressions of humanitarian sympathy for the plight of the African are common. But the major economic effort of the governing minority has been directed to the aims set out above. The preoccupation with these objectives and the channelling of economic life to achieve them may not, in all circumstances, produce conditions which would satisfy the second criterion of economic development. A conflict may thus arise between the interests of the governing group and the economic improvement of the indigenous population.

Premises towards Government of the African Population

Although the overriding objective of policy in the Rhodesias has been the expansion of European settlement, it was still essential to achieve a *modus vivendi* with the African population. From the beginning, the indigenous peoples were on the scene in force. To European settlers, their presence was at once a liability and an asset. They were a nuisance in that they occupied land coveted for European occupancy and in that their numbers presented a potential threat to European supremacy. But the presence of the African was advantageous in the sense that his labour could contribute to the expansion of the money economy. The native administrator was expected to formulate and execute a policy which would secure the advantages while minimizing the disadvantages of this situation.

Reconciliation of these objectives has never in practice been perfect and the forms of native administration have been in a continuous process of evolution. Initially, considerations of expediency and expense largely determined the manner in which native administration was organized. Both recommended a system which would build, wherever possible, on existing native institutions and prevent a radical departure from traditional practices. Administration along these lines could be reasonably effective. Moreover, it was cheap; the meagre resources of the European community could not tolerate any substantial drain for the purpose of administering the African community.

Retention of tribal institutions as the instruments of rule, however, did not imply that the tribal authorities were allowed much scope for decision. Instead they were the channels through which the European governing officials communicated their instructions. A Southern Rhodesian committee put the point in 1911, recommending:

That it is desirable to control the natives as much as possible through their own chiefs and headmen. The power of arbitrament amongst their own people at present exercised by chiefs should be recognized; such powers should be exercised under the control of the Native Commissioner or other District Officer.[1]

European administrators held the ultimate authority and had

[1] *Report of the Native Affairs Committee of Enquiry, 1910–11*, p. 8.

the power to appoint and dismiss the salaried chiefs and head-men. In the strict sense, the pattern of rule was direct; but the use of the chiefs and headmen as the agents made the governing process itself an indirect one.

This approach to native administration stands in contrast to that expounded elsewhere in British colonial Africa. Lugard in Nigeria and Cameron in Tanganyika argued for a view of indirect rule which involved more than the mechanics of day-to-day administration. It implied as well the use of tribal institu-tions as the foundations upon which higher forms of government with wider responsibilities could be built. In that setting, it was a philosophy of political development in which traditional institutions of government formed the base for political advancement of the indigenous peoples. Outwardly, the two approaches have much in common; in both, European officials maintained overall supervision. But the spirit animating them was quite different. The Lugard-Cameron view presupposed self-government by the indigenous peoples as the ultimate goal. It is this theory which has been applied, for example, in Ghana and Nigeria.

This latter interpretation of native administration was alien to the intentions of the original governing minority in the Rhodesias. Even if it had been desired, the circumstances of the Central African tribes at the turn of the century were hardly favourable for its development. The tribal structure in Southern Rhodesia had been shaken in the fighting which put down the last resistance to European rule in the 1890s. In most of Northern Rhodesia and Nyasaland, the incursions of the slave trade and inter-tribal warfare had destroyed the cohesion of traditional institutions. Only in Barotseland (in the present Northern Rhodesia) was European penetration confronted with a traditional governing authority flourishing and function-ing intact. The success of the Barotse peoples in retaining to the present day a degree of political autonomy unique in Central Africa testifies to the strength of their established institutions. In most of the remainder of Central Africa, it was necessary to improvise. The tribal structure was rehabilitated and recast in such fashion as to insure its responsiveness to European direction.

In Southern Rhodesia, the pattern of native administration

has undergone remarkably little change. Officially, the government accepted the principle of African local self-government in the Constitution of 1923. Little was done to implement this before legislation in 1937 allowed Native Councils to make rules and regulations within their own areas. The results of this concession to African administrative autonomy have been limited. The reluctance of the Southern Rhodesian Government to promote a sense of political responsibility among its Bantu peoples is indicated by its delay in granting to Native Councils any financial responsibilities. Not until 1943 were they given any funds to spend.

Under Colonial Office rule, Nyasaland and Northern Rhodesia have made a more substantial departure from the initial form of native administration. In both, attempts have been made to stimulate political training of the indigenous peoples by applying the indirect-rule philosophy. Legislation towards this end was passed in Northern Rhodesia in 1929, although it was not until 1936 that provision was made for Native Treasuries. These steps had been taken in Nyasaland in 1933. In the two northern territories, the official aims of these policies were to prepare Africans for broader political participation.[1] Such expectations were nurtured in Nyasaland particularly. The hostile reception of federation in Nyasaland is not unrelated to this phenomenon.

Whether the systems latterly adopted are described as direct (more accurately, intermediary) rule or indirect rule, two features of the relationship of the European governing authorities to the African peoples are common to both Rhodesias. In neither, regardless of the differing rationale of the approach to native administration, has the African achieved any substantial voice in the political process. The major issues of policy are still almost exclusively determined by Europeans. Secondly, both official approaches to native administration presuppose the survival, in some form, of the traditional bases of authority in the indigenous society. Both are obliged to rely upon the indigenous system for the maintenance of law and

[1] For a review and criticism of the powers permitted to Native Councils in Southern Rhodesia, see Percy Ibbotson, *Report on Native Councils*, March 1952 (published by the Federation of African Welfare Societies in Southern Rhodesia, Bulawayo). Hailey, op. cit., contains a useful discussion of the status of Native Councils in the Colonial Office territories.

C

order; it could not, therefore, be allowed to collapse completely under the shock of European contact.

Governmental Policy and Economic Opportunities for Europeans

Viewed in purely economic terms, the Rhodesias could not expect to expand their European populations substantially unless they could offer prospective immigrants higher real incomes than would be available to them elsewhere. But international movements of labour cannot be accounted for in economic terms exclusively, any more than the doctrine of the rational economic man can be used without qualification to explain all human behaviour. The motives of the original European immigrants to Central Africa were complex. The spirit of adventure or missionary zeal, in some cases, outweighed the prospect of material gain. But many of the measures subsequently designed to attract European settlers to Central Africa (or, in some circumstances, to discourage the emigration of those already there) have appealed to their economic ambitions.

The allocation of the land in Central Africa has been one of the most powerful reinforcements of this policy. In the Rhodesias, lands most suitable for commercial use have been reserved for Europeans. The dimensions of this problem loom largest in Southern Rhodesia. Of the total area of the colony, roughly half is assigned to Europeans, predominantly in the fertile High Veld. Approximately 42 per cent. of Southern Rhodesia is for African use.[1] The bulk of the indigenous population, however, has been compressed into Native Reserves comprising about 22 per cent. of the total acreage. Native Purchase Areas, where Africans of demonstrated agricultural ability may acquire rights of individual tenure, account for another 8 per cent. The allocation and use of this land is regulated by the government and, as yet, much of it remains unoccupied.[2] The remainder of the African area is designated

[1] Land distribution data are obtained from the *Reports of the Director of Native Agriculture*, Southern Rhodesia.

[2] One of the factors retarding a more rapid utilization of this land is explained by the Chief Native Commissioner: 'The number of applications for farms in the Native Purchase Area continues to outstrip the number surveyed and made ready for allocation each year; ... the willingness of the applicants to undergo suitable courses of training is an indication of the eager competition for farms. Staff is again the limiting factor in this problem', *Report of the Chief Native Commissioner*, 1954, p. 4.

as 'Special Native Areas'. This category of land allocation, created in 1950, has expanded the total acreage available to Africans largely by reducing the area previously unassigned to either race. As the Special Native Areas include much of the arid and tsetse-infested zone, their African population is light. Of the total African area, much is officially classified as waste land and only about 15 per cent. is regarded as suitable for cultivation.

In Northern Rhodesia, the European area is quantitatively less significant, accounting for less than 6 per cent. of the total.[1] The European area, however, absorbs about 16 per cent. of the land not infested by tsetse fly (which at present makes habitation unattractive in more than 69 per cent. of the colony). The remainder is African in Native Reserve and Native Trust Lands and in Barotseland. The relative distribution in Nyasaland is still more favourable to the indigenous peoples. Only 5 per cent. of the total area is held by Europeans while Native Trust Land accounts for 87 per cent. of the total. The smaller total land area of Nyasaland, however, means that — in absolute terms — the area treated there as Native Trust Land is smaller than the Native Reserve Areas of Southern Rhodesia. Qualitatively, the land available for exclusive African occupancy in Nyasaland is generally superior to that in Southern Rhodesia. But the indigenous population of the former is roughly a quarter greater than that of the latter.[2]

In the Rhodesias, the government's power to determine land distribution has guaranteed the availability of land for European settlement. By comparison with most agricultural export countries, however, these territories are at a disadvantage because of the low natural fertility of the soil. To some extent this handicap could be offset by making land available to the settler in volume and at negligible cost. In some cases, outright grants of land were made to prospective settlers. But when land

[1] In Northern Rhodesia, Africans are not legally debarred from acquiring Crown lands (i.e. those assigned to the European area). By 1960, however, no African had 'successfully applied' for a farm on Crown land. See *Survey of Developments since 1953* (Report by Committee of Officials), Cmnd. 1149, 1960, p. 241.

[2] For discussions of land policy in Northern Rhodesia and Nyasaland, see *The Central African Territories: Comparative Survey of Native Policy*, Cmd. 8235, 1951, Hailey, op. cit., and *Survey of Developments since 1953* (Report by Committee of Officials), Cmnd. 1149, 1960.

was sold, the governing authority placed little more than a token price upon it.

These steps, however, have not always been enough to achieve the aim of acquiring a steady influx of European immigrants. In the conditions of Central Africa, land for agricultural purposes is not a free good even when given away. Considerable expenditure is required to clear and stump it and to provide water before the land can be productively used. To minimize these problems for the European settler, the government was again prepared to assist. The technique applied has differed at various points in time, but government has generally been prepared to subsidize these development costs in some form. In Southern Rhodesia, the creation of a Land and Agricultural Bank was one of the first acts after self-government. Its function has been to provide credits at attractive rates of interest for the European agricultural community. More direct assistance has been a feature of later government policy in both Rhodesias. Subsidies or grants have been made to European farmers for the building of dams, the sinking of boreholes, and soil conservation. European agriculture has, in fact, been made a sheltered industry.

These encouragements to a settled agricultural community alone, however, could not shelter the European farmer completely. His economic fortunes still depended upon favourable weather and upon profitable markets. The government could insulate him from the full shock of the poor seasons by granting direct assistance in the drought years. But its ability to shield the European settler from the effects of a collapse in the prices of his product was more limited. It could nevertheless ameliorate his plight.

The Rhodesian response to the slump in world agricultural prices in the early 1930s illustrates one of the effects of settler supremacy on the relationship of the African to the money economy. Faced with declining prices for its products, the European farming community in the Rhodesias reacted in much the same fashion as did agricultural producers elsewhere. It sought to divorce itself from the prices determined by the market and to obtain a supported price for its product. In the Rhodesias, these devices were necessarily more complicated than in most of the other agricultural countries in which they were attempted. Agricultural production for market was not exclusively in the hands of Europeans. African farmers also participated, although to only a limited extent. Precise estimates of their contribution to total sales are not available before 1931. But it was generally recognized that their sales of maize, the principal cash crop at that time, were sufficiently large to threaten the maintenance of a supported price applied solely to the European-grown crop. This form of competition was felt most acutely in Southern Rhodesia and to a lesser extent in Northern Rhodesia.

With governmental sponsorship, Southern Rhodesia established a Maize Control Board in 1931. It was organized on co-operative lines and controlled by European farmers. The object was clearly consistent with the policy of supporting permanent European settlement. A report of an official committee reviewing the agricultural situation in 1934 stated the case explicitly:

The issue that has to be faced is whether it is possible to build up a white Colony on any basis other than a white agricultural population.[1]

If the price support scheme was to serve this purpose, it was necessary to dispense its benefits to European growers and, if possible, to deny them to Africans. The difficulties in framing a programme, which would achieve both, were apparent to the committee appointed by the government in 1931 to draft recommendations for the control of maize. Its proposals, which formed the basis for the original control programme, called for a two-price system. In the home market, maize would be sold at a supported price; the unsold surplus would then be disposed of on the international markets for whatever it could command. Roughly the average price of the total maize sales would be distributed at the end of the season to the European members of the pool. But the African-grown product presented an obstacle to the tidy administration of the scheme. African maize was generally regarded as of low quality and unfit for export as grain. Normally, African sales of maize were used only for consumption within the territory.

If maize sold by Africans continued to be distributed in the

[1] *Report of the Committee of Enquiry into the Economic Position of the Agricultural Industry of Southern Rhodesia*, C.S.R. 16, 1934, p. 1.

usual fashion the purposes of the price support scheme would be wrecked. The African would get the full benefit of the supported price while more of the European crop would be sold abroad than might have been the case otherwise. Commenting on this possibility, the 1931 Committee of Enquiry made the cautious observation that native-grown maize, if left uncontrolled, would 'at once become the most prominent factor in the matter'.[1] It was, therefore, determined that the marketing of African-grown maize also be brought under the jurisdiction of the Board. The price paid to the native producer would be determined by the government and the proceeds of African sales would be accounted in a separate pool. The African grower would not be paid the full market value for his product. The difference between the supported price and what the African received was placed in a government fund 'for the benefit of the natives of the area from which the maize had been supplied'.[2]

The operational formulae applied by the Maize Control Board underwent numerous changes in the 1930s, but throughout the period a bias against African sales was consistently maintained. Even so, the barriers to maize sales by Africans did not fully satisfy the European agricultural community. More rigorous market segregation was called for in 1934 with the recommendation that 'no native-produced article should be sold in the European area and vice versa except under permit.'[3] The case for excluding Africans from the domestic market completely was well summarized in the views of the chairman of a 1934 official committee of inquiry:

The native, owing to free land and labour, low standard of living, methods of farming can produce at a cost under recent overseas parity . . . It therefore appears equitable to treat native grown maize as export maize.[4]

This view has persistently been widely held by the European farming community in the Rhodesias. Since the war, it has recurred in a different context. The government's price supports have been calculated on the basis of costs of production in European agriculture. Some European farmers have main-

[1] *Report of the Maize Enquiry Committee*, C.S.R. 2, 1931, Southern Rhodesia, p. 10.
[2] Ibid., p. 18.
[3] *Report of the Committee of Inquiry into the Economic Position of the Agricultural Industry of Southern Rhodesia*, C.S.R. 16, 1934, p. 27.
[4] Minority report of the Chairman, Max Danziger, loc. cit., p. 11.

tained that the African is not entitled to subsidized prices because he has 'no costs of production'. The views of the European farming community in Northern Rhodesia have been similar. But, with smaller numbers, their weight has been less influential in marketing policy. A maize marketing organization was formed in the depression years on the pattern of the Southern Rhodesian Maize Control Board. Its formation, however, came later and it did not begin operating until 1935.

While the organization of the marketing system has handicapped the African farmer's entry into the money economy, his exclusion has never been as complete as the extremists among European farmers would have desired. Although he was discriminated against in price in the depression years, he nevertheless was enabled to dispose of part of his production for cash. The colour bar of the 1930s on agricultural marketing has subsequently been relaxed in the Rhodesias. But several other forms of discrimination against African entry into the money economy through the sale of agricultural products persist. This applies in particular to the sale of profitable export crops in the post-war years — notably, Virginia tobacco. European farmers increasingly have concentrated their production on this commodity; the high price it commands in the Commonwealth market has made it highly profitable to do so. The resulting shift in the emphasis of European production away from maize is one of the factors accounting for the reduced resistance to African sales of agricultural products for home consumption.

But the African producer is still largely blocked from taking advantage of the boom in export crops. Marketing of Virginia tobacco in the Rhodesias is dominated by an association of European producers and African production is not welcomed. In the view of the marketing association, the reputation of the Rhodesian product in international markets cannot be risked by permitting an 'inferior' African product to carry its label.[1] In this respect, Nyasaland again must be differentiated from the Rhodesian pattern. Africans have been encouraged to produce cash crops for export and have been able to surpass, in the post-

[1] In order to qualify for access to marketing facilities for Virginia tobacco, growers must be registered with the Tobacco Marketing Board. Of 3,117 growers registered in 1958, eight were Africans. African production of the less profitable Turkish tobacco has been given some encouragement by governments in the Rhodesias.

war years, the output of the Protectorate's European plantations in the production of tobacco and cotton. Tea and tung
production, however, remain almost exclusively in the hands of
the European producers.

While the Rhodesian territories have generally regarded
European farmers as the most stable settlers, they alone could
not swell the size of the European community sufficiently.
Another type of policy was required to provide further economic
inducements to European immigrants. The fundamental
economic attraction of the Rhodesian territories to the outside
world — their mineral wealth — was a gift of nature and not
directly subject to government policy. Government, however,
could take steps to insure that the exploitation of mineral resources was conducted in a manner consistent with the maximum inflow of European settlers; or, conversely, it could devise
policies to check an exodus of the European population. In
Southern Rhodesia, direct governmental action has concentrated in recent years on the latter objective. With less
abundant mineral wealth than its northern neighbour, Southern Rhodesia has historically relied on a relatively large number
of small gold mines as a major source of export revenues. But
the fortunes of the gold-mining industry have declined. The peak
output of recent times was achieved in 1940 and the number of
producers has since shrunk rapidly. The government has
employed a number of devices, with varying success, in an
effort to keep the small-worker in operation. It has attempted to
lower his costs by making equipment available to him at a subsidized rental. It has attempted to increase the efficiency of his
operations by providing a government-owned plant for processing low grade ores.[1] And it has even attempted to increase the
income of the small-worker by subsidizing the price of gold.[2]

[1] The Roasting Plant at Que Que began operations in 1937 with equipment
for treating sulphide ores for the recovery of gold. In most years, the plant has
operated at a loss; its operating deficits must be regarded as a subsidy to the gold-
mining industry. See *Annual Reports of the Roasting Plant, Que Que* Southern
Rhodesia, and *Report of the Commission of Inquiry into Certain Aspects of the Operation
of the Roasting Plant, Que Que, Southern Rhodesia*, C.S.R. 39, 1953.

[2] This practice was short-lived. After less than two years of the operation of the
subsidy system, the government was forced to abandon it because of objections by
the International Monetary Fund. The devaluation of sterling in 1949 gave an
additional fillip to the industry. See *Reports of the Chief Government Mining Engineer,
Southern Rhodesia, 1947-49*.

But of wider significance is the manner in which the Rhodesian political and social structure has operated to provide artificial supports to the economic position of Europeans who are not self-employed (like the farmer or small-worker in mining) but are wage employees. The practices followed are not solely a matter of governmental policy. They have their roots in the prejudices and the social beliefs of the community. These are sometimes expressed directly in legislation but they may exert a profound influence without it.

Whatever its basis, the industrial colour bar is consistent with the objective of encouraging and promoting the inflow of a permanent European population. Through this device, technical skill has remained a monopoly of the European. It has kept the African out of highly paid positions and has acted as a magnet for drawing Europeans into them. But it need not follow that all members of the European working force are highly trained or that the gap between their wage scales and those of Africans could be maintained in a competitive labour market. There is no conclusive evidence on these points. Two recent studies, however, throw indirect light on the problem. One is an analysis comparing the occupational distribution of European males in Southern Rhodesia with the male labour force in Britain. Census returns for 1951 formed the basis of comparison. Because the definitions employed in the two censuses were not identical, European occupations in Southern Rhodesia were reclassified into the categories used in the British census. These adjustments brought out a striking contrast. Whereas 13 per cent. of the male labour force in Britain was engaged in 'unskilled' occupations, only 0·6 per cent. of the European males in the working force of Southern Rhodesia could be classified in this category. Similar comparison of the 'partly skilled' jobs in the two countries indicated that 16·4 per cent. of the British male working force fell within this category compared with 2·7 per cent. in Southern Rhodesia.[1] These comparisons are not flawless but they do suggest that the bulk of employed European males — well over 90 per cent. in fact — in Southern Rhodesia held positions which are officially regarded as skilled. It might be argued that the European labour

[1] Colin Leys, *European Politics in Southern Rhodesia* (Oxford University Press, 1959), pp. 82–83 and Appendix I.

force of Southern Rhodesia constitutes a highly selected *élite* with proportionately more abundant talents and training than could be found among British workers. In this case, the divergence in occupational patterns might be the result of natural economic forces. But a study prepared in 1952 fails to lend support to this view. The findings of the Rhodesian Teachers' Research Committee from an intelligence survey of a complete school year at the age of eleven-plus revealed that the mean intelligence of the Rhodesian pupil was approximately the same as that found from similar studies in Britain.[1] This conclusion is hardly a definitive basis for judging the aptitudes of the European labour force in Southern Rhodesia. But it does cast doubt on the view that the economic performance of Europeans there is as far superior to that of the British labour force as the comparison of the occupational distribution would indicate. And it further suggests that the heavy weighting of the European labour force towards 'skilled' occupations in Southern Rhodesia may not be based on merit alone, but that it may be a reflection of artificial conditions in the labour market.

In Southern Rhodesia, the industrial colour bar has been bolstered by legislation. Enactment of the Industrial Conciliation Act of 1934, reaffirmed in 1945, was specifically intended for this purpose. According to its provisions, fixed rates of pay were established for all jobs subject to trade union organization in the urban areas of the colony. Technically, an employer had a free choice in selecting whom he might engage without regard to race. But he was obliged to pay whomsoever he engaged for skilled and semi-skilled work at the stipulated wage, i.e. at the artificially high wage rate set for Europeans. In practice, this has meant, with only a few exceptions, that Africans have been debarred from climbing the industrial ladder. The stipulated jobs have been held by Europeans almost exclusively. A secondary feature of the Act was that its terms allowed only Europeans to bargain collectively. No African industrial organization could be officially recognized as a legitimate trade union. This did not prevent African employee organizations from being formed. But it did deny them the ability to conduct wage negotiations through the normal machinery of collective

[1] See *Report of the Rhodesian Teachers' Research Committee, 1952* (Bulawayo, 1955, mimeographed).

bargaining. In the post-war years, some African employee groups have been well enough organized to conduct strikes and make work stoppages effective. But such actions, although drawing attention to the grievances of African employees, were not technically legal.[1]

The industrial colour bar is practised with almost equal effect in Northern Rhodesia, but it draws its strength from different sources. It is neither sanctioned nor supported by legislation. The pattern of social behaviour which has developed in the territory, centring particularly around the copper-mining industry, has given discrimination in employment a considerable status. The enforcement of discrimination, however, stems primarily from the power of the European Mine Workers' Union in the Copperbelt. The mine operators, on the other hand, have long pressed for reforms which would permit African employees to advance. Thus far, their efforts have met with limited success. In August 1955 an agreement was negotiated with the European Union which brought the first breach in the colour bar. It marked a victory for the principle of African advancement, but its practical effects have been modest. Only about 1,000 African employees in an African labour force of over 35,000 in the copper-mining industry were directly affected by the new agreement in its first five years of implementation.

Meanwhile the European Mine Workers' Union has attempted to extend a rigid industrial colour bar to all other forms of employment in the territory. It has succeeded in imposing conformity to its standards on all contractors engaged for construction work by the mining companies. This has taken the form of a provision in the contract between the mining companies and European Mine Workers' Union known euphemistically as 'the fair wages and conditions clause'. Under the terms of this clause, the European Union can determine the job classifications for contract work and can insist on rates of pay 'being comparable with the emoluments of similar daily paid employees in the Copper Mining Industry'. Moreover, the preservation of the colour bar is assured by the provision that 'contractors shall observe established practices in the

[1] The legal position of Africans in trade unions was modified by the Industrial Conciliation Act of 1959; see discussion below.

Copper Mining Industry in regard to the following: methods and hours of work, [and] employment of qualified artisans; . . . by methods of work is meant accepted practices on the job covering work performed by tradesmen and others'.[1] The European Mine Workers' Union has also been engaged in an effort to organize a European Industrial Union which can apply its standards to all forms of industrial employment in Northern Rhodesia.

The Northern Rhodesian case differs from that of Southern Rhodesia in another respect. African trade unions have not been denied legal recognition in the former as they have in the latter; in fact, one African union has been organized with governmental assistance. The formation of an African Mine Workers' Union dates from 1949. Although its operations have been handicapped by the lack of personnel experienced in trade union negotiation, it has organized strike actions with efficiency on several occasions during its brief life. Its effectiveness as a bargaining instrument is still limited. While the African union has succeeded in raising the pay scales of the African mine employees, it has not itself taken the lead in attacking the colour bar. The limited degree of African advancement thus far achieved has stemmed largely from the initiative of the mine operators.

Apart from Nyasaland, where the volume of industrial employment is insignificant, the institutions of the Central African territories are thus designed to provide support to the economic position of European workers and to place an artificial ceiling to the status attainable by Africans in wage employment. The unfortunate economic effects of this system have been repeatedly pointed out by outside observers of the Rhodesian economic structure. As early as 1930, the industrial colour bar was attacked in a report prepared at the request of the Southern Rhodesian Government. As its author, Professor Henry Clay, argued:

> Even if in some occupations the Native does displace the white man, now that he is able to earn more he can demand more, and so offers a market for an increased output of goods in general in which additional white labour will find employment . . . These fears

[1] Based on material extracted from the files of the Northern Rhodesia Chamber of Mines, Kitwe, 10 November 1955.

are, indeed, based on the fallacy that there is a limited amount of work to be done, and that if the Native does it the white man cannot do it. This fallacy, if it were true, would constitute an equal objection to the admission of any more white men to the country, for fear they should take away the work of those already in the country.[1]

But the pattern is a persistent one and the social and political forces which support it have yielded little to the attacks of their critics. The effects of the colour bar in industrial employment have been conspicuous and readily subject to comment. But the industrial aspect of racial discrimination in the economic life of Central Africa is only a small part of the whole. As conventionally defined, the colour bar may be regarded as 'a process whereunder the African worker is prevented from (1) acquiring skill, (2) exercising skill, and (3) obtaining the full reward for the exercise of skill'.[2] This definition can be appropriately applied to a range of social phenomena much broader than industrial employment alone. Policies towards the allocation of land and towards the marketing of agricultural products have tended to draw a colour line through all aspects of economic life.

Governmental Policy and Economic Opportunities for the Indigenous Population

While the expedient and inexpensive method of administering and governing the African population called for the preservation of traditional society, some disturbance in its structure was required if the labour demands of the money economy were to be satisfied. Thus, it was inevitable that the economic and political aspects of the doctrine of settler supremacy should push native policy in conflicting directions. Yet the contradiction was not complete. A certain amount of male labour could enter the money economy without risking a disruption in the traditional system. Indeed, it has often been argued that part-time employment of adult males would have a wholesome effect. The Chief Native Commissioner of Southern

---

[1] Henry Clay, *Report on Industrial Relations in Southern Rhodesia*, C.S.R. 3, 1930, para. 123.

[2] W. J. Busschau, *Report on the Development of Secondary Industries in Northern Rhodesia* (Government Printer, Lusaka), 1945, p. 24.

Rhodesia took this position in 1900, maintaining that African men 'must be given work to be kept out of trouble'.[1]

At the same time, it was generally believed that there was an upper limit to the amount of absenteeism which the indigenous system could tolerate. The critical ceiling, however, could not be precisely determined. Arbitrarily, the figure of roughly 50 per cent. absenteeism among the adult males has usually been treated as the allowable maximum. This figure was imported into native administration in Rhodesia from South Africa. In his report for 1919, for example, the Chief Native Commissioner cited as applicable to Southern Rhodesia the following passage from the Report of the South African Native Affairs Commission of 1903–05:

> The number of natives available for paid labour at any one time [is] a percentage of 50·6 of the total male population between the ages of 15 and 40.[2]

The assumptions on which this calculation is based have never been made explicit. But the same implied premise apparently has continued to underlie the thinking of the Native Affairs Department in Southern Rhodesia.[3]

In the early years of expansion in the European's money economy, the problem of administration was not one of keeping absenteeism within bounds. Rather, it was the reverse. The number of African males responding to the new opportunities for wage-earning fell well short of employers' demands and the Native Commissioners launched a campaign to induce more Africans to accept wage employment. The early results were disappointing. The Administrators of the British South Africa Company in Southern Rhodesia applied their full powers of persuasion, supplemented by threats of force and expropriation, to draw forth larger numbers of African workers into the nascent money economy. The methods adopted — which

---

[1] Letter from the Chief Native Commissioner to the Colonial Office, 26 May 1900, *Correspondence Relating to the Regulation and Supply of Labour in Southern Rhodesia*, Cmd. 1200, July 1902, p. 36.

[2] *Report of the Chief Native Commissioner of Southern Rhodesia*, 1919, p. 5. Earlier, the 1910–11 Committee on Native Affairs in Southern Rhodesia had taken the same position.

[3] This view appears in the manner in which the availability of native labour for wage employment is discussed: e.g. *The Report of the Commissioner of Native Labour*, Southern Rhodesia, 1947.

attempted to push the subsidized chiefs into the role of recruiting agents — caused concern in the Colonial Office and stirred the Colonial Secretary to register his disapproval of any form of 'compulsory labour' in a letter to the directors of the British South Africa Company.[1]

The story is a familiar one in the settler communities in Africa. The resistance of the traditional society to rapid adaptation and to absorption into the money economy did not, however, provoke in the Rhodesias a remedy employed elsewhere. In the sugar plantations of Natal and in the construction of the Uganda Railway, for example, Indian workers had been imported. At one point in Rhodesian history, however, the issue hung in the balance. Faced with a possible disruption in mining operations owing to a 'shortage' of African labour, the British South Africa Company inquired in 1900 into the feasibility of introducing indentured Asiatic labour into the country.[2] But the matter was resolved without resort to this expedient. What the positive attractions to African labour — cash wages and imported goods — could not alone achieve was accomplished through the negative inducement of compulsory taxes which could only be paid in cash.[3] When the two in combination failed to produce the required quantity of indigenous labour, recruiting of Africans from outside the colony was called upon to fill the gap.

With wider exposure to the money economy through time, the African has responded more readily to its positive inducements and in greater numbers. But the economic opportunities open to Africans are still severely qualified in the Rhodesias. The colour barrier restricts their entry into many categories of employment. Africans can seldom aspire to jobs requiring

[1] Letter from the Colonial Office to the B.S.A. Company, 23 December 1899, loc. cit., p. 26.

[2] See letter from the British South Africa Company to the Colonial Office, 18 August 1900, loc. cit., pp. 45–46.

[3] One loophole in the Southern Rhodesian tax system was quickly closed. In the early years, some natives settled their tax obligations in raw gold. This practice was the subject of a protest from the Salisbury Chamber of Mines to the Chief Native Commissioner in 1900. The mining organization observed that 'it would greatly facilitate the settlement of the labour question if the Hut-Tax had to be paid in current coin, for in order to obtain same the native would have to more frequently enter into the service of the settler'. The Administration indicated that this method of payment would no longer be allowed. See B.S.A. to the Colonial Office, 29 November 1900, loc. cit., p. 62.

advanced skills, even if they possess them. Nor are they given equal opportunities with Europeans to acquire skills. This is strikingly apparent in the approach of the Rhodesian social structure to public education. While it is obviously to the advantage of the European community to equip the native population with training which enables its members to perform efficiently in the money economy, the educational system is not designed to impart skills on a scale which might challenge the monopoly position of European skilled workers. Moreover, education for Europeans is assigned priority for another reason: to assist them in maintaining their initial economic advantage. The case is summarized in the words of a Committee which examined the question in Northern Rhodesia in 1948:

Generally speaking, the work of the European is supervisory in character. He is at present called upon to provide professional and skilled workers, while the African provides manual labour and semi-skilled or skilled workers, and however rapidly the African develops, this is likely to be true for some considerable time to come. It is important, therefore, that the European should receive a sound general education to as high a standard as he is able to achieve so that he may be capable of carrying out these functions, relying upon intelligence and ability rather than upon artificially created conditions of employment.[1]

This position is reinforced by an education policy toward the African the aim of which is not to turn out 'skilled artisans to compete in the open labour market'.[2] This negative objective was stated explicitly in 1925, but the view it represents has been persistent in the Rhodesias. As was noted in a 1951 survey of education for Africans in Southern Rhodesia:

The majority of school children enjoy, at the most, two years of school life which, whatever small value they may have for the future life of the child, will not, in the opinion of most of our witnesses, ensure the retention of any degree of literacy even in the vernacular.[3]

[1] *Report of the Committee Appointed to Investigate European Education in Northern Rhodesia*, May-July 1948 (Government Printer, Lusaka, 1948), p. 4.

[2] *Report of the Commission Appointed to Enquire into the Matter of Native Education in All its Bearings in the Colony of Southern Rhodesia*, C.S.R. 20, 1925 (Government Printer, Salisbury), p. 103.

[3] *Report of the Native Education Inquiry Commission, 1951*, C.S.R. 6, 1952, (Government Stationery Office, Salisbury), 1952, p. 14.

Educational policy in Nyasaland has departed from the aims established in the Rhodesias. As early as 1925, the objectives of the Protectorate's programme were set out as follows:

We have aimed largely to meet the European demand for educated skilled labour ... The results have been that all the responsible posts that can be held by Natives are held by our educated Natives, overseers, engineers, car-drivers, interpreters, and clerks.[1]

By 1939, the Native Welfare Committee could report of Nyasaland that 'the percentage of the population which is literate in the vernacular is higher than in any other British Tropical dependency and 'that there is a higher percentage of local native skilled and semi-skilled labour than in any other Colony in East and Central Africa'.[2] Even so, the resources which have been available for educating the African population have been too small to yield impressive results.

Indirectly, but no less forcefully, the behaviour of Africans as wage employees has been conditioned by the segregation applied to land ownership in the Rhodesias. With only a few limited exceptions, Africans are thereby precluded from acquiring security of tenure in European areas and cannot contemplate permanent residence there. Although an African may be absent for prolonged periods, the government still regards him as a member of his original community and subject to its jurisdiction. This approach to native administration may be out of touch with real conditions. But its retention has, for the governing minority, two recommendations: it preserves the simplicity of native administration and, perhaps more importantly, it can be used as a defence against proposals to allow Africans in wage employment a substantial voice in European political affairs.

The administrative application of this doctrine of separation differs in the three territories. Since 1930, it has been backed by the force of law in Southern Rhodesia, although it was well established by convention from the beginning. The Land Apportionment Act of 1930 divided the geographical area of the colony into European and Native areas and granted a member

---

[1] Letter from the Head of Blantyre Mission, contained in C.S.R. 20, 1925, p. 103.
[2] *Memorandum on Native Policy in Nyasaland, January 1939*, Native Welfare Committee (Government Printer, Zomba, 1939), pp. 12–13.

D

of each race, with a few minor exceptions, exclusive rights in his own areas. This legislation specifically provided that no African 'shall acquire, lease, or occupy land in the European area'.[1] In the territories administered by the Colonial Office, policy has been less rigid. The practice in Northern Rhodesia, however, is not significantly different from that in Southern Rhodesia, although there is no specific statutory bar to acquisition of urban property by Africans. The extent of urbanization in Nyasaland is still slight; the question of the nature of African tenure in the urban areas has little practical significance.

The traditional arrangements in the Rhodesias have, in effect, denied the African wage-earner any permanent identification with the money economy. He could enter it, but officially only as a temporary sojourner. His movements and even the provision of his necessities of life had to be administered and regulated. Because the property-holding restrictions normally prevented him from providing for his own requirements, housing had to be organized on his behalf. This could be done by his employer directly. But the more widespread practice — and the one most often encouraged in the Rhodesias — is the housing of African employees in locations owned and supervised by the local authorities. The employer choosing this alternative spares himself the capital outlay of building his own location; but he is normally held responsible for the payment of rentals to the municipality. Apart from the large mining companies (which generally construct their own townships), the standard solution in the Rhodesias is to rely on the municipalities.

The procedures of the municipal authorities illuminate an important aspect of policy towards the African in wage employment. Southern Rhodesia, the territory with the heaviest volume of wage employment, presents the most interesting case. In their approach to housing, the municipal authorities are limited both by the territorial legislation covering the residence of Africans in the European areas and by the financial resources available to them. The law obliges them to site African locations in areas segregated from European residential districts and

[1] Before 1930, Africans technically had equal rights with Europeans to acquire land outside the reserves. These rights were removed with the passage of the Land Apportionment Act. The principle of strict geographical segregation which it embodied had been recommended by a Commission in 1925. See *Report of the Land Commission, 1925*, C.S.R. 3, 1926.

charges the local administrations with the maintenance of good order and of reasonable standards of public hygiene in the African settlements. But financial considerations impose a more serious limitation on their operations. In general, the municipal housing authorities are under pressure to maximize the total number of African workers they can accommodate with the limited funds at their disposal. This tends to place the emphasis on the construction of accommodation for single men to the neglect of housing for married men and their families.

This bias against the married African employee is apparent in the ratios of single to married men with families accommodated in the more important municipalities of Southern Rhodesia. In 1955, for example, only one African worker in seven could expect to have his family living with him in the municipal townships in Salisbury. In Bulawayo, the ratio of single to married housing units was nearly five to one; the situation in Umtali was easier with a four to one ratio.[1] The ratios differ slightly; but that a disproportionate number of employees must be separated from their families applies generally throughout the publicly administered locations in the Rhodesias. The reason is readily apparent. The capital cost of providing a home for a worker and his family is roughly six times that required to accommodate a single man in dormitory fashion. The economic incentive to concentrate construction on accommodation for single men has been given even greater emphasis since legislation in 1951 called for the municipal authorities to charge the same rent for each employee. Employers have been billed according to the number of employees housed in the townships, without differentiation according to the type of accommodation occupied. On the basis of this rental pooling arrangement, the municipalities have been able to obtain a profit from the housing of single men but have incurred losses on family accommodation. In the Salisbury municipal townships, it has been estimated that the ratio of 6·3 single to every married native housed must be maintained if the finances of the locations are to be balanced.[2]

[1] Based on correspondence and interviews with the Directors of Native Administration in the municipalities of Southern Rhodesia.

[2] This situation was outlined by the Director of Native Administration of Salisbury at the Thirteenth Annual Conference of the Municipal Association of Southern Rhodesia, May 1954. See mimeographed minutes of the conference.

The practical effect of these arrangements is to prevent the African from acquiring a permanent foothold in the European area, even though he may spend most of his productive life in wage employment. Some relaxations in the uncompromising view of strict geographical segregation are now in the process of being made. As yet, however, they are not of sufficient magnitude to modify the general pattern. All but a handful of African wage-earners are obliged, whether they would prefer otherwise or not, to retain an identification with the traditional society.

Recent Amendments in Social Policy

Particularly since the formation of the Federation and the introduction of the official doctrine of partnership which came with it, numerous amendments in the traditional dualism of the Rhodesian social structure have been made. If not removed, many of the more irritating disabilities under which Africans have lived have at least been relaxed. The pass laws and the liquor control laws have been softened; segregation in Post Offices has been banned; Africans have been allowed to compete for posts in the Civil Service from which they had formerly been excluded and an African has been appointed to a junior cabinet post in the Federal Government. Perhaps the most significant change on the social scene has been the foundation of a University College which opens its doors to members of all races. These are clear signs of progress and they stand in marked contrast to the hardening of the colour line which has occurred simultaneously in the Union of South Africa.

Modifications in the attitude of the governing minority towards the provision of economic opportunities for Africans have also transpired. In agricultural marketing, for example, the present climate is far removed from that of the 1930s when African farmers were discriminated against in price. A differential between the prices paid to the European and African producers has remained, but its purpose has changed. The rationale is no longer primarily the discouragement of African marketing. Instead, lower prices are paid to Africans in order to accumulate funds for the improvement of African agriculture. Since 1950 in Southern Rhodesia, the coverage of the official marketing board has been extended from maize to include other small grains, with the government fixing prices for all grains which the Minister of Agriculture shall deem subject to control. The Grain Marketing Act of 1950, however, makes it possible for the board to drop as well as to extend controls, although if marketing is freed, the board remains the buyer of last resort. In the post-1950 years, it has occasionally been the case that the price guaranteed by the government has been below the price which might have been obtained under free marketing. This situation has generated demands from some sections of the European agricultural community for removal of governmental controls. The official reply to one of the these requests shows the shift in emphasis from the marketing policies of the 1930s:

It [the Grain Marketing Board] recognizes that Native agricultural development is very largely dependent on the levies collected ... by the Board on Native grains passing through the Board's hands. Divestment does not enable the levies to be collected and it would thus be inconsistent with the essential purpose of control.[1]

In Southern Rhodesia, the government has also given long overdue attention to reform in African agriculture in other ways. A Native Land Husbandry Act, passed in 1951, calls for the elimination of communal holdings and the allocation of freehold plots to African families. The implications of this Act will be examined in detail in subsequent chapters. It is at least clear, however, that the Act reflects an interest in improved performance by indigenous agriculture — an area of economic activity which had been largely ignored by government before the war.

The plight of the African wage-earner has also been altered by modifications in two of Southern Rhodesia's long-standing pieces of restrictive legislation. Amendments to the Land Apportionment Acts now permit some Africans to acquire leasehold tenure to urban housing and the government has undertaken to underwrite long-term mortgages for qualified home owners. In addition, a new Industrial Conciliation Act was passed in 1959 which would permit African workers to join trade unions (which had formerly been exclusively for Europeans) and to allow them to receive European rates of pay. The effects of this legislation (which came into force on 1 January 1960) cannot easily be foretold. Some commentators anticipate

[1] *Report of the Grain Marketing Board, Southern Rhodesia, 1952–53*, p. 5.

that it will mean the end of the colour bar in urban employments. Whether or not this will in fact be the case will be determined primarily by the membership of the European trade
unions. The amended Industrial Conciliation Act does not out-
law the exclusion of qualified Africans from European employments, nor does it require existing unions to accept African
members. Its terms are drawn to permit 'branches' of trade
unions to be organized on a racial basis. It is not yet clear what
this will mean in practice.[1]

All of these modifications indicate a degree of flexibility on
the part of the governing minority. To date, only a small
fraction of the indigenous population has been directly affected
by the reforms which have been undertaken. While the basic
fabric of Rhodesian society has not been fundamentally altered,
such piece-meal changes could mark the beginnings of a substantial departure from the traditional pattern of settler supremacy. But it would be rash to suppose that the essential props to
the dualistic structure have yet been dismantled or that fundamental reforms must inevitably follow from the promising
changes which have been made. Effective political control in
the Rhodesias is still in the hands of a settler minority which has
displayed little disposition to share power with Africans. The
franchise has indeed been extended to permit a larger number
of Africans to register on the electoral rolls, both territorial and
Federal. The arrangements governing the eligibility of African
voters are complex and differ between the various levels of
government.[2] In each case, however, the franchise requirements
(which are drawn in terms of minimum income, property-
holding, and educational qualifications) are such that only an
insignificant number of Africans are entitled to the same vote
as Europeans. The influence of the United Kingdom Govern-

[1] It also remains to be seen what the implications of this apparent move towards
non-discrimination will be for the employment of Africans in skilled positions. In
effect, this legislation may reinforce one of the European artisans' traditional
defences — 'equal pay for equal work'. While this slogan has an egalitarian ring,
its practical effect has been to check African advancement. Few Rhodesian
employers are likely to hire skilled Africans if they are obliged to pay them at the
artificially-inflated scales set for Europeans.

[2] For a detailed analysis of the franchise question at both the Federal and
territorial levels, see Philip Mason, *Year of Decision: Rhodesia and Nyasaland* in *1960*
(Oxford University Press under the auspices of the Institute of Race Relations,
1960) and Colin Leys, op. cit., esp. chap. VII.

ment has not been unimportant in the recent moves towards widening the franchise. But the complex electoral apparatus which has emerged has not yet threatened European control, although it does permit an increasing number of Africans to participate in the political process.

CHAPTER III

THE CHARACTER OF THE INDIGENOUS ECONOMY

O F the two distinct economies within the economic system of Central Africa, the indigenous economy has a natural claim to priority in consideration. It has preceded the money economy in time, and moreover, the majority of the inhabitants of these territories still retain a stake in its fortunes. A thorough comprehension of the functioning of the economic system as a whole is impossible without an insight into major structural characteristics of indigenous economic organization.

The Traditional Form of the Indigenous System

In original form, the economic life of the indigenous communities in Central Africa was carried on in closed and largely self-sufficient units. Trade in goods, with but a few exceptions, was negligible. Part of the explanation for the lack of organized exchange lay in the general poverty of the area. As a result, the early forms of commerce which developed concentrated not on commodities but, through the slave traffic, on men. The situation was aptly summarized in E. A. G. Robinson's observation: 'Having nothing else to sell, the African has sold himself.'[1]

The absence of any sizeable exchange was also partially accounted for by the relatively uniform resource endowment of the African interior and the physical barriers to the movement of goods. The former limited the opportunities for advantageous exchange, and the latter, for isolated communities, recommended self-sufficiency as the least hazardous objective of economic activity. For the area as a whole, this type of organization was the most usual one. There were a few exceptional cases — notably the Lozi people of Barotseland.[2] Their physical

---

[1] E. A. G. Robinson, 'The Economic Problem', contained in *Modern Industry and the African* (J. Merle Davis, ed., Macmillan & Co., Ltd., London, 1933), p. 135.

[2] The unique character of Lozi life has been well described in Professor Max Gluckman's studies; e.g. 'Economy of the Central Barotse Plain', *Rhodes-Livingstone Institute Paper No. 7* (1941); 'Essays on Lozi Land and Royal Property', *Rhodes-Livingstone Institute Paper No. 10* (1943).

environment, with fertile flood plains for cultivation and access to rich fishing grounds, has differentiated them from the normal pattern. With these advantages, the Lozi successfully resisted the encroachments of the slave trade and were themselves able to develop a limited exchange beyond their own jurisdiction.[1]

It was more generally the case in Central Africa that the economic life of the indigenous peoples functioned within self-contained systems which were bound to the land. The land resources available to them, however, were not richly productive. Soil fertility was soon exhausted. But the abundance of available land made some compensation for this deficiency. In most areas, a form of shifting cultivation (known as the *chitemene* system) evolved. The details of the *chitemene* practice were adjusted to the natural conditions; within Northern Rhodesia alone, twenty-one variations of this agricultural practice have been distinguished by classifying the length of period of cultivation, acreages involved, and varieties of crops grown.[2]

The common characteristic of this almost universal practice was the abandonment of exhausted lands and their substitution by new areas brought into cultivation by clearing bush, burning it, and allowing the ash to fertilize the soil.[3] The destructiveness of the traditional form of *chitemene* has been much criticized. But the alternative before the coming of the European is not clear. As Lord Hailey noted in 1938, shifting cultivation was 'less a device of barbarism than a concession to the character of the soil'.[4] The more recent judgement of a Northern Rhodesian agricultural officer is also instructive: 'African agricultural practice is very closely adapted to local conditions and . . .

[1] Elizabeth Colson notes that the Lozi traded hoes and other iron goods in pre-European days to the Tonga peoples of Northern Rhodesia; the latter 'seem to have paid with ivory and slaves'. 'The Plateau Tonga of Northern Rhodesia', in *Seven Tribes of British Central Africa*, Elizabeth Colson and Max Gluckman, eds. (Oxford University Press, 1951), p. 107.

[2] See C. G. Trapnell and J. N. Clothier, *The Soils, Vegetation and Agricultural Systems of North-Western Rhodesia* (Government Printer, Lusaka, 1937) and *The Soils, Vegetation and Agriculture of North-Eastern Rhodesia* (Government Printer, Lusaka, 1943).

[3] Barotseland, where natural conditions permit settled cultivation, again contrasts with the general pattern. See Gluckman, op. cit. and William Allen, 'African Land Usage', *Rhodes-Livingstone Journal*, vol. iii (June 1945) p. 17.

[4] Hailey, *An African Survey* (second edition, Oxford University Press, 1945), p. 879.

represents a high degree of development within the limits imposed by the general cultural level of the people.'[1]

As a general rule, the level of output which could be obtained from the traditional agricultural system was seldom much above the consumption requirements of the population. Nor was there much incentive to expand production beyond this point. Specialization of production for exchange, as opposed to purely subsistence output, was rarely a real possibility. And, given the hazards of the climate and the prevalence of pests, the accumulation of surpluses from current production to be held as stocks was hardly attractive. Thus the omnipresent possibilities of crop failure made famine conditions a constant threat. When the rains failed, the population was obliged to improvise a minimum diet from what nature herself provided.[2]

Within the economic unit of the closed community, some division of labour and specialization occurred. Normally, this was along well-established lines with a division of function according to sex. The adult males in the community were responsible for the construction of shelters and for the clearing and preparation of new lands. Their role, in other words, was essentially one of providing the development works of the community. The male's role also included the regulation of the community's relationship with animals — i.e., trapping and hunting for game or, in areas free of tsetse fly, the care of cattle herds. To some extent, the latter function could be passed to juveniles. Most of the routine tasks in peasant agriculture, on the other hand, were the lot of the women upon whom the burdens of sowing and cultivating were placed. The techniques with which these tasks were performed were crude by Western standards and had not advanced beyond the technology of the hoe before European intervention.

Under the traditional system, standards of real income, of necessity were low. There was little net saving, apart from that required to accommodate increases in the population, for the channels into which investment (in real terms) could be directed were limited. An extension of the land area through

---

[1] J. M. Winterbottom, 'The Ecology of Man and Plants in Northern Rhodesia', *Rhodes-Livingstone Journal*, vol. iii (June 1945), p. 38.

[2] Audrey Richards describes such a reaction to crop failure in her study of the Bemba of Northern Rhodesia in the 1930s. See *Land, Labour, and Diet in Northern Rhodesia* (Oxford University Press, 1939), especially pp. 35–37.

additional clearing was one of the few possibilities, and, in some Central African tribes, surpluses in current production were translated into this type of capital formation. The recipient of a bountiful harvest could transform his surplus into land clearance by preparing a feast at which the guests would be expected to assist him with a particular project. The sociable nature of this institution was not always compatible with economic efficiency. Even so, the amount of effort which could profitably be directed into land clearance was limited by the available techniques and the reliance upon the family as the unit of production. The most popular alternative form of real accumulation — common in the areas free from trypanosomiasis — was the increase in cattle herds. Although rarely prized for the potential real income stream which they might yield, cattle were convenient as a store of value.[1] Within the confines of the restricted system, it was indeed rational to store wealth in this fashion — at least as rational as the hoarding of gold at some stages in Western economic history. Cattle represented a highly liquid asset and one which bore interest without effort on the part of the owner. Moreover, cattle served the social function of conspicuous display and the size of the herds, not their economic quality by Western standards, became the badge of rank and the mark of prestige.

As a general approximation, the pattern of the indigenous Central African economy in its traditional form is one in which real output and real income remain low, productive capital formation is geared to the size of the population, and techniques are static. Given the internal division of labour under which it is organized, the system can continue to function as an economic unit as long as fresh lands are available to replace those exhausted by cultivation. In addition, the system was sustained by patterns of tastes which were simple, easily satisfied, and extended little beyond physiological requirements.

Judged by Western standards of economic performance, these indigenous economies were highly inefficient. Within them was a considerable volume of concealed unemployment.

---

[1] The persistence of this view of cattle, even among peoples well advanced in contact with the money economy has been noted by Colson, 'The Role of Cattle among the Plateau Tonga of Mazabuka District', *Rhodes-Livingstone Journal*, vol. xi (1951), pp. 12–46.

This applied particularly to male labour which, apart from its part-time employment in keeping the productive capital of the agricultural economy intact, made little contribution to output. The temporary absence of male labour could thus be tolerated without any short-term sacrifice in real product. But within the isolated indigenous economy, the narrowly circumscribed pattern of tastes offered little incentive for more sustained exertions.

The significance of the male's role in the traditional economic structure was quickly appreciated by the early European settlers in the Rhodesias. The money economy which they brought with them required labour and they turned to the indigenous economy to find it. Recognizing the character of the demands placed upon African men in their tribal community, prospective employers were prepared to engage African workers on a temporary basis. Three months of wage employment per year from each adult male was regarded as adequate to satisfy requirements in Southern Rhodesia shortly before the turn of the century.[1] Even so labour was not readily forthcoming in the desired amounts.[2] Inevitably, a time lag was required before the African could adjust his economic incentives to new circumstances.

Even the exposure to the wider horizons of the European's money economy and the novel assortment of goods which he brought with him did not in the early years result in a dramatic departure of African tastes from their well-established patterns. Some new consumption goods, of course, were introduced into the system by those Africans who became wage-earners. More remarkable was the extent to which their expenditure patterns were directed to the accumulation of goods which could be easily fitted into their traditional system. No precise statistical data are available on African money expenditure in the early years after European contact. But several items of qualitative information are illuminating. In Southern Rhodesia, the territory in which the impact of the money economy was heaviest, the increase in the number of African-owned cattle

---

[1] *Correspondence Relating to the Regulation and Supply of Labour in Southern Rhodesia*, Cmd. 1200 (July 1902), p. 7.

[2] Cf. discussion in chapter II of the measures adopted to accelerate the flow of African labour into wage employment.

and ploughs in the early years was impressive. Total African wage income (net of tax) was small. In 1900, it was estimated at £155,000 per annum.[1] By 1914, however, direct tax revenue collected from the native population had exceeded £248,000 and it was estimated that the native population purchased about £460,000 worth of 'imported goods'; (the latter calculation included only purchases of 'overseas' goods and excluded an unknown volume of expenditure on imports from South Africa).[2] Between 1902 (the earliest year for which estimates were compiled) and 1914, the number of African-owned cattle in the colony increased more than sevenfold — from roughly 55,000 to over 400,000. During the same period, African ownership of the plough, an implement unknown before Western contact, was estimated to have reached a figure exceeding 5,000.[3] Quantitative estimates of the same coverage were not prepared in the early years for the two northern territories. But the impressions of observers of the initial impact of the money economy in Northern Rhodesia and Nyasaland testify to the same phenomenon. Almost universally, the acquisition of money was accompanied by the introduction of the plough. The use of money for the purchase of cattle was precluded, of course, in the areas dominated by the tsetse fly. Where cattle culture had been a part of the traditional way of life, however, a significant share of money income was directed to accumulation in this traditional form. In part, the prevalence of this phenomenon is accounted for by the ravages of rinderpest which, shortly before European intervention, had decimated the herds of the cattle-keeping peoples of Central Africa.

While the initial introduction of the money economy was perhaps as much an instrument for the gratification of traditional wants as for the satisfaction of new ones, it did involve a partial alteration in the techniques of the peasant economy. The plough could be easily assimilated into the technology of the agricultural community and the effects of its use were far-reaching. The land area which could effectively be brought

---

[1] The Chief Native Commissioner calculated money income at £180,000 and hut tax paid to the government at £25,000. See letter to the Colonial Office from the Chief Native Commissioner, 26 May 1900, Cmd. 1200 (July 1902), p. 36.

[2] See *Annual Report of the Chief Native Commissioner of Southern Rhodesia, 1914*, especially p. 7.

[3] *Reports of the Chief Native Commissioner, passim.*

under cultivation was vastly increased. Formerly, the total
acreage under crops had been primarily a function of the size of
the population. The plough, however, made more extensive
farming a possibility. In the Southern Rhodesian case, the
impact of this new technique is demonstrated in the estimates
of acreages under cultivation. While the method of estimation
was admittedly crude and the absolute figures subject to a wide
margin of error, the trend revealed is unmistakable. According
to these estimates, the acreage under African cultivation more
than doubled in the first two decades of this century — a rate
of extension far in excess of even the highest estimates of population growth.[1]

The opportunities offered by the money economy for the
injection of capital into indigenous agriculture were not, however, reflected in corresponding increases in output. The
accumulation of cattle, although serving some economic as
well as non-economic purpose, was not primarily undertaken
out of consideration for the addition to the real income stream
which might accrue. Nor did the real capital formation through
land clearance and the use of the plough expand agricultural
productivity commensurately. For, while cultivation was more
extensive with the change in techniques, the increased area
could not be tilled with the same efficiency by the family
productive unit. As the Chief Native Commissioner for Southern
Rhodesia noted in 1917, the increase in scale of operations, in
some instances, meant that the cultivators were 'unable to give
the lands proper attention'.[2] The same tendency was commented upon by an official (later the director), of the Native
Agricultural Department in Southern Rhodesia who observed
in 1929 that 'we have the admission of Natives that higher
yields were obtained from hand-hoed lands. The misguided use
of the plough does not improve Native farming, but only
increases the acreage of poorly tilled lands'.[3] More recently, the
same difficulty has upset the calculations of the Northern
Rhodesia Agricultural Department in its attempts to implement a programme of improved African farming. The pro-

---

[1] *Annual Reports of the Chief Native Commissioner, 1902–1920, passim.*

[2] *Annual Report of Chief Native Commissioner, 1917*, p. 8.

[3] E. D. Alvord, 'Agricultural Life of Rhodesian Natives', *Southern Rhodesian
Native Affairs Department Annual, 1929*, p. 9.

gramme was primarily designed to encourage rotation practices and bonuses have been offered to African farmers adopting the Department's recommendations. A 1954 survey of an area in which the improved farming system had been partially intro-duced, produced the unexpected result that the yields of maize — the major crop in the area — were lower on the 'improved' farms than on the ones in which the recommended rotation had not been applied. Attempting to account for this result, the report commented:

It appears that a more or less direct relationship exists between the yield per acre and the number of acres planted with maize. The tendency exists for the maize yield to decrease with an increase in the area planted with maize, or conversely, for the highest yield per acre to be found on those farms where a relatively small acreage was planted with maize. One can deduce from the above that there is definite limit to the area that an African and his family can cultivate thoroughly and that where an African over-reaches this limit his crop inevitably suffers. This limit has been over-reached proportionately more often in farms in our improved group and consequently the average yield per acre of maize for the group as a whole has suffered.[1]

The initial impact of the money economy could thus occasion a shift in techniques within the indigenous agricultural com-munities. Some economies in the use of labour were thereby permitted, but it did not necessarily follow that real output of the family group advanced substantially. Larger acreages could be cultivated but at the expense of a reduction in output per acre.

The Indigenous Population and Land

In the Central African environment, the balance between population and land is clearly crucial to an analysis of the prospects and potentialities of the indigenous economy. Two aspects of this issue are relevant for consideration: one concerns the changes which the indigenous agricultural economies might

[1] A. M. Morgan Rees and R. H. Howard, *An Economic Survey of Commercial African Farming Among the Sala of the Mumbwa District of Northern Rhodesia* (Type-script), p. 32.

have been obliged to undergo even if they still remained in their isolated state; the other is concerned with the extent to which the circumstances of the indigenous agricultural economies have been altered as a result of the introduction of an external money economy. Empirically, these elements of the problem cannot be effectively separated. Formally, however, there is a legitimate distinction to be drawn between internal and external stimuli for change in the indigenous economic structure.

Investigators of population change in Central Africa are faced with formidable difficulties. Compared with most Western countries, the basic data are notoriously defective. No comprehensive census of the indigenous peoples in these territories has yet been undertaken. The available data — even for the period since 1930 — consist largely of well-informed estimates by the various native commissioners and a few sample population surveys. They are useful for the purposes of illustrating the long-term trends, although they cannot be profitably refined with elaborate statistical precision.

The problems of simple enumeration are serious enough in these territories; but there are also difficult problems of interpretation. The concept of the indigenous population is not entirely free from ambiguity in this context. It can be treated as the number of people legally regarded as resident within a particular territory, regardless of whether they are in fact present (i.e. the *de jure* population); or it may be defined as covering the *de facto* population, excluding those who are absent from the area in which they are officially registered; or, conceivably, the *de facto* population may be defined as composed of all Africans actually present within one territory including those who are technically aliens. In practice, the administrative arrangements of the Central African territories are best adapted to work with the legal concept of population. Every adult male is registered for tax purposes in one of the districts of his territory of origin. Although he may be absent from both the district and territory and in wage employment elsewhere, his official status usually remains unchanged unless residence in the territory of immigration is regarded as permanent.

The calculation of the number of adult male taxpayers has generally been the base upon which estimates of the total population have been constructed. The enumeration of the number of eligible taxpayers can, in most cases, be regarded as fairly reliable.[1] Serious error, however, may occur in the estimate of the population as a whole. The usual practice has been to inflate the number of indigenous taxpayers by a given factor, treating the result as a first approximation of the size of the total population which can then be adjusted in light of other information. But the factor used for this purpose has been altered from time to time.[2] This is a legitimate procedure, for there is no *a priori* reason to suppose that the number of eligible male taxpayers should remain a constant proportion of the total population. For the later years, some reassurance about the validity of these crude methods of estimation is supplied by the relative consistency between the results of sample censuses of population undertaken in the two Rhodesias and the independent estimates of the native commissioners.[3] No sample census of the same type has been conducted in Nyasaland. Systematic enumeration, apart from the annual estimates prepared by the Provincial Administration, has been undertaken on occasion; the most recent census attempts were made in 1931 and 1945.[4] Subject to the reservations already noted, the officially reported

[1] During war years, when the effectiveness of administration was reduced by shortages of staff, the estimates prepared are less reliable.

[2] In Southern Rhodesia, for example, the estimate of the indigenous population published for 1936 was lower than that shown for 1935. Pointing out that no real decrease had occurred, the Chief Native Commissioner noted: 'For many years, we have estimated the native population by a rule of thumb method which is now found to be inaccurate. In 1926, we had the same primitive method of estimating as in 1935' (*Report of the Chief Native Commissioner, 1936*, p. 2).

A further adjustment in procedure was made in 1949 after analysis of the results of the sample population survey made by the Central African Statistical Office.

[3] In Southern Rhodesia, the sample census result in August 1948 for the *de jure* population was 1,619,000 (fiducial limits of 44,800 at the 5 per cent. level of significance); this compares with the estimate of the Department of Native Affairs of 1,630,858 as of 31 December 1947. *Report of the Demographic Sample Survey of the African Population of Southern Rhodesia*, (The Central African Statistical Office, Salisbury, July 1951). The Northern Rhodesian comparison for 1950 is less close. The results of the sample survey indicated a *de jure* population of 1,837,000 (fiducial limits of 43,000 at the 5 per cent. level of significance); the comparable estimate of the Provincial Administration was 1,674,000. *Report of the 1950 Demographic Sample Survey of the African Population of Northern Rhodesia* (Central African Statistical Office, Salisbury, April 1952).

[4] The Nyasaland censuses, although marking a distinct advance from the approximations prepared in the other two territories, are far from flawless. Enumeration was made by inadequately trained native personnel. For a detailed criticism of the methods employed, see R. R. Kuczynski, *A Demographic Survey of the British Colonial Empire*, vol. ii (Oxford University Press, 1949), pp. 522–32.

changes in the African populations legally resident in the three territories may be observed in Table I.

TABLE I

ESTIMATED 'DE JURE' AFRICAN POPULATION IN SELECTED YEARS (000S)

	Southern Rhodesia	Northern Rhodesia	Nyasaland
1931	986·9	1,372·2	1,599·9
1936	1,088·7	1,366·0	1,620·1
1945	1,473·7		2,178·0
1946	1,546·8	1,547·7	
1950	1,755·6	1,674·0	2,340·5
1953	2,003·9	1,771·7	2,514·2
1957	2,282·8	1,947·1	2,660·0

Sources: Southern Rhodesia: *Annual Reports of the Chief Native Commissioner*; Northern Rhodesia: *Annual Reports on African Affairs*; Nyasaland: *Censuses of Population, 1931 and 1945; Annual Reports of the Provincial Commissioners.*

Although these estimates are subject to a considerable margin of error, particularly in the earlier years, a rapid rate of increase of the indigenous population of Central Africa is unmistakable. Southern Rhodesia presents the most striking rate of growth, with the African population apparently more than doubling itself in roughly a quarter of a century. The actual rate of increase during this period may be somewhat overstated in these estimates. The number of indigenous males on the tax registers has expanded at a rather slower rate. Although the methods for estimating the total population have been altered, the tax rolls have remained the foundation for the calculation of the aggregate. Present trends, however, are consistent with a high rate of growth in the African population of Southern Rhodesia. This was brought out in the 1948 sample census which provided data for the first time on birth and death rates. The results indicated a rate of natural increase of 2·81 per cent. per annum, a rate at which the population would be approximately doubled in 25 years.[1]

The rate of expansion in the Northern Rhodesian African population has proceeded at a less accelerated pace, but the contrast with Southern Rhodesia is probably less marked than a direct comparison of the 1931 and 1957 estimates would suggest. The earlier figure in Northern Rhodesia was probably

[1] See *1948 Demographic Sample Survey*, especially p. 8.

overstated and was subsequently adjusted downwards in later years; the estimate of the Provincial Commissioners in 1936, for example, represents a slight reduction on the total population reported for 1931.[1] In the later years, on the other hand, the official estimate may understate slightly the total size of the population. The results of the sample census of 1950 indicate that this may have occurred. Nevertheless, the rate of growth is probably slower than in Southern Rhodesia. The calculations prepared in the Report on the 1950 sample census indicated a natural increase at that time of 2·5 per cent. per annum which, if sustained, would double the indigenous population in 28 years.[2]

Because of the lack of uniformity in the methods of calculation, direct comparison of population change in Nyasaland and in the other two territories cannot be attempted in detail. The crude estimates of the total population in Nyasaland indicate a steady growth at a somewhat slower pace than in Southern Rhodesia although slightly higher than in Northern Rhodesia.[3] Part of this increase is accounted for by the influx of Africans from Portuguese territory for permanent settlement. Despite the Nyasaland Government's effort to check this flow, the numbers classified for census purposes as members of tribes from Portuguese East Africa increased by 61 per cent. between 1931 and 1945. (In absolute numbers, this represented an increase of about 145,000 between these years.) The influence of this factor in inflating the population of Nyasaland was more marked in the decade following the First World War. For the years between 1921 and 1931, the director of the census in Nyasaland ascribed roughly half of the increase in the total population to this immigration.[4] The extent to which the high volume of migration to wage employment outside Nyasaland

[1] For a devastating critique of the haphazard and frequently inconsistent methods used in estimating the African population of Northern Rhodesia in the 1920s and 1930s, see Kuczynski, op. cit., especially pp. 402–37.

[2] See *Annual Reports on African Affairs, Northern Rhodesia; Report on the 1950 Demographic Sample Survey of the African Population of Northern Rhodesia*, especially p. 8.

[3] It is interesting to note that these estimates of Central African population growth contrast sharply with the calculations prepared for the East African territories. Evidence presented to the East Africa Royal Commission suggested that the annual rate of increase in these territories between 1931 and 1948 was between 1 and 1·75 per cent. Cf. *Report of the East African Royal Commission, 1953–1955*, Cmd. 9475, pp. 31–32.

[4] *Reports of the Census, Nyasaland, 1931 and 1945; Annual Report of Native Affairs, Nyasaland, 1932*, p. 5.

may have lessened the natural increase in the population cannot be adequately ascertained. The census figures reflect the numbers whose legal domicile remains in the territory, and permanent absentees are thus excluded. As the 1945 census did not indicate an abnormal ratio of males to females in the population, there is some indication that the degree of permanent emigration is slight. This evidence, however, is hardly conclusive, as in the later years it is probable that a higher proportion of migrant workers taking extraterritorial employment have been accompanied by their families. The influence of temporary male migration for periods of two-year employment on the birth rate cannot, of course, be determined.

Although the quality of the statistical material on population in Central Africa is uneven and imprecise, the conclusion that a relatively rapid rate of growth has occurred is inescapable. This rate of growth, in itself, would imply some modification in the traditional agricultural systems, even in the absence of European settlement. To some extent, the upsurge in population and the presence of the European are causally related. One of the proudest boasts of the colonial administrator is that sound government and internal stability have removed the natural checks to population expansion which prevailed in pre-colonial Africa.[1] Without question, the abolition of the slave traffic, the prevention of inter-tribal warfare, and the introduction of European medicine and sanitation have eliminated some of the most serious restrictions to population growth. But, whatever its causes, the significant increase in the numbers of the indigenous peoples presents a new set of conditions and problems.

In the discussion of the balance between the size of population and the land resources available to it, no simple criteria of

---

[1] At the same time, European intervention may have imposed some limitations of an unfamiliar type on the expansion of the population. As the Social Security Officer of Southern Rhodesia pointed out in 1944: 'The evidence submitted on health matters points to a widespread incidence of bilharzia and hook-worm among the natives in particular, which it would appear (although statistics to prove it are non-existent) European occupation has done little to diminish, and unwittingly a great deal to increase. The artificial conditions of life imposed on the natives in employment have led to a great apparent increase in venereal disease which again cannot be measured, but about which every individual and society in contact with the problem has not the slightest doubt. The beginnings of tuberculosis are already evident . . . ' (*Report of the Social Security Officer, Southern Rhodesia, 1944*, Part I, p. 4.)

the conditions of an 'optimum' can usefully be employed. Certainly no static or universally applicable formula can be expected to contribute significantly to the analysis of the problem in Central Africa. Crude estimates of the density of population on the land can be prepared for the various territories. In Nyasaland, average density is much higher than in the Rhodesian territories. The 1931 census returns revealed an average density of nearly 43 inhabitants per square mile; in one district, density reached 297 per square mile. By the time of the 1945 census, the average of the *de facto* population alone had reached nearly 56 persons per square mile with the most densely settled district recorded with 310 persons per square mile.[1] Northern Rhodesia's much larger land area produces a figure for average density in the range of 6 inhabitants per square mile for 1950, using the sample census results as a guide to the *de jure* African population.[2] Concentrations of population in some districts are, of course, much heavier. It must be remembered that less than half of the total area of the territory is free of tsetse fly. In Southern Rhodesia, 1953 comparisons of the African population (*de jure*) with the areas assigned for African use indicate an average density of roughly 33 per square mile. If the native reserves alone are examined, the results obtained push the average density of the *de jure* population up to nearly 57 per square mile.[3]

These calculations are intended only for general comparisons. With imprecise population estimates, no exact assessment can be attempted. In any case, statistical averages, which obscure differences in the fertility of the soil and in rainfall, are independently of little value. As a general observation, however, it is apparent that there is a limit to the size of population which can

[1] Based on the *Reports of the 1931 and 1945 Censuses, Nyasaland*. The 1931 census enumerated only the *de jure* population. Average density, on a *de jure* basis, in 1945 was more than 59 per square mile. The computation of the averages was made officially on the basis of the total population (i.e. both native and non-native). The non-native population was less than 3,600 in 1931 and only just above 5,200 in 1945. The two calculations differ slightly in the measures of land area used; the 1945 census used a figure roughly 3 per cent. below that reckoned in 1931.

[2] Derived from the *Report on the 1950 Demographic Sample Survey of the African Population of Northern Rhodesia*, especially Table I, p. 14.

[3] Derived from *What the Native Land Husbandry Act Means to the Rural African and to Southern Rhodesia* (Government Printer, Salisbury, 1955), Tables XIII and XIV, pp. 29–30.

be accommodated within a restricted land area under the traditional forms of agricultural organization. For the *chitemene* system presupposes the availability of fresh areas for cultivation. If this condition ceases to hold, the African agricultural community will be forced to make some adaptations in its customary practices. This is not to suggest that there is any absolute standard against which 'overpopulation' or 'underpopulation' can be measured. On the contrary, these concepts are relevant only within a particular context and when the variables are assumed to be constant. If the limits of the *chitemene* system are reached, the indigenous agricultural community might adapt to new circumstances by shifting its technology, by introducing different varieties of output, or by altering its customary division of labour.

With but a few exceptions, the capacity of the unmodified *chitemene* system to accommodate population increase is approaching or has reached its limit in Central Africa. Nyasaland was the first territory in which the pressure was acutely felt.[1] Although its climate and physical environment are more hospitable to agricultural production than most other parts of the African interior, its total land area is far more restricted. In the more densely populated districts the government was early obliged to promote the substitution of settled for shifting cultivation. There was little alternative. By 1939, the situation on Native Trust Lands in the Southern Province had reached the state that eviction of tenants from private European estates was difficult because there was no room for them elsewhere.[2] The situation has deteriorated still further in the post-war years.

In Southern Rhodesia, the smaller population and the more extensive land area have delayed the abandonment of traditional agricultural practices. In the first few decades of colonization, fresh lands were still abundant and the system could continue with little interference. In fact, as has been noted, land

---

[1] On this point, the *Report of the Post-War Development Committee, 1945*, Zomba, observed (p. 111): 'The facts of rapidly increasing population and rapidly declining soil fertility have already been sufficiently emphasized to make it clear that the country's capacity for supporting its own people is under increasing strain. Study of a population map of Nyasaland and adjoining territories shows that the population density is already far greater in this country than in any of its neighbours. . . . '

[2] See *Report of the Provincial Commissioner, Southern Province, 1939*, p. 13.

brought under cultivation expanded dramatically with the importation of the plough. From 1930 to roughly 1950, the acreage estimated under African cultivation in the colony continued to expand, but at approximately the same rate as the increase in population.[1] Acreage estimates prepared by the Department of Native Agriculture have indicated little increase, and in some years a decrease, since 1950. (The reliability of these estimates is questionable.) Sample surveys of African agriculture taken in 1948–49 and 1954–55 indicated that, for the colony as a whole, acreage cultivated by Africans was continuing to expand at roughly the same rate as the population.[2] In some individual districts, however, further expansion had been checked. Northern Rhodesia stands out as the exceptional case in Central Africa. Quantitatively, land resources have been adequate to cope with an uncompromising form of shifting cultivation.

The above outline of the general situation can be misleading unless the demands placed upon the available land resources by European settlement have been drawn into account. While it is accurate to characterize the present situation in Central Africa at large as one in which population pressure on the land available for African cultivation will soon dictate agricultural adaptations, it is not the case that the increase in the indigenous population is alone responsible. In one sense, the 'shortage' of land is artificial. The most attractive agricultural lands in the Rhodesias have been denied to Africans and reserved instead for Europeans.

In varying degrees, European settlement has thus increased the urgency of a reformation of the customary agricultural systems by reducing the land areas available for cultivation in each of the territories. To a limited extent, this reduction has been compensated for by the application of European capital and skill to an expansion of the amount of land which could effectively be brought under productive cultivation. The eradication of the tsetse fly in some areas and the provision of water have both served this purpose. But, on balance, there can be

---

[1] *Reports of the Chief Native Commissioner, 1930–1954, passim.*

[2] *Report on the Sample Census of African Agriculture of Southern Rhodesia, 1948–49* (Central African Statistical Office, Salisbury, 1951). As yet, the results of the second survey have not been published. Information noted above has been supplied by the Director, Central African Statistical Office.

little question that the restriction in the available land areas has had the more pronounced effect.

Difficulties created by European claims are of course, most acute in Southern Rhodesia, the territory in which European settlement is heaviest. The implementation of the land segregation policies set out in the Land Apportionment Acts required restrictions not only to the expansion of African cultivation, but also the physical re-location of some established indigenous communities. In 1933, the Chief Native Commissioner of Southern Rhodesia estimated that 132,000 natives were within the European area as demarcated by the Act of 1930.[1] Compliance with the terms of the Act required their resettlement in the Native Reserves by 1937. Even at this relatively early date, officials of the Native Affairs Department were under no illusions about the practicability of resettlement. The Reserves were already well filled; the Native Affairs Department expressed doubts as to whether, in fact, it would be possible to accomplish the transfer to the Reserves as they then existed and indicated the need for development expenditure to improve their carrying capacity. By 1944, the position had worsened. As the Chief Native Commissioner reported:

> Implementation of the provisions of the Land Apportionment Act presents a problem of some magnitude. Not only are some of the Native Reserves and some of the Native Areas over-stocked, but some of both are overpopulated, and until it is possible to find and develop water supplies in a number of Reserves and Native Areas, the overflow of population and the removal of natives from the European area will not be possible.[2]

The post-war reports on native agriculture have been even less qualified. According to the calculations of the Southern Rhodesian Department of Native Agriculture, all five native provinces of the colony were overpopulated by 1954 and all but one were overstocked. Within the provinces, however, a few individual reserves are still regarded as capable of supporting a slightly larger population, but they are negligible in number.[3]

---

[1] *Report of the Chief Native Commissioner, Southern Rhodesia, 1933*, p. 2.
[2] Ibid., 1944, p. 162.
[3] See *Report of the Director of Native Agriculture, Southern Rhodesia*, 1954, esp. Chart VIII.

Adaptations in Indigenous Agriculture — Pressures and Possibilities

That pressures for fundamental reform in the traditional agricultural systems of Central Africa are now building up is abundantly apparent. But terms such as 'overpopulation' and 'overstocking' are relative and subject to differing interpretations. The basis on which the calculations for Southern Rhodesia have been prepared is itself of interest in reflecting the position which has now been reached. The official formula is derived, first, by assessing the total acreage of the native areas; from this, waste and unusable land is deducted. The remainder is regarded as alternatively for grazing or for arable cultivation. An estimate is then made of the number of people dependent for their living upon this land by subtracting the numbers of indigenous Africans resident in the urban areas from the estimated size of the total population. In effect, it is the *de facto* population on the land which is derived by this method. The combination of these calculations into an estimate of the degree of overpopulation presupposes criteria for determining the allocation of the available land between grazing and arable cultivation. The Director of Native Agriculture set out the procedure in 1946, stating that 'under present conditions, the minimum number of cattle or equivalent in small stock required per family to provide manure and compost to maintain fertility year after year on a small area of 6-10 acres of tilled land is six head'.[1] In other words, the techniques demanded by the introduction of settled cultivation require livestock to maintain the productivity of the soil; and livestock, in turn, compete with crops for the available land. Allowance is made in the official calculations for variations in the grazing possibilities by climatic areas. Thus, ten acres are regarded as the minimum for the maintenance of one beast in the high rainfall areas; thirteen and one-third acres in the medium rainfall areas; and sixteen and two-thirds acres in the low rainfall areas. These calculations yield the result that the minimum grazing requirement per family is 60, 80, and 100 acres respectively in the three rainfall areas.[2]

---

[1] Ibid., *1946*, p. 51. It may be noted that five goats or sheep are regarded as the equivalent of one head of cattle for these purposes.

[2] Ibid., pp. 48–49.

These computations of overpopulation and overstocking highlight the seriousness of the situation which is developing in the Native Reserves of Southern Rhodesia. But these estimates, in one respect, fail to provide a complete picture of conditions. They are based on a concept of practices which 'ought' to be followed, not on those actually used in African agriculture. Official thinking has long favoured the abandonment of shifting cultivation and concern has often been expressed about its destructive effects — particularly the erosion of soil which is encouraged by the burning of natural cover.[1] Settled agriculture has been officially recommended as the alternative, both as a means of preserving natural resources and of increasing the carrying capacity of the reserves. But before 1951, only a small-scale effort was directed towards improving the agricultural methods of the African. Even by 1954, when extension services for African agriculture had undergone a major expansion, only 25 per cent. of the African cultivators of the colony were believed to have been 'influenced by demonstrators' engaged in extension work; by 1957, this figure was still only 26 per cent. of the total.[2] Despite pressure on the land, primitive methods are still used by the bulk of the agriculturalists in the Native Areas of the colony.

The adoption of settled agriculture, at the minimum, will require a major departure from the techniques which have formerly characterized African agricultural practice. It may also alter the sexual division of labour within the indigenous agricultural community. Maintenance of soil fertility, which formerly took the form of clearing new land, must now be performed with the use of animal fertilizer. It is too early to judge the effects which this may have on the role of the adult male in the indigenous economy. Under the traditional arrangement, his function was well-defined. It may well be that the task of offsetting soil depletion will continue to be his responsibility. But, under different conditions, the discharge of this function may require more continuous exertions than formerly.

---

[1] See, for example, *Report of the Commission to Enquire into the Preservation, etc. of the Natural Resources of the Colony* (Government Printer, Salisbury, 1939).

[2] *Report of the Director of Native Agriculture* (published in the *Report of the Chief Native Commissioner*, 1954), Chart V, p. 29; 1957, Table IV, p. 52.

It must also be noted that the assumption of settled agriculture, which underlies the official estimates of the degree of overpopulation, itself implies that techniques, once changed, become static. Conceivably, the total land area available for cultivation could be extended by a further change in techniques — e.g. by substituting commercial for animal fertilizers in maintaining the productivity of the soil. This would imply the replacement of non-monetary by monetary forms of gross investment. But this can be a real possibility only when money income can be earned through sales of agricultural surpluses. The volume of marketable production above the consumption requirements of the family which can be achieved from six to ten acres of tillable land has obvious limits.

While the opportunities of earning a money income from agricultural production are restricted, the assumption of fixed techniques in African agriculture may be a realistic one. But no static assumption is appropriate to the consideration of population change. Its continued expansion makes more urgent either a further alteration in agricultural techniques, an expansion of the available land area, or the provision of employment for the population outside the African areas. The Southern Rhodesian Government has attempted to counter this problem with a radical revision in the pattern of African agriculture in the Native Land Husbandry Act of 1951. Under this legislation, the traditional system of communal land tenure is being scrapped and individual ownership put in its place. The size of the allowable individual holdings is based on the criteria examined earlier for establishing the extent of overpopulation — the standard holding in the high rainfall areas is six acres of arable and sixty acres of grazing land, with adjustment upward in this basic calculation in the less favoured districts. The Southern Rhodesian Department of Native Agriculture describes these holdings as 'economic units'.[1] Whether this is in fact the case may be open to question; but what is clear is that larger standard units were physically impossible without a large-scale dispossession of the indigenous agricultural population. That the definition of an 'economic unit' was adjustable to these realities was explicitly pointed out

[1] See *What the Native Land Husbandry Act Means to the Rural African and to Southern Rhodesia*, esp. p. 5.

in a discussion of the Native Land Husbandry Act which appeared in a 1958 official publication:

One of the basic concepts of the Act is the 'economic unit' which is deemed to be that allocation of arable and grazing land, varying with climate, soil, and other criteria, from which a family may be expected to derive a reasonable livelihood ... Had the act been applied ten years ago allocation could have been based on an average of 9 acres of arable land and 90 acres of grazing land. Had it been delayed another ten years the average would have come down to 4 acres of arable land and 45 acres respectively. As it is, the average today is about 6 acres of arable and 60 acres of grazing.[1]

It must be recalled that these calculations have been based on the estimates of the *de facto* population in African agriculture. The actual number of Africans indigenous to Southern Rhodesia is, of course, much larger. With only minor exceptions, the legal residence of all of the colony's Africans is still in the Native Areas. The discrepancy between this fact and the assumptions on which the Act had been planned has led to unforeseen difficulties. As the Under-secretary of the Department of Native Agriculture and Land Husbandry noted in his report for the year 1957:

By the end of 1956 the need for immediately stabilizing the number of people entitled to rights became apparent. Apart from the normal annual increase in cultivators in areas where the Act had still to be applied, as the Act became known many natives who originally had no intention of taking up land were flocking to the reserves and special native areas to put a plough or hoe into the ground so that they would be entitled to farming rights. If this process was allowed to continue unchecked it would mean that in many areas where it was possible to give every cultivator an economic

---

[1] 'African Economic Development in Southern Rhodesia', *Native Affairs Department Annual, 1958*, p. 47. Even the standard of six acres of arable and sixty acres of grazing land cannot be met in all cases. In these circumstances, the Department of Native Agriculture describes its procedures as follows: 'Under conditions of overpopulation the solution adopted has been to allocate on the basis of existing holdings, providing of course that no one gets more than the standard right (provision is made for variation in regard to chiefs, headmen, polygamous families, etc.). In such areas, there may therefore be many holders registered with small uneconomic units ... ', *What the Native Land Husbandry Act Means to the Rural African and to Southern Rhodesia*, p. 5.

holding it would no longer be possible to do so if the application of the Act was delayed.[1]

In face of this development, the scheduling of administrative work was rephased. The original plan had been to complete all phases of work — including surveying, demarcation and classification of soils, provision of soil protection works, and allocations of plots to individual owners — in one zone before proceeding to the next. This scheme was soon scrapped. Instead the Act was applied by proclamation to cover all Native Areas with the provision that farming rights were to be 'restricted to those persons who were cultivating land when the Act was applied to the area'.[2] This step was taken before the initial survey work had been completed.

The full effects of the Native Land Husbandry Act cannot yet be judged. But it should at least prevent a further fragmentation of the available acreage. Land rights may be sold or transferred, but no single African cultivator will be permitted, at least in the early stages, to acquire title to more than three standard holdings. Whichever effect predominates in the coming years — the prevention of fragmentation or permission of aggregation — it is apparent that with present techniques, little of the natural increase in the population can find room in the Reserves.

In Nyasaland, population pressure came to a head earlier, but the factors responsible were quite different. The much smaller area of the territory itself has been the primary cause. European occupation has claimed but little of the available land resources. And, on the land alienated for European ownership, a working compromise has been evolved to accommodate part of the overflow of population from African areas. This has taken the form of African tenancy agreements on European estates. The practice was brought under regulation and given official blessing in 1928. By 1945, 211,394 Africans were classified as resident on private estates, with more than 80 per cent. of them in the Shire Highland districts.[3] The tenants pays rent to the landlord in cash or in kind, an obligation not required of African cultivators in the Native Trust Lands. The

[1] *Annual Report of the Undersecretary, Department of Native Agriculture and Land Husbandry* (contained in the *Report of Secretary for Native Affairs*, 1957), p. 32.
[2] Ibid., p. 32.　　　[3] See *Nyasaland Census*, 1945.

social effects of this practice have not always been salutary. But it has at least minimized the competition between Europeans and Africans for the land resources of the Protectorate.

Much of Nyasaland's indigenous agriculture is now distinguished by the fact that population growth has meant a breakdown in traditional techniques. In the most densely populated sections of the Southern Province, for example, population density was estimated to be as high as 700 per square mile in 1955. This has meant, in turn, that the average size of family holding is no more than one to two acres in many districts. In districts of the less fertile Northern Province, however, the average family holding is still as much as 15 acres.[1] These conditions have obliged a break from the traditional form of *chitemene*. Continuous cultivation is now common in the most densely populated areas, although an alternation between crop and fallow periods is still possible in the less fertile northern regions. In the judgment of Nyasaland's Director of Agriculture however, 'the ratio of resting land to crop is inadequate to maintain fertility and is widening fast'.[2] Nor is soil fertility being maintained in the areas where settled cultivation has set in. The pressure of population and its demands for cropping land have all but eliminated grazing areas. In many parts of the Southern Province, 'grazing land is insufficient for more than a handful of livestock (the total cattle population of the province is 27,000 amongst 1¼ million people) and there is therefore practically no addition of organic manure to the land'.[3]

In Northern Rhodesia, circumstances are quite different. The quantity of land there is sufficient, in general, to permit an uncompromising form of *chitemene* to continue. But soil quality on average is unusually poor. As population continues to grow, pressures for change — which to date have appeared in only a few small districts — will intensify. One of the exceptions to the general rule is in the Northern Province about which the Department of Agriculture commented in 1956:

It is essential that agriculture should be stabilized in the Province within a reasonable period, because the indigenous system of *chitemene* cultivation is able to support only a very sparse population.

---

[1] *Outline of Agrarian Problems and Policy in Nyasaland* (Government Printer, Zomba, 1955), p. 1.

[2] Ibid., p. 2.   [3] Ibid., p. 2.

There are already signs of the system breaking down in certain areas, notably the Inamwanga triangle of Isoka district, where rather-above-average soil conditions have permitted too frequent cutting over of the bush.[1]

Time and European contact together are bringing or have brought fundamental changes to the balance between population and the land resources of Central Africa. But the impact of the money economy upon the organization of the indigenous agricultural communities cannot be measured in terms of these relationships alone. Introduction of the money economy has widened the economic horizons of the indigenous communities and afforded opportunities for increased real incomes. It will be recalled that the governing minority in the Rhodesias has not always been receptive to crop sales by Africans. Within the limits imposed by the system, African sales of cash crops have shown an upward trend in the past several decades. Marked fluctuations in sales occur, depending on the season, but the trend over the long period has been towards increased sales volume. Nevertheless, the basic subsistence character of the bulk of African agricultural production has not radically altered. The consumption requirement of the family is still the primary objective of production, and it is the surplus above immediate consumption which is made available for market. The substantial variation in sales between favourable and unfavourable seasons reflects this phenomenon.[2]

Market opportunities, however, are far from being evenly spread throughout the indigenous communities. In many cases, remoteness from marketing centres still rules out extensive crop sales. In the Rhodesias, the main arteries of the transport and communications network have been planned to link the

---

[1] *Annual Report of the Department of Agriculture, Northern Rhodesia*, 1956, pp. 10–11.

[2] On this point, the Native Production and Marketing Branch of the Native Affairs Department, Southern Rhodesia, has commented: 'It is necessary to stress ... that native agriculture is still predominantly for subsistence. The average annual production of all food crops by natives for the 4 years 1944–47 was 3,904,000 bags of which the average sales were only 538,000 or 13·7 per cent. In a year of good crops, the average sales are, of course, higher. [In 1948] it is estimated that 4,889,000 bags of foodstuffs were produced and 912,000 or 18·7 per cent. sold ... While it is true that in years of low yield the percentage sales drop, they do not disappear as the Native producer must realize some part of his crops for his cash needs' (published as a section of the *Annual Report of the Chief Native Commissioner, 1948*, p. 98).

European centres with the sea. Road systems in the African areas
have received low priority in the allocation of public expenditure. At times, it has even been questionable whether the
inadequate roads in the reserves have even been maintained.
This situation was vividly brought out for Southern Rhodesia by
its Chief Native Commissioner in 1954:

> It has now become quite impossible to cope with these com-
> munications on the small amount of money available ... Most
> Native Commissioners indicate a general deterioration in the
> condition of roads and in view of the fact that these, apart from
> being so essential to Native settlement and economy, are closely
> linked with the problem of soil conservation, it is obvious that more
> money will have to be made available to reclaim and improve the
> position.[1]

In the past few years, heavier appropriations have been made
for road work in African areas. But much yet remains to be done
before crop sales can be regarded as a genuine alternative open
to indigenous producers.

General Properties of the Indigenous Economy

While change is under way within the indigenous economies
of Central Africa, much that is familiar from the customary
structure of the days before European intervention still remains.
Moreover, despite local differences in detail, several important
features of indigenous organization are common throughout the
three territories. In all of them, the family unit is the basis of the
productive structure and self-sufficiency in its minimum consumption requirements is still the first target of its efforts. Each
of the indigenous communities in Central Africa has also been
obliged to work with soils which are not richly productive in the
first instance and which lose their fertility rapidly when tilled.
Traditional organization had worked out its own technique —
shifting cultivation — for overcoming this handicap. This, in
turn, produced a unique division of labour within the family
unit and called for a specialization of functions according to
sex and age.

New circumstances are now in the process of destroying the
foundations upon which the indigenous agricultural system was

---

[1] *Report of the Chief Native Commissioner, Southern Rhodesia, 1954*, p. 13.

originally built. But only in Nyasaland has a clear break with shifting cultivation yet been made. In Southern Rhodesia, the day is fast approaching when the old technique for maintaining soil fertility will no longer be possible. Plans for reform are now under way. A large gap still remains, however, between the practices recommended and promoted officially and those which are actually followed in African agriculture.

F

CHAPTER IV

THE ECONOMIC BEHAVIOUR OF
THE INDIGENOUS POPULATION

SOCIAL and political aspects of dualism in Central Africa (and most forcefully in the Rhodesias) do not provide unrestricted access to the indigenous peoples for participating in the opportunities created by economic expansion. But growth of the money economy has opened up channels through which Africans may improve their real income through contact with it. In order to appreciate whether or not the second criterion of economic development — i.e. that *per capita* real income for the indigenous peoples should grow through time — can be fulfilled, an assessment of the African's response to those opportunities which are open to him is appropriate.

One body of opinion has held that the peoples of underdeveloped economies tend to be indifferent to novel opportunities for economic improvement. This view is frequently expressed, for example, by European employers in the Rhodesias. Many of them have come to regard African workers as shiftless, lazy, and inefficient. The African is often held to have much stronger preferences for leisure than for the goods which can be acquired with a money income. Scepticism has therefore been voiced about the relevance of conventional assumptions on rational economic behaviour in such an environment.

Some professional economists have given their blessing to this view by citing a backward-sloping supply function for labour as a characteristic of underdeveloped economies. More recently, however, a quite different aspect of economic behaviour in the poorer countries has been emphasized. In place of preoccupation with the lack of response to economic advance, the argument has been made that the more basic problem may be an overly enthusiastic emulation of novel and higher levels of living on the part of poor peoples. The 'demonstration effect',[1] as Professor Nurkse has termed it, may lead the developing

[1] Ragnar Nurkse, *Problems of Capital Formation in Underdeveloped Countries* (Blackwell, Oxford, 1953), pp. 58 ff.

country — in the absence of controls — into serious balance
of payments difficulties and may mean that all or most of the
gains from higher incomes will be used for consumption and
little or none for capital formation.

It is clear that these two interpretations of the reception
given to economic change by indigenous peoples are not
ideally compatible. In order to establish more clearly the type
of assumptions about economic behaviour which are relevant
in Central Africa, an inspection of the response made by the
African peoples to opportunities for improvement in their real
income will be worth while. At the outset an important qualification concerning the type of the evidence which may bear
on this issue must be recognized. Empirical inquiries, by their
nature, are confined to subject matter which is measurable.
Legitimate scepticism may greet any of the social sciences — and
particularly economics — should claims to a 'scientific' account
of the mainsprings of human behaviour be offered. Motivations
cannot be satisfactorily measured nor can hypotheses concerning them be completely verified. Only behaviour (which is not
at all the same thing as motivation) can be observed. It is
nevertheless possible to draw inferences about motives from
observed behaviour and to formulate hypotheses on this basis
about the response which might be expected in new situations.
While these hypotheses cannot be conclusively tested, they can
at least be checked against subsequent observation.

Growth and expansion in the economy have opened two
significant channels through which Africans may increase their
real incomes: the sale of agricultural products and the sale of
labour to wage employers. The essential point is to establish the
way in which the indigenous peoples have responded to these
opportunities. But it must be remembered that these two
methods of acquiring money income are not always options
which are simultaneously open to members of the indigenous
community. In some circumstances, the African who seeks to
acquire money income may effectively have only one choice.
The physical barriers to the movement of goods and, at times,
a discriminatory bias in marketing arrangements may effectively preclude the acquisition of substantial sums of cash
through the sale of agricultural products. He then has only one
option: the sale of his labour. But these avenues into the money

economy may still be legitimately regarded as alternatives in the sense that that they compete for productive labour. The possible effects of this competition must now be considered.

From the preceding examination of the character of traditional agricultural systems, it is apparent that this problem is much more complex than some of the simplified models of economic theory would suggest. In the agricultural community, the division of labour by sex and age implies a specialization of function within the productive unit of the family. But the type of labour for which the money economy creates a demand has generally been restricted to one component of this productive unit — the adult male. Because his essential contribution to the production process does not occupy him fully, the effects of his withdrawal on the productivity of the agricultural community will depend on the length of his absence, the natural fertility of the soil, and the customary practices of his tribal group. Within Central Africa, the traditional theme of *chitemene* has afforded scope for numerous variations upon it. Piecemeal extensions to the land area can be made annually, while like amounts of land are retired from production. Alternatively, a larger area can be worked to exhaustion and the entire site of the kraal moved after several years.[1] Whatever the arrangement, adult man-power can hardly be spared from the traditional system for more than two to three years without a serious setback in output.[2] Despite local differences in practice, it is possible in any

[1] The piecemeal extensions practice is believed to be common among the tribes in Southern Rhodesia; (see *What the Native Land Husbandry Act Means to the Rural African and to Southern Rhodesia*, p. 1). An illustration of the other extreme may be provided from the experience of the Western Province in Northern Rhodesia: 'Where a form of *chitemene* is practised, an absence of more than two years on the part of the man has a serious effect upon the food supply of the family, since it is the man's work to fell the trees and gather branches, in the ashes of which the millet or kaffir corn is planted', *Report on the Western Province*, contained in the *Report on African Affairs, Northern Rhodesia, 1947*, p. 14.

[2] In areas in which contact with the money economy has produced alterations in the traditional sexual division of labour, a drain of more than half of the adult man-power still appears to reduce agricultural output. William Watson's study of the Mambwe people in Northern Rhodesia provides an interesting illustration. His studies of the Mambwe indicate that both men and women now use the hoe and that few specialized tasks remain. Even the lopping of trees (which is done only by adult males) is now often performed by co-operative work parties for the village as a whole. Nevertheless, roughly half of the adult man-power must be available in order to sustain production. Watson's conclusion is that a 'critical point is reached when there are more than two women to each man in the village:

case for the adult male to take temporary wage employment without reducing real agricultural output.

It would be erroneous to describe this situation as one of 'disguised unemployment', in the usual sense of the term. The marginal product of the adult male is not zero or negative, even though the short-term effects of his absence are negligible. Over the longer term, the indispensability of his contribution to total product will be felt — for the *chitemene* system depends for its longer-term viability upon his efforts. The practical arrangements of the labour market in Central Africa have partially attempted to reconcile the requirements of the money and indigenous economies for male labour. If a system of migration between the two economies functions perfectly, it can work to the economic advantage of both. The indigenous agricultural community can continue to operate as an economic unit and, further, its real income is supplemented by cash receipts. To the wage employer, the transient character of the labour force made available by these arrangements may not be desirable. But he is compensated for this inconvenience by his ability to obtain labour at a lower wage rate than would be the case if the labourer and his family, not just the labourer himself, were dependent on money wages for their livelihood.

But it is also possible that the African male may increase the real income of his family while remaining in the indigenous agricultural community. This might occur if he were prepared to extend himself more fully and to make a continuous contribution to agricultural production. Surpluses might then be produced for market. Under the original closed conditions of the indigenous economy, there was little incentive for this additional effort. But the fresh opportunities of the money economy may call forth this response. It must be restated, however, that access to markets for agricultural crops is not uniform throughout Central Africa.

In an examination of the effects of contact between the indigenous and money economies, it would be useful to establish empirically the variations in output of the indigenous agricul-

anything higher than this disrupts both the economy and social life . . . ', see William Watson, *Tribal Cohesion in a Money Economy: a Study of the Mambwe People of Northern Rhodesia* (Manchester University Press for the Rhodes-Livingstone Institute, 1958), p. 34.

tural systems with particular reference to the effects of migrations of male labour upon it. The statistical data required for a precise demonstration are lacking. Crude estimates on output in African agriculture have been prepared for Southern Rhodesia, but they are subject to a wide margin of error. The most reliable clue to output changes is probably to be found in an examination of the volume of cash sales of African-grown production. Although not free of ambiguity, the sales estimates are at least much more accurate than the output statistics.

An indication of the types of response which have been made to the money economy in Central Africa can be obtained by analysing the administrative provinces within each territory and by assessing their relative contribution to the total sales of cash crops and to total wage employment. The selection of administrative provinces as the basis for classification is not ideal; the large areas covered by each can conceal considerable local variations within the province. But the data available dictate the use of provincial units. Nor do the available data illuminate identical time periods in all three territories. Given the limitations of the material, no definitive conclusions can be sustained. But the relationships revealed may provide a basis for some tentative hypotheses.

Wage Employment and Agricultural Sales in Northern Rhodesia

Of the three territories, Northern Rhodesia presents the simplest case. The districts in which agricultural production for market is possible are limited to a relatively small proportion of the total African area of the territory, primarily to the land adjacent to the line of rail. Maize is the major cash crop and its marketing is controlled by a government-sponsored control board. Effectively, this means that marketing opportunities are concentrated primarily in the Southern and, to a lesser extent, Central Provinces.[1] In the Eastern Province, some African-grown maize is sold and in recent years ground-nuts have been produced for sale under governmental encouragement. But the isolation of the Province rules out a heavier concentration on

[1] Operations of the Maize Control Board, the principal buyer of African maize, are concentrated in the Railway belt — i.e. the Southern and Central Provinces; see *Reports of the Maize Control Board, Northern Rhodesia.*

production for market.[1] In agricultural production, as in almost every other respect, Barotseland stands out as unique in Central Africa. Although opportunities for market production are limited by the lack of communications, its more favourable natural endowment and higher real income standards — factors which have permitted the Barotse peoples to retain a unique degree of political autonomy — place the province in a separate economic classification.

The distribution and the relative concentration of agricultural production in Northern Rhodesia is well reflected by the official estimates, by province, of the numbers of agricultural implements and of cattle. The provinces which have been able to enter the money economy through the sale of cash crops virtually monopolize the holdings of these forms of agricultural capital. The number of ploughs in use in the most favoured area (the Southern Province) increased nearly fivefold, for example, between 1947 and 1954. Still more striking is the fact that the Southern Province consistently claimed roughly 70 per cent. of the total number of ploughs in the entire territory throughout this period.[2] The other province adjacent to line of rail, the Central Province, is less well favoured for profitable agricultural production. The accumulation of agricultural equipment there, however, has proceeded at roughly the same rate, but the aggregates involved are considerably smaller. The late introduction of the possibilities of commercial agriculture into the Eastern Province is revealed in the same data. Market outlets have only recently been opened. While the aggregate accumulation of agricultural implements there is still small, the rate of increase in recent years has been rapid. Barotseland and the Central Province stand roughly on par with one another in the accumulation of implements, although the former concentrates more heavily on cattle as an asset, being exceeded in its holdings only by the Southern Province. In the remaining provinces of

[1] Market opportunities for African maize production in the Eastern Province have increased substantially since 1950, although local sales have tended to drop recently 'mainly through European Farmers becoming more self-sufficient . . . The large surplus gives some cause for concern . . . The distances of the Eastern Province from railhead are great — Lusaka 250 to 350 miles and Salima 150 to 250 miles — and there is a possibility of difficulty in the future in disposing of the surplus at an economic price', *Annual Report of the Department of Agriculture, Northern Rhodesia, 1954*, p. 4.

[2] *Annual Reports on African Affairs, Northern Rhodesia, 1947–1954.*

the territory, both the accumulation of agricultural capital and sales of cash crops are negligible.[1]

In an assessment of the extent to which the various provinces supply wage labour, two types of estimates can be cross-checked against one another. For selected years since 1941, estimates by the Provincial Administration and the Northern Rhodesian Department of Labour have been prepared. These are designed to indicate the average numbers of male taxpayers at work for wages from each of the provinces. The basis of estimation is hardly precise, but the results provide some indication of the relative orders of magnitude. For 1950, these can be compared with the independent estimates brought out in the sample census of the African population.

The results of the Northern Rhodesian Government's estimates since 1941 are shown in Table I. The pre-1951 and post-1951 estimates for the Western and Northern Provinces are not comparable because of boundary redefinitions with the creation of the North West Province. In other respects, the geographical areas described are roughly uniform throughout the period.

A comparison between this form of estimate by province and the results of the 1950 sample census reveals a high degree of consistency in the pattern. The definitions employed in the two calculations are not identical but are sufficiently uniform to warrant comparison in Table II. The Provincial Commissioner's estimates are based on the average number of male taxpayers employed for wages; the sample census results, on the other hand, distinguish the numbers of males over puberty in the *de jure* and the *de facto* populations. The difference between these two magnitudes is expressed below as a percentage of the *de jure* population and can be regarded as a rough index of the number of adult males absent in wage employment on census day.

As a tentative generalization, it would appear that in the areas in which agricultural production for market can be carried on successfully the absence of male labour for wage employment is relatively lower than in the provinces in which agricultural production is a less profitable alternative. Clearly this is the case in the Southern Province. It is at the top of the scale in cash crop production and at or near the bottom in the

[1] *Annual Reports on African Affairs, Northern Rhodesia, 1947-1954.*

relative number of wage earners it supplies. Its only rival in the latter respect is Barotseland where agricultural production is attractive, if not for a cash market. The Eastern Province, where opportunities for sale of cash crops are of recent origin, has generally exported labour in volume. But the migration into wage employment tended to show a decline after market

TABLE I

ESTIMATES OF THE PERCENTAGE OF MALE TAXPAYERS AT WORK
FOR WAGES FROM THE VARIOUS PROVINCES OF NORTHERN RHODESIA
FOR SELECTED YEARS

	Central Province	Eastern Province	Southern Province	Barotse Province
1941	49	62	33	44
1944	55	71	39	48
1947	52	55	33	45
1950	52	57	38	41
1952	63	53	41	37
1954	60	58	38	38
1957	61	61	39	42

	Western Province	Northern Province	North West Province
1941	35	40	
1944	36	43	
1947	43*	43*	
1950	47	52	
1952	46	59	36†
1954	55*	59*	45
1957	56	59	51

Sources: Calculated from Northern Rhodesian *Reports on African Affairs* and *Labour Department Annual Reports*. For 1941 and 1944, data on the Kaonde-Lunda Province have been consolidated with that for the Western Province. The former was officially merged with the latter in 1947.

* Two districts from the Northern Province were shifted to the jurisdiction of the Western Province in 1947; the same two districts were transferred back to the Northern Province in 1953.

† North West Province was created from outlying areas of the Western Province in 1951.

opportunities, though still limited, appeared. In the Northern and Western Provinces, almost no entry into the money economy through the sale of agricultural products is possible, both because of the poverty of the soil and the absence of communications. These provinces, in recent years, have been near the top of the scale of absentee males. The insulation of these districts from the influences of the money economy is indicated by the relatively low rates of absenteeism from these remote districts in the earlier years. The Central Province might at first inspection appear a departure from the pattern. Much of the province has the advantage of proximity to the line of rail.

TABLE II

COMPARISON BY PROVINCES IN NORTHERN
RHODESIA, 1950, OF THE PERCENTAGE OF
MALE TAXPAYERS AT WORK FOR WAGES
(PROVINCIAL COMMISSIONERS' ESTIMATES)
AND THE PERCENTAGE OF MALES OVER
PUBERTY ABSENT (SAMPLE CENSUS
ESTIMATES)

	Provincial Commissioners' estimates	Sample census
Central	52	58
Eastern	57	56
Southern	38	40
Barotse	41	38
Western	47	43
Northern	52	53

Sources: Calculated from the *Report on the Demographic Sample Survey of the African Population of Northern Rhodesia*, 1950, and Table I.

But apart from the few localities in which cash crop production is undertaken, the soil conditions of its African areas are poor.[1] Thus, for the province as a whole, the high rate of absenteeism is not inconsistent with localized production for market.

Wage Employment and Agricultural Sales in Nyasaland

The analysis of this problem in Nyasaland becomes a more complex matter. The data are not completely comparable with the types of material available on the Rhodesias and more qualitative and indirect methods of assessment are required. The locus, by provinces, of production of cash crops and of the distribution of population presents few difficulties. But the distribution of wage-earners by province of origin cannot be ascertained with even the same limited degree of certainty. Some guides to the province of origin of labour seeking employment outside the territory are available. But a complete picture must also draw into account African wage-earners employed

[1] See *Report of the Land Commission, Northern Rhodesia, 1947*, p. 18.

within the territory. Their provincial origin, apart from a relatively few years, cannot readily be established. In terms of total volume of wage employment given to the indigenous peoples of the territory, however, external employers are numerically more important than employers of wage labour within the Protectorate.[1]

Among the three provinces of Nyasaland, neither population nor commercial agricultural activity is uniformly distributed. The estimated total population (*de jure*) of the territory is divided roughly as follows:

Northern Province:	14 per cent.[2]
Central Province:	37 per cent.
Southern Province:	49 per cent.

Agricultural production for market is heavily concentrated in the Central Province. The high-value African crop for export, tobacco, is largely grown in this province, with the Southern Province contributing a small share of the total. Since 1949, the Central Province has dominated the sale of food crops in the post-war years. Agricultural production for the money economy in the Northern Province, on the other hand, has been negligible. The Southern Province occupies a middle position. Its principal source of money income is from cotton production. But even with its denser and larger population, its aggregate cash earnings cannot rival those of the Central Province.[3]

Within Nyasaland, employment opportunities by province are also disproportionate. The bulk of the European estates and enterprises are situated in the Southern Province. Roughly 80 per cent. of the wage employment within the territory has been offered there.[4] In the average post-war year, the Central Province has provided approximately 15 per cent. of the local wage-earning opportunities. Wage employment in the Northern

[1] Based on a comparison of the estimates of Nyasaland labourers employed inside and outside the Protectorate as reported in the *Colonial Annual Reports, Nyasaland*. Both sets of estimates are highly imprecise. The figures for local employment for wages are crude assessments based on voluntary returns submitted by employers of ten or more Africans showing their labour requirements in the peak periods of the year.

[2] Based on the *Census Report, 1945* and subsequent *Annual Reports of the Provincial Commissioners, Nyasaland*.

[3] *Reports of the Department of Agriculture* and *Annual Reports of the Provincial Commissioners, Nyasaland*.

[4] *Reports of the Labour Department, Nyasaland*.

Province is of little consequence; the government is almost the only wage employer in the province. Only a crude estimate can be made of provinces of origin of locally employed wage labour. Calculations have been prepared by government labour officers but they do not indicate the areas of origin of all wage employees; instead they cover only those adult male employees in regular employment in the peak periods of the year. This leaves unaccounted for some 20 per cent. of the wage labour force which is casually employed. Nevertheless, these estimates are broadly consistent with the pattern of provincial location of employment. Although there is some inter-provincial migration into wage employment within the Protectorate, the proportion of local wage employees drawn from each province is approximately the same as the share of total employment offered within each province.[1] Thus, three-quarters to four-fifths of the indigenous workers employed for wages within the Protectorate are from the Southern Province.

For the consideration of the provincial origin of Nyasaland wage-earners taking employment outside the territory, two types of data are available. One is the estimates based on the 1945 census which classified the absent males over 18 years of age by province. The results indicated that just under one-third of the total adult male population of the territory was absent from the Protectorate. Proportionately, the Northern Province was most significant: 65 per cent. of its adult males were regarded as absentees. This was followed by the Central Province with 32 per cent. absentees and the Southern Province with 24·6 per cent.[2] Some indication of the post-1945 trend in emigration is afforded by the annual issues of identification certificates to emigrants leaving the territory for employment outside. These returns, however, can provide only a qualitative guide to the trends; the possibilities of evasion are such that they cannot be regarded as measuring the full extent of emigration. Nor — and this is a more serious flaw in the data — can they offer any indication of the degree of permanence of absenteeism. It can hardly be safely assumed that the duration of extra-territorial employment will be uniform for the various provinces.

[1] Based on data contained in the *Reports of the Labour Branch of the Provincial Administration* and the *Reports of the Department of Labour, Nyasaland.*
[2] *Census of Population, 1945, Nyasaland.*

The provincial classification of adult males to whom passes were issued for work outside Nyasaland, reveals several developments of interest. The returns are shown in Table III.

TABLE III

ISSUES OF IDENTIFICATION CERTIFICATES FOR EMPLOYMENT
OUTSIDE NYASALAND, BY PROVINCES, 1942–57

	Northern	*Central*	*Southern*
1942–7	6,912	14,267	13,147
(average exodus)			
1948	6,856	13,749	13,315
1949	6,473	13,883	12,046
1950	6,151	14,914	11,316
1951	6,304	23,404	12,993
1952	8,849	26,277	18,345
1953	8,024	26,682	18,091
1954	8,130	30,402	23,134
1955	7,246	31,976	26,964
1956	7,387	31,298	33,619
1957	7,384	33,152	33,810

Sources: *Reports of the Labour Branch of the Provincial Administration* and *Reports of the Department of Labour.*

As the table indicates, the Northern Province which, relative to its population, was the main supplier of wage employees for work outside the territory up to 1945, has maintained a fairly steady rate of emigration in the post-war years. The fact that the proportion of wage-earners outside the territory has been high in relation to its population is, in part, the result of official policy. When recruiting of Nyasaland males for employment in Southern Rhodesia and South Africa was given official sanction in 1935, the government specified that recruiting organizations would be permitted to operate only in the Northern Province. This did not prevent some natives of the Southern Province from travelling northwards to sign labour contracts. But the numbers taking this course were not believed to be large.[1] No barrier existed to the exodus of labour from any province on a voluntary basis; only the organized recruiting of labour on long-term contracts was localized.

The trend toward higher rates of exodus in the post-war years is notable in the other two provinces, especially in the Central Province. This, at first glance, appears surprising. It might have been expected that the Northern Province, where opportunities

[1] See *Report of Provincial Administration, Southern Province, 1938*, p. 16.

for acquiring money income locally are extremely limited, would continue to contribute a higher proportion of total absentees than its share of the population. Similarly, the Central Province, with the most favourable prospects for cash crop production, would supply a lower proportionate share of the wage employees. The Southern Province should occupy a middle position, if it is to be maintained that cash crop production in fact competes with wage employment.

Although a precise quantitative judgement cannot be reached, closer inspection indicates that the apparent inconsistency may not in fact be a real one among the provinces of Nyasaland. In interpreting the statistics on rates of exodus, it must be remembered that the duration of absenteeism is likely to be greater in the Northern Province than elsewhere. This is due to the concentration of organized recruiting in this province. Labour engaged on fixed contract is more likely to be absent for longer periods than that which emigrates on an informal basis. Thus, while the turnover (as measured by the issues of passes to emigrate) may be higher in one province, it does not follow that the percentage of males in external employment is also higher. Moreover, in the case of the Northern Province, it is necessary to recall that the percentage of males in external employment was initially much higher than in the other two provinces; in 1945, 65 per cent. of the adult males were treated as absent. As a result, the possibilities of accelerating the flow of emigrant labourers have been much more restricted. Thus, it may yet be that the Northern Province still contributes more than its proportionate share to total wage employment.

The apparent discrepancy in the relative position of the Central and Southern Provinces must now be considered. The former contains the heaviest concentration of cash crop production and has a lower population than the latter. But the estimates of emigration into wage employment indicate that the Central Province has in many years surpassed the Southern. In an interpretation of this phenomenon, the availability of local wage employment must be drawn into account. As has been noted, the breakdowns available for post-war years on the province of origin of Nyasalanders employed regularly for wages within the territory reveal that 75 to 80 per cent. are from the Southern Province. The statistics available do not permit a detailed aggregation of the contribution of each province to total wage employment (including both internal and external). But the data suggest that a higher proportion of the population of the Southern Province is employed for wages than in the Central Province. The dominance of the former in home employment for wages more than offsets the slight apparent lead which the latter has at times maintained as a supplier of external wage employees.

As a tentative hypothesis, the generalization that wage employment and agricultural sales vary inversely can be retained for Nyasaland. But this judgement can only be supported by some qualitative interpretations and must remain open to amendment pending the availability of more satisfactory data.

It remains to explain the accelerated rate of emigration from the Central and Southern Provinces in recent years. This exodus has occurred during a period of record prosperity for the producers of cash crops in the territory. It is likely that this paradoxical phenomenon is accounted for in large measure by the high population densities of the two provinces in which cash crop production is attractive. Owing to the crowding on the land, the population has in fact been forced into wage employment. A closer analysis of this factor will be taken up in later discussion.

Relationships between Wage Employment and Agricultural Sales in Southern Rhodesia

Of the three territories, Southern Rhodesia is the most complicated and the most interesting case. Lines of demarcation between the provinces selling agricultural products and those in which cash sales are negligible cannot be as clearly drawn as in the other two territories. In favourable seasons, each province acquires some money income through agricultural marketing. But an additional complicating feature is the considerable variation in the types of product offered in the various provinces.

For administrative purposes, Southern Rhodesia is divided into five native provinces. Each indigenous African is regarded as maintaining a legal residence in one of them, even though he may have settled in wage employment in the urban centres.

Applying this *de jure* concept of population, two independent estimates of the inter-provincial distribution of the population are available. One is based on the 1948 sample census of the African population; the other on the 1950 estimates of the Native Affairs Department. As shown in Table IV, the two are reasonably consistent with one another.

The assessment of the contribution of each of these provinces to the aggregate sales of agricultural output must be conducted in two stages. The first will deal with the sale of food crops; later, the marketing of cattle will be considered. From 1948 to 1954, sales returns through the government marketing organization are available for the five principal food crops: maize, munga, rupoko, ground-nuts, and kaffir corn. With the excep-

TABLE IV

PERCENTAGE DISTRIBUTION OF THE 'DE JURE'
AFRICAN POPULATION OF SOUTHERN RHODESIA BY
PROVINCES

	1948 *Sample census*	*1950* *Native Affairs* *estimates*
North Mashonaland	25	26
South Mashonaland	17·5	17
Midlands	22·5	21
Manicaland	15	15
Matebeleland	20	21

Sources: Calculated from *1948 Sample Census*; 1950 Estimates of the Native Affairs Department, Southern Rhodesia, as calculated from the *Official Yearbook of Southern Rhodesia, 1952*, p. 107.

tion of maize (which has been marketed through official or quasi-official channels since 1931), earlier estimates of the provincial contributions to sales are not reliable. The post-1948 figures, although adequate to establish the general trends, are still unsatisfactory in several respects. Estimates of the total value of African produce sold have been prepared by the governmental marketing boards. These, however, are based on a marketing year ending in May and do not distinguish the province of origin of the produce sold. The later deficiency is remedied by the calculations prepared by the Marketing Branch of the Native Affairs Department, but its estimates are prepared on a calendar year basis. As a result, there are some minor discrepancies in the aggregate sales figures from the two sources. In most years, the divergence is not serious, and the two types of data can be reasonably combined to provide a broad breakdown of the distribution of money income from crop sales between the provinces. It should be noted that the data do not permit a detailed adjustment to allow for the differences in prices paid to producers due to quality variations. Working with average values of marketed production, therefore, implicitly assumes that quality of production is reasonably

TABLE V

VALUE OF FIVE PRINCIPAL CASH CROPS SOLD BY EACH PROVINCE IN SOUTHERN RHODESIA, 1948–54
(£000s)

	North Mashonaland	South Mashonaland	Midlands	Manicaland	Matabeleland
1948	656	228	245	135	77
1949	219	118	306	98	55
1950	918	210	344	216	53
1951	287	133	111	77	13
1952	1,214	382	482	198	28
1953	1,411	504	487	507	151
1954	1,376	333	383	261	105

Notes and Sources: These results have been derived by calculating the average value per ton for maize, munga, kaffir corn, rupoko, and ground-nuts for each year from data reported by the Native Production and Marketing Branch in its *Annual Reports* and in *What the Native Land Husbandry Act Means to the Rural African and to Southern Rhodesia*, Table XVIII, p. 30. Aggregate values by province have then been calculated from the returns, by province, of quantities sold as shown in the *Annual Reports of the Production and Marketing Branch, Department of Native Affairs, 1948–54*. These returns are based on the records of the Grain Marketing Board, as adjusted to a calendar year.

uniform throughout the territory. In any case, the quality variations which may occur are not likely to cause significant distortion to a general analysis of income distribution by provinces.[1]

For the seven-year period 1948–54, the approximate distribution of the money values of the five principal cash crops has been calculated as shown in Tables V and VI.

Because of the seasonal variations which have unevenly affected

---

[1] A further qualification must be noted. The statistical evidence available refers to the value of crops sold which is not the same as the income received by the African producer. Levies are deducted from the sale price to cover marketing costs and contributions to the Native Development Fund. The rate of levy, however, is standardized throughout the colony. Moreover, the levy, as a proportion of the total value of the product sold, has been roughly the same for each of these crops during this period.

G

the agricultural production of the various provinces, a more accurate general picture of the position of each can be obtained

TABLE VI

PERCENTAGE OF THE ANNUAL AGGREGATE MONEY VALUE OF THE FIVE PRINCIPAL CASH CROPS ATTRIBUTABLE TO EACH PROVINCE OF SOUTHERN RHODESIA, 1948–54

	North Mashonaland	South Mashonaland	Midlands	Manicaland	Matabeleland
1948	49	17	18	10	6
1949	28	15	38	12	7
1950	53	12	20	12	3
1951	46	21	18	12	2
1952	53	16	21	9	1
1953	46	16	16	17	5
1954	56	14	16	11	4

Notes and Sources: Calculations are derived from the sources shown in Table V. Percentages shown have been rounded.

by aggregating the sales of the main cash crops over the seven-year period. The contribution of each province to the total marketed value from 1948 to 1954 appears as follows:

TABLE VII

PERCENTAGE OF THE AGGRE-GATE VALUE OF THE FIVE PRINCIPAL CASH CROPS ATTRI-BUTABLE TO EACH PROVINCE OVER THE SEVEN-YEAR PERIOD 1948–54

North Mashonaland	49
South Mashonaland	15
Midlands	19
Manicaland	12
Matabeleland	4

Sources: as shown in Table V.

The striking features in this allocation of money income from the sale of cash crops are the predominant position of North Mashonaland and the negligible contribution from Matabeleland. The other three provinces display a generally uniform pattern; the ordering of their contribution to cash sales corresponds to their relative shares of the total population.

In Southern Rhodesia, money income may also be acquired by African agriculturists through the sale of livestock, primarily of cattle. To the African community, however, this method of entering the money economy is different in character from the sale of surplus foodstuffs. In large measure, cattle are still regarded in the traditional sense; i.e. as a store of value and not as a source of income. Voluntary sales of cattle occur in the years of bad harvests when disinvestment is made to acquire the minimum current requirements of cash. The extent to which this view persists is borne out in the trends in cattle sales. For the years since 1930, crude estimates of cattle marketings have been prepared annually for Southern Rhodesia. Without exception, the years of poor crops have been associated with an increase in cattle sales.[1] But in recent years, the main factor influencing the increasing volume of African cattle sales has been non-voluntary. The government has imposed a programme of de-stocking which, in effect, has meant compulsory marketing. Although not always welcomed, this has supplemented the money income of the agricultural African population. As a regular source of income, the African farmer generally prefers to sell crops rather than cattle. Even with compulsory de-stocking, the aggregate of cattle sales in the post-war years of good harvests has run at roughly one-third the total value of marketed crops. The pattern alters in unfavourable crop seasons. Then the African taps his emergency reserves, cattle sales expand and can exceed crop sales in value.

The provincial allocation of money incomes from cattle sales cannot be precisely established. In part, this is a consequence of the manner of marketing. That portion of the total which is bought by the government's Cold Storage Commission and the value of sales enforced through the implementation of compulsory de-stocking are reliably recorded. But some sales of African-owned cattle are made directly to private butchers and to European farmers who purchase feeder stock from Africans. The latter transactions escape accurate accounting, although the Native Affairs Department estimates the numbers involved. In an attempt to establish the role of the various provinces in the cattle trade, only crude approximations are thus possible. The relative position of the provinces is probably reasonably represented by the estimates of the Department of Native Agriculture of the average number of cattle held per resident

[1] This conclusion is apparent from a comparison of the variations in cattle sales with the sales of cash crops as estimated in the *Reports of Chief Native Commissioner*.

family in each of the provinces. In 1954, for example, this can be established as follows:

North Mashonaland	—	3·3 cattle per family[1]
South Mashonaland	—	4·2 ,, ,, ,,
Midlands	—	4·85 ,, ,, ,,
Manicaland	—	2·9 ,, ,, ,,
Matabeleland	—	7·5 ,, ,, ,,

To the extent that this pattern of distribution of cattle holdings corresponds to the sales of cattle by province, it would be expected that Matabeleland would be the major seller, followed by the Midlands and South Mashonaland. Cattle sales would be lowest in North Mashonaland and Manicaland.

In the provincial returns of the weight and grade sales organized by the government, this general pattern appears to hold. In 1954 and 1955, for example, the sales in Matabeleland were well in excess of those in any other province. South Mashonaland and the Midlands occupied a middle position. North Mashonaland and Manicaland were minor contributors to the national aggregate.[2] The coverage of this data, of course, is not complete. But the consistency of the pattern suggests that some adjustments are appropriate in the initial estimate of the provincial allocation of money income from agricultural production. With the inclusion of money income from cattle sales, it appears that the provincial distribution of income based on crop sales understates the proportionate shares of Matabeleland, South Mashonaland, and the Midlands. Similarly, the relative shares of North Mashonaland and Manicaland are probably somewhat overstated.

With these amendments, a comparison can now be made between the provincial distribution of money income and the distribution of population. North Mashonaland, with a quarter of the total population, is, by any reckoning, the richest of the group. Even when its commanding position in crop sales is adjusted downward, its leadership in total income is not

[1] Calculated from data contained in the *Report of the Director of Native Agriculture, Southern Rhodesia, 1954*, especially Charts VIII and VIII-A, pp. 38–40 (published as part of *The Report of the Chief Native Commissioner, 1954*).

[2] *Report of a Commission of Inquiry on the Marketing of Cattle for Slaughter and the Distribution and Sale of Beef in Southern Rhodesia*, C.Fed. 31, 1956, Appendix II, p. 30.

challenged. At the other end of the scale, Matabeleland is still relatively the poorest with one-fifth of the *de jure* population. Its poor showing in crop sales is partially offset by its leading position in cattle sales. But its regular share of total agricultural income is probably still considerably lower than its share of the population. Of the three provinces in the middle position with respect to crop sales, the considerations introduced by the sale of cattle indicate that Manicaland is probably relatively poorer than the other two. With 15 per cent. of the population, it earns roughly 12 per cent. of cash-crop income; but its relative total income figure is actually less because of its minor contribution to cattle sales. South Mashonaland with 17·5 per cent. of the population and the Midlands with 22·5 per cent. claimed 15 and 19 per cent. respectively of the income from crop sales. In each case, the share of total agricultural income is probably larger as both have relatively higher proportions of the income from cattle sales.

It is now necessary to compare this outline of the provincial distribution of agricultural income with the contribution of each province to total wage employment. The general pattern established for the other Central African territories indicates that wage employment was lowest where agricultural income was highest. If this relationship is to hold in Southern Rhodesia, it should follow that Matabeleland would have the highest proportion of absentees to its male population and North Mashonaland the lowest. The other three provinces should lie in an intermediate position with Manicaland showing a somewhat higher proportion of absentees than South Mashonaland and the Midlands.

The estimates of the degree of absenteeism in the various provinces, unfortunately, are fragmentary, but it is nevertheless useful to check the consistency of the results obtainable against the pattern which might be expected. To obtain an indication of the extent of absenteeism, it is necessary to rely on calculations of the 1948 sample survey of the African population. As was the case in the Northern Rhodesian sample census of 1950 (which was conducted along the same lines), an index of the extent of absenteeism can be constructed by comparing the difference between the number of adult males in the *de jure* population and the number in the *de facto* population in each of the provinces. This approach, however, is deficient in that it cannot indicate the length of absenteeism from each of the districts. Instead the census figures show only the number of absentees at the time of the census. But it may not be far from the mark to treat the relative positions of the various provinces, as brought out in the 1948 data, as a generally fair represent-ation of the importance of each as suppliers of wage labour. This view is supported by the results of the more limited sample survey taken in Southern Rhodesia five years after the original survey. The coverage for 1953 was only partial.[1] But for the administrative districts (within provinces) for which data are comparable in the two samples, analysis reveals a remarkable stability in the relative degree of absenteeism for both periods.[2]

Using the 1948 statistics as the basis of calculations, the pattern shown in Table VIII emerges. The percentage of male absentees from each province is defined for this purpose as the difference between the number of adult males in the *de jure* and *de facto* populations, divided by the total number of adult males (*de jure*) for each province.

TABLE VIII

PERCENTAGE OF ABSENTEEISM
OF ADULT MALES FOR THE
VARIOUS PROVINCES OF
SOUTHERN RHODESIA, 1948

North Mashonaland	55
South Mashonaland	41
Midlands	48
Manicaland	51
Matabeleland	60

Sources: Calculated from the *1948 Sample Census, Southern Rhodesia.*

With one exception, these results conform to the pattern ex-pected from the analysis of agricultural income distribution by provinces. Matabeleland has the lowest agricultural income and, for its population, is the highest contributor to wage

[1] The smaller coverage of the second survey was partly accounted for by the deliberate exclusion of areas in which forced resettlement of the population had occurred. Through these omissions, it was intended to avoid bias arising from 'the hostility of the people'; see *Preliminary Report of the Second Demographic Survey of the Indigenous African Population of Southern Rhodesia, 1953* (Central African Statistical Office, Salisbury, May 1954), p. 1.

[2] Ibid., pp. 6–7.

employment. It would also be expected that Manicaland would have a higher ratio of male absentees than South Mashonaland or the Midlands. This is also confirmed in the above ratios of absenteeism. But from the agricultural income calculations, it should follow that North Mashonaland would have the lowest ratio of male absentees if the general hypothesis is to hold. In fact, it is a surprisingly high contributor to wage employment, being second only to the poorest province in its ratio of male absentees.

What can account for this deviation in the case of North Mashonaland from the norm? In searching for an explanation, several considerations are relevant. This province is adjacent to the heaviest concentrations of European settlement in the territory. As a result of its geographical situation, agricultural marketing is less hampered by poor communications than is the case in the more remote African areas. Moreover, it is favoured by more abundant rainfall than any of the other provinces.[1] The available historical data indicate that the leadership of this province in agricultural sales has been a persistent phenomenon and is not limited to the period 1948–54. As comprehensive data are not available for all cash crops before 1948, this conclusion is based on the marketing of maize exclusively.[2]

In part, the more advanced degree of exposure to the influences of the money economy may account for the unique position of North Mashonaland. This may have led to more radical changes in tastes than in the more isolated areas and, in consequence, additional inducements to the acquisition of money income may have been present. This could account for the increased production of agricultural crops for market, or for the higher ratio of male absenteeism. Some other explanation must be sought when both occur simultaneously. The answer may lie in the manner in which population pressure on the land is felt in this province. This cannot be subjected to precise quantitative measurement. Several considerations, however,

[1] The Department of Native Agriculture adopts four classifications for rainfall in the reserves: good, variable, medium, and low. The area of North Mashonaland classified in the first category is proportionately much higher than in Matabeleland, Midlands, or South Mashonaland. Manicaland is more favoured than the latter three provinces, but less so than North Mashonaland. See *Annual Report of the Director of Native Agriculture, 1954*, Chart VIII, pp. 38–40.

[2] See *Reports of the Maize Control Board, Southern Rhodesia, 1931–1948.*

point to the conclusion that population pressure in North Mashonaland, despite its agricultural prosperity, is more advanced than in the other provinces of Southern Rhodesia. The sample census of African agriculture undertaken in 1949 indicated that North Mashonaland was almost at the bottom of the scale of average acreages per cultivator by provinces. Only one province had a lower average acreage and the difference between the two was slight.[1] A similar relative position for North Mashonaland is brought out in the Native Agriculture Department's annual estimates of the amount of usable acreage per family of five resident in each of the provinces.[2]

Perhaps a more accurate reflection of the extent to which the African himself feels the pressure on the land can be obtained by examining the numbers of dependants, not just male wage-earners, absent from the native areas. In this regard, the position of North Mashonaland is unequivocal. The results of the 1948 census establish it as the only Southern Rhodesian province in which the number of absent males is exceeded by the number of absentee women and children.[3] This provides a rough index of the degree of permanence of absenteeism; the larger the number of African dependants resident in the European area, the more permanent the settlement in wage employment is likely to be. Thus, the strikingly high ratio of absentee dependants from North Mashonaland (in relation to the other provinces) provides *prima facie* evidence that population there is being forced off the land and into permanent wage employment at a relatively faster pace. This phenomenon is occurring also in the more densely populated districts of Nyasaland.

Conclusions on the Economic Behaviour of the Indigenous Population

From the foregoing analysis of the indigenous agricultural economies of Central Africa, it would appear that the tentative hypothesis advanced on the relationship between agricultural

[1] *Report of the Sample Census of African Agriculture of Southern Rhodesia, 1948–49* (Central African Statistical Office, Salisbury, 1951), Table IV, p. 9. It should be noted that the average acreage per cultivator shown in these calculations is based on the *de facto* agricultural population in each province.

[2] Calculated from data shown in the *Annual Report of the Director of Native Agriculture, 1954*, Chart VIII.

[3] Calculated from the *1948 Demographic Sample Survey*.

income and wage employment can generally be sustained from the observed reactions in these three territories. But there is an apparent exception to this uniformity. It has emerged in districts where population pressure on the land has been heavy. In these circumstances, additional labour can not be accommodated on a restricted agricultural area, with existing techniques, without a reduction in *per capita* output. In areas where this has happened, male labour may be pushed out of the indigenous economy. A high rate of exodus into wage employment and a relatively high volume of agricultural sales may then occur simultaneously.

But it is also clear that the indigenous economies have passed through two earlier stages before this situation has evolved. The first is their condition before Western contact. The indigenous economy was then organized to be self-sufficient; real income and output were low and tastes were modest. Until recently, some of the remoter districts of Northern Rhodesia were still in this state of isolation.

The second stage is inaugurated by the introduction of the money economy from outside. Because of the narrow horizons of the traditional society, the response of the indigenous peoples to unfamiliar opportunities for increasing their real incomes may be delayed. Historically, a prodding from the tax-collector has been required. But, after a period of adjustment, they have attempted to acquire cash either through the sale of agricultural surpluses or through the sale of their labour. At this stage the productive relationships within the indigenous economy have an important bearing on the terms of contact with the money economy. The traditional division of labour does not require the continuous presence of the adult male to maintain its conventional level of production. His employment for wages, on a temporary basis, can increase the real income of the family. But wage earning is attractive only when it increases the total real income — in other words, it must supplement more than it subtracts from the non-monetary income achieved through agricultural production. Most of the indigenous economies in Central Africa are now in this stage.

These circumstances have two important consequences for the relationship between the indigenous and the money economies. One is that the customary division of labour within the indigenous economy permits its male members to be employed at a low real wage. To attract them into wage employment, the employer in the money economy need not offer a wage high enough to support both the worker and his family. For his family remains in the indigenous economy and its minimum requirements are met there. These circumstances also mean that the low real wage which suffices to obtain male labour initially would no longer be adequate to attract wage-earners if their absence would reduce the output of indigenous agriculture. Even though it is not a continuous one, the contribution of the adult male is vital. The indigenous economy cannot continue to function as an economic unit without the maintenance and renewal of its most important agricultural asset — the land. This is the task which its male members perform. Their absence for prolonged periods would cause output to fall. Effectively, this imposes a limit to the quantity of manpower which the indigenous economy would voluntarily be prepared to spare at the conventional level of real wages. The critical rate of absenteeism may vary with the local conditions. As a rule of thumb guide for these territories as a whole, the ratio offered by the Native Administrators may not be altogether misleading. Their calculations worked from the assumption that the integrity of the indigenous social system required the presence, at the minimum, of 50 per cent. of its able-bodied male adults. This figure is not precise; but the assumption of a ceiling to the tolerable volume of absenteeism has genuine support in the economic realities of the indigenous economy. It may be recalled that in recent years the proportions of adult males employed for wages has exceeded 50 per cent. in some districts. A closer inspection of this phenomenon will be made in a later chapter.

The third stage in this evolution is now apparently being reached in some sections of Nyasaland and in one province of Southern Rhodesia. At this stage the growth of population presses on the land resources so severely that *per capita* agricultural incomes would decline with the absorption of more man-power. These circumstances might produce results quite different from those of the second stage. When the indigenous economy can continue to function on its traditional lines, only a certain proportion of its adult man-power can be attracted into wage employment without a rise in real wages. Pressure on the land may alter this relationship. If average returns in the indigenous economy are falling, a higher proportion of the total man-power may be available at the same real wage rate.

The analysis of this chapter also supports the general conclusion that the African has tended, at least in recent years, to order his contacts with the money economy in a manner which would maximize his real income. It would be idle to pretend that the African's response to the money economy has always been so. In the early years, coercion in various guises was often required to induce him to acquire cash. But the evidence on his recent economic behaviour suggests that, when appropriate allowance for his special circumstances has been made, he acts as a rational economic man. In general, two avenues have been available for increasing his real income. But, in particular cases, only one has been genuinely open. The opportunities for selling agricultural surpluses are neither uniform nor universal throughout Central Africa; isolation rules out the prospect of earning a sizeable cash income from crop sales for a high proportion of the indigenous population. Where access to markets has permitted the sale of surpluses, it would appear — subject to the qualifications discussed earlier — that the African has intensified his efforts as a farmer, produced more, and acquired a money income thereby. These areas, in general, have offered a lower proportion of their adult males for wage employment. The districts in which this avenue into the money economy has been closed have apparently supplied higher percentages for wage employment.

These relationships indicate a rationality in the economic behaviour of the African. But it would be mistaken to expect him to conform, in Central African conditions, to European standards of rational economic behaviour. The social system, especially in the Rhodesias, expects and conditions different codes of conduct from the two races. It has tended to place an upper limit to the African's economic aspirations. Most Africans still have little opportunity to acquire, for example, such expensive items of consumer capital as urban housing and electrical equipment. And, so long as they are obliged to confine their tastes within restricted bounds, it is not irrational to adjust receipts of money income accordingly. European employers often observe that employees drawn from an indigenous society which has had more than a half-century's contact with the money economy are still remarkably indifferent to its opportunities. Within the confines of the social structure, this apparent indifference may, be rational.

But it is not only this aspect of the social environment in the money economy which produces a different form of behaviour from the African wage employee. His conduct is also governed by his situation as a member of two communities and two economies. The African who enters wage employment is still a member of indigenous society and must retain a stake within it. His absence from indigenous agriculture has a crucial bearing upon its production. In these circumstances, the rational course may be a division of his time between the two economies. In striking a balance between them, he may be enabled to maximize his real income. Continuity in wage employment — without a substantial rise in the real wage rate — may fail to achieve this objective of rational economic behaviour.

CHAPTER V

THE MONEY ECONOMY:
AN AGGREGATIVE VIEW

O F the two economies within Central Africa's dualistic economic structure, the money economy is clearly the more dynamic. It has been the locus of the stimuli which have set off economic expansion there. Not only has the introduction of the money economy succeeded in bringing the African interior into the international trading network and thereby opened up opportunities for enlarged production and exchange, but it has also brought with it new technologies and modes of economic organization. While many of the institutions of the money economy are reproductions of those developed in metropolitan countries, the Central African system also possesses important properties which differentiate its operations from those of more advanced economies. In part, these stem from the presence of the indigenous economy. But the character of the money economy has also been conditioned by its direct dependence on external contacts. Movements of capital and labour from abroad have played a strategic role in its expansion. By the same token, the major force governing the generation of money incomes in Central Africa has been the state of foreign demand for its exports.

In order to appreciate the nature of the economic expansion which has taken place, an examination of the relevant data is appropriate. At best, such statistics can convey only part of an economic system's story. Even the part they can tell is not always perfectly recorded in Central Africa. But a survey of data available can at least yield further insights into the significant characteristics of the money economy.

Measurement of the Money Economy's Performance

One of the consequences of dualism is that the conventional techniques of national income accounting cannot readily measure the *national* income. Instead they are designed to include only that portion of economic activity which has been monetized and to which a value has been assigned by the market place. This procedure means that some economic functions are excluded from the national income aggregate in any country: the unpaid services of housewives, for example, are not covered, although they may contribute enormously to a nation's economic welfare. Such omissions do not distort seriously the national income accountant's statement of economic activity in North America or in Western Europe. But the same guiding principle — the exclusion of non-marketed goods and services — rules out a sizeable volume of total national income in an underdeveloped country. Most of the production of the indigenous economy is thereby automatically excluded. As a result, the national accounts effectively measure, not the national income, but the size of the money economy.

Attempts have been made to incorporate non-monetized indigenous production into the national economic aggregates. But the problem is far more complex than it might appear. Reliable information on the volume of non-marketed production is seldom available. Even if physical output data were obtainable, the problem of its valuation would remain. To assign the prices prevailing in the money economy to non-marketed output would be to assume identical tastes and preferences in both sections of the community. Moreover, this solution would rest on the implicit assumption — which is hardly warranted — that market prices would be unchanged if the large volume of non-marketable output were actually offered for sale.[1]

A more defensible practice is to confine the measurements of the national income to market activity and to admit the impossibility of incorporating non-marketed production into the national income aggregate. But to suggest that all market activity can be included in the national income estimate is still too sweeping. As a practical matter, only transactions which

[1] Phyllis Deane has attempted to construct national accounts which include a valuation of non-marketed production for Northern Rhodesia and Nyasaland for the years 1938 and 1945; see *The Measurement of Colonial National Incomes* (C.U.P., 1948); and *Colonial Social Accounting* (C.U.P., 1953). These calculations require the implicit assumptions noted above. A similar approach has been employed for Nigeria; see A. R. Prest and I. G. Stewart, *The National Income of Nigeria, 1950–1951*, Colonial Research Studies, No. 11 (H.M.S.O., London, 1953).

take place in the organized markets of the money economy can be measured. It is possible that sales of agricultural produce, for example, may take place between the indigenous peoples in their own areas. In Central Africa, the volume of these exchanges is not believed to be large. No exact information is available on this subject, however, and those transactions are not brought into the national income calculations. These omissions mean that the resulting measure of the money national income understates the total income of the community and the results must be interpreted in the light of this qualification.[1] For the purpose of assessing the scope and size of the money economy, the procedure is adequate. It affords a quantitative measure of the changes in the money economy through time and can be used as a rough indicator of the extent to which the indigenous economy becomes monetized through the sale of labour and of agricultural surpluses.

The openness of the underdeveloped economy calls for further modifications in conventional accounting practice. It is misleading to depict the total net value of output within the underdeveloped territory as its national income. More accurately, this is the net geographical product. Included within it is the contribution of factors supplied from abroad. When the income paid to these factors has been excluded, the residual is a truer representation of the national income of an under-developed economy.[2]

Estimates along these lines have been prepared for the Federal area (the three Central African territories collectively) for the years since 1950. These calculations indicate the approximate magnitude of the expansion which has taken place in the

[1] An alternative procedure is to add a nominal figure to the money national income to represent the value of non-marketed output. The entry has no absolute significance, but is a useful reminder of the omissions in the national income as stated. This practice has often been employed in the calculations of the Central African Statistical Office. In its 1959 publications, the Central African Statistical Office has attempted to value non-marketed output by Africans. It is carefully noted, however, that 'the estimates of the subsistence income of Africans represent only a very rough approximation to what is believed to be the correct order of magnitude. An independent estimate has not yet been made for each territory of the Federation . . . ', (*Monthly Digest of Statistics, Supplement*, vol. vi, no. 3, p. 15).

[2] A wide selection of terms is available to identify the 'net geographical income' concept. The Central African Statistical Office has employed 'net domestic product'; Phyllis Deane uses the expression 'taxable income'; alternatively, 'net territorial product' is sometimes used. Arbitrarily, 'net geographical product' will be adopted in the remainder of this study.

money economy. Before the slump in international demand for
non-ferrous metals, the Federation's money economy was indeed
growing at a rapid pace. Expansion has been retarded since 1956,
but the improvement recorded since 1950 is still impressive.

Among the three territories, the prime mover in the expansion
of the Federal area, of course, has been Northern Rhodesia.
The rate of growth there since the war has been especially
striking. Southern Rhodesia has also enjoyed a substantial
growth, although at a slower rate. Aggregative estimates for
Nyasaland are much less satisfactory, but a sizeable expansion
in the money economy has also been recorded there. By comparison with the Rhodesias, however, the absolute size of
Nyasaland's money is still very small.

Foreign Trade and the Generation of Money Income

The overwhelming importance of export receipts in the
generation of money incomes can be seen at a glance by comparing them with the net geographical income. (See Tables
I–V.) For the Federal area as a whole, the ratio of exports to net
geographical income has often been well over 50 per cent. The
proportion, however, dropped in 1957 and 1958 when the
export bill was declining. Both the net geographical income
and export receipts were reduced, but the former fell more
sharply than the latter. Similar relationships can be established
for the individual territories in the years before Federation.
Comparisons by territories, however, are not possible since 1953
because the compilation of foreign trade statistics on a territorial
basis was discontinued with federation.

Of the three territories, the money economy of Northern
Rhodesia has been proportionately the most closely tied to
export production. Before federation, the ratio of domestic
exports to the net geographical income was consistently in
excess of 80 per cent. and reached 90 per cent. in two post-war
years. Similar results were revealed about a pre-war year from
the pioneering national income estimate prepared by Miss
Phyllis Deane for 1938.[1] Her definition of national income

---

[1] Phyllis Deane, *The Measurement of Colonial National Incomes* (National Institute
of Economic and Social Research Occasional Papers XII, C.U.P., 1948), Tables
XL and XLI, pp. 64–66. The adjusted calculations shown above have been derived
by deducting the value of subsistence incomes and of income received from abroad
from Miss Deane's estimate of 'the total taxable national income at factor cost'.

included the value of non-marketed production by Africans. When her data are adjusted to conform to the present definitions of aggregate income in the money economy, it would appear that the net geographical income of Northern Rhodesia in 1938 was approximately £11,588,000 and the net national income in the money economy roughly £6,700,000. The value of domestic exports for the year amounted to more than 88 per cent. of her net geographical income calculation. It is interesting

TABLE I

MEASURES OF AGGREGATE MONEY INCOME IN RELATION TO EXPORTS, FEDERATION OF RHODESIA AND NYASALAND, 1950–59 (£000,000s)

	Net geographical income	*Net national income*	*Value of exports (f.o.r.)*	*Ratio of exports to net geographical income*
1950	156·4	130·4	92·9	59
1951	191·4	158·9	110·2	58
1952	220·4	189·9	134·3	61
1953	248·9	218·7	147·6	59
1954	269·3	234·2	153·4	57
1955	314·6	275·1	179·3	57
1956	356·2	308·3	188·1	53
1957	345·8	305·1	163·0	47
1958	338·7	308·1	142·6	42
1959	395·9	354·7	193·9	49

Notes: Export aggregates since 1954 are based on the trade returns of the Federation of Rhodesia and Nyasaland. The Central African Statistical Office has derived the figures for the earlier years by consolidating the individual trade returns of the three territories and eliminating all inter-territorial trade. The results are therefore comparable throughout. All export values are f.o.r. Gold exports have been treated as merchandise exports.

Sources: *Monthly Digests of Statistics* and *Annual Economic Reports, Federation of Rhodesia and Nyasaland.*

to note that, for the years covered by aggregative estimates of the money economy in Northern Rhodesia, the value of domestic exports has always been greater than the net national income.

In Southern Rhodesia, export revenues have formed a much smaller proportion of the net geographical income. Estimates of the Central African Statistical Office since 1939 indicate that a ratio of roughly 40 per cent. has been steadily maintained. Earlier estimates, prepared by Professor S. H. Frankel and Mr. H. Herzfeld covering the years 1924–43, suggest that

H

the proportion may then have been somewhat higher. Their calculations yield ratios varying between 45 and 56 per cent. Differing methods of computation, however, account for part of the variation in the results of the two series. The Frankel and

TABLE II

MEASURES OF AGGREGATE MONEY INCOME IN RELATION TO EXPORTS, NORTHERN RHODESIA (£000,000s)

	Net geographical income	Net national income	Net national income at 1949 prices	Value of exports, (f.o.r.)	Ratio of domestic exports to net geographical income
1945	13·7	11·4	13·4	11·5	84
1946	16·1	12·3	14·1	12·8	80
1947	25·5	15·2	16·3	21·1	83
1948	32·0	20·5	21·6	28·3	88
1949	41·0	27·4	27·4	32·9	80
1950	54·9	32·9	31·9	49·4	90
1951	81·4	54·2	49·7	66·4	82
1952	90·1	64·4	56·0	81·7	90
1953	107·7	83·7	70·4	93·7	87
1954	117·8	—	—	—	—
1955	144·4	—	—	—	—
1956	156·7	—·	—	—	—
1957	126·6	—	—	—	—
1958	107·2	—	—	—	—
1959	153·1	—	—	—	—

Notes: The official estimates of 'net national income' are not consistently defined throughout the period shown. Before 1951, undistributed profits of the large mining companies were included in the net geographical income, but excluded from the net national income. Beginning in 1951, the legal residence of these companies has been transferred to Northern Rhodesia. When their registrations have been changed, they have been treated as local companies and their undistributed profits incorporated into the net national income.

Following federation in 1953, detailed national accounts and foreign trade statistics have not been compiled for the Central African territories independently. Adjustment of the net national income to 1949 prices has been calculated from the consumer price index of Northern Rhodesia. This affords only a crude measure of changes in the real national income. The consumer price index is based on the budgets of European households exclusively; no calculation of price changes affecting the African in the money economy has been officially prepared for most of this period.

Sources: *The National Income and Social Accounts of Northern Rhodesia*, Central African Statistical Office; *Monthly Digests of Statistics, Federation of Rhodesia and Nyasaland*.

Herzfeld estimates, although described as calculations of net national income in the money economy, in fact approximated more closely the concept of net geographical income; no allowance was made for income transferred to externally supplied factors of production and none was made for income

received in Southern Rhodesia from abroad. Nor was the extent
of the money economy fully represented; the value of African

TABLE III

MEASURES OF AGGREGATE MONEY INCOME IN RELATION TO EXPORTS, SOUTHERN
RHODESIA (CENTRAL AFRICAN STATISTICAL OFFICE ESTIMATES) (£000,000s)

	Net geographical income	*Net national income*	*Net national income at 1939 prices*	*Value of exports, (f.o.r.)*	*Ratio of domestic exports to net geographical income*
1939	27·4	25·2	25·2	10·2	38
1940	28·9	26·4	25·6	13·4	46
1941	31·2	28·6	26·8	13·5	43
1942	32·2	29·9	26·4	15·2	47
1943	33·0	30·8	25·9	13·9	42
1944	35·1	32·8	26·4	14·3	41
1945	39·3	27·1	29·2	15·8	40
1946	45·8	43·7	33·2	18·6	41
1947	53·3	50·4	37·3	20·8	39
1948	64·7	62·9	43·6	25·6	40
1949	73·6	71·1	46·5	29·6	40
1950	94·0	90·7	54·6	40·8	43
1951	102·1	97·6	54·9	42·0	41
1952	121·1	117·0	61·3	51·1	42
1953	133·6	125·1	63·2	54·0	40
1954	138·3	—	—	—	—
1955	157·6	—	—	—	—
1956	179·8	—	—	—	—
1957	198·7	—	—	—	—
1958	209·8	—	—	—	—
1959	218·9	—	—	—	—

Notes: The net geographical income estimates differ from the approach of Frankel
and Herzfeld (shown in Table IV) in that African sales of produce are counted as
part of the money economy; also the incomes of service personnel are included.
(See the comparison of method discussed in the *Economic and Statistical Bulletin,
Southern Rhodesia*, 21 June 1947, p. 10.)

For the period 1939–45, the incomes of statutory boards and commissions were
excluded, but are included in the calculations for the later years. Their omission
in the earlier years does not seriously affect the comparability of the two sets of
figures, as the net incomes of statutory bodies were negligible between 1939 and
1945. The net income of the Rhodesia Railways (which were transferred from
private to public ownership in 1947) has been included throughout; it appears as
company income from 1939–45 and, for the later years, is included in the incomes
of statutory bodies.

Adjustment of the net national income to 1939 prices is based on the consumer
price indices of Southern Rhodesia; these calculations are subject to the qualifications noted in Table II.

Sources: *The National Income and Social Accounts of Southern Rhodesia*, Central
African Statistical Office; *Annual Statements of External Trade, Southern Rhodesia;
Monthly Digests of Statistics, Federation of Rhodesia and Nyasaland.*

agricultural produce sold, although not large, was not included.

Nyasaland has been relatively neglected by the national
income accountants but, by any reckoning, its money economy

TABLE IV

ESTIMATES OF THE 'NATIONAL INCOME' IN THE
MONEY ECONOMY OF SOUTHERN RHODESIA, 1924–43
PREPARED BY PROFESSOR S. H. FRANKEL AND
H. HERZFELD (£000s)

	Net money 'national income' (current prices)	Net money 'national income' constant prices (1929 base)	Ratio of domestic exports to net money 'national income' (current prices)
1924	10,636	11,161	48
1925	10,209	10,758	47
1926	12,042	12,879	45
1927	13,884	14,553	45
1928	14,009	14,309	47
1929	13,978	13,978	47
1930	13,098	13,124	43
1931	8,796	9,124	50
1932	9,688	10,576	55
1933	11,144	12,736	53
1934	13,276	15,366	56
1935	14,549	17,016	55
1936	16,749	19,751	55
1937	19,247	21,872	56
1938	20,696	22,996	51
1939	21,536	23,823	47
1940	25,643	27,995	52
1941	26,474	27,780	51
1942	30,148	29,673	50
1943	30,882	28,594	45

Notes: The method employed by Frankel and Herzfeld approximates the 'net geographical income' more closely than the 'net national income'. No allowance was made for income transferred to factors of production supplied from abroad or for income received in Southern Rhodesia from abroad. Internal transfer payments were excluded; payments to service personnel were treated as transfers in the war years. The value of agricultural produce sold by Africans was not included.

The aggregates were compiled by the method of valuing the output of each of the sectors of the Southern Rhodesian economy (with the exception of African produce marketed); i.e. European agriculture, mining, manufacturing, and services. To arrive at an estimate of the net value added, deductions were made from the gross calculations according to formulae developed in national income calculations in South Africa.

Source: *Report of the Commission of Enquiry into the Mining Industry of Southern Rhodesia* (Salisbury, 1945), Appendix A, pp. 68-70.

is small. Calculations by the Central African Statistical Office for 1950–53 have been constructed on a net national income basis only. Discussion of the position of export revenues in its money economy cannot therefore be strictly comparable with the net geographical income approach adopted for the Rhodesian territories. It is apparent, however, that export earnings are the dominant element in the money income stream. For the years 1950–53, the value of domestic exports was more than 70 per cent. of the estimated net national income.

TABLE V

MEASURES OF AGGREGATE MONEY INCOME IN RELATION TO EXPORTS, NYASALAND (£000,000s)

	Net geographical income	*Net national income*	*Value of exports (f.o.r.)*	*Ratio of domestic exports to net national income*
1950	—	6·9	5·0	72
1951	—	7·9	5·8	73
1952	—	8·6	6·2	72
1953	—	10·0	7·1	71
1954	16·1	—	—	—
1955	17·5	—	—	—
1956	19·2	—	—	—
1957	20·4	—	—	—
1958	21·6	—	—	—
1959	23·9	—	—	—

Notes: Estimates of net geographical income before 1954 and of net national income after 1953 have not been published by the Central African Statistical Office.

Sources: *Monthly Digests of Statistics, Federation of Rhodesia and Nyasaland; Reports of the Customs Department, Protectorate of Nyasaland.*

Phyllis Deane's estimates for 1938 suggest that the ratio was lower in that year. Her calculation of the net national income, when adjusted to exclude the imputed value of non-marketed goods and services, yields a figure of approximately £2,100,000 for the money economy compared with exports valued at slightly under £1,000,000 in 1938.[1]

Comparisons of the net national income in the money economy with export revenues do not, of course, provide an ideal measure of the importance of the export earnings in the generation of money incomes. The cases of the two Rhodesias

[1] Calculated from Deane, op. cit., Tables 71 and 73, pp. 90–91, 93.

illustrate the point. The ratios calculated for the two territories reveal that before federation the share of export revenues in the net geographical income was roughly twice as great in Northern as in Southern Rhodesia. But it does not follow from these data that the money economy in Southern Rhodesia succeeded to a much greater degree in detaching itself from dependence on exports. On the contrary, export earnings have remained the strategic element in the generation of money incomes. Secondary forms of income which the Southern Rhodesian economy has developed are largely dependent on the prosperity of the export industries. There is a further weakness in these calculations. National income aggregates and export statistics involve concepts of different orders. The former measures 'net' magnitudes, based on the value added within the confines of a particular economic system; the latter is a gross measurement and may include the value of inputs which have been imported. To the extent that domestic exports have an import content, the importance of exports in the generation of money incomes is overstated in these comparisons. This problem arises slightly in Southern Rhodesian exports of recent years which have included some manufactured goods processed from imported materials. But the magnitude of this difficulty is not sufficiently great to produce serious distortion.

Despite their inadequacies, these methods of measurement indicate that the activity of the money economy in Central Africa has been largely governed by the fortunes of the export trade. And, like other countries in this position, these territories have been vulnerable to fluctuations in international demand for their products. The contribution of Central African producers to world trade in its export products has generally been too small to permit them any unilateral control over prices.[1]

---

[1] Only in recent years, with the post-war expansion of the Copperbelt, have the Central African territories made a substantial contribution to international trade in any primary product. By 1956, the Northern Rhodesian copper industry was the second largest producer of the metal in the Free World, exceeded only by the production of the United States. Generalizations from quantitative comparisons exclusively can, however, be misleading. As the Northern Rhodesian copper companies are externally owned and controlled, their price and output policies are not locally determined. Companies with interests in Northern Rhodesian mining also have extensive mining investments elsewhere. With this interlocking financial structure, some degree of synchronization is achieved in price and production policy internationally.

Two commodities exported from these territories, however, were brought into international cartel arrangements in the 1930s. These restriction schemes (which were intended to stabilize prices of copper and tea) brought little benefit to Central African exporters.[1]

Changes in world market conditions have had a formidable influence on the activity of the money economy in all three territories. This was most painfully apparent in the trade slump of the 1930s. The shock of collapsing prices for primary products was felt by each, although in differing degrees. Southern Rhodesia's export revenues did not recover their 1929 position until 1934, and a more prolonged contraction in export receipts was avoided only because the colony was a gold producer. Recovery was much slower in Nyasaland. As an exporter of agricultural products exclusively, its export income has varied with the season as well as with the state of international markets. It was only in 1938 that Nyasaland's exports of domestic produce surpassed the level achieved in the peak pre-depression year of 1927. The slump had an entirely different effect in Northern Rhodesia. The new mines of the Copperbelt were just coming into production when the crash occurred. Further expansion plans were checked and output was held below capacity as a result of the international cartel restrictions. Even so, the additional output of the new mines enabled export revenues of the territory to grow even through the depression years.

More active demand for primary products in the war years brought expanding revenues to Central Africa. But the major expansion has come since the war. From 1945 to 1953 (the last year for which territorial trade statistics were compiled), Southern Rhodesian export earnings expanded by more than three and a half times; Northern Rhodesia's export income rose more than eightfold; the same calculation for Nyasaland indicates a growth of roughly 400 per cent.

In the past several years, the Rhodesias have again been forcefully reminded of the instability of export earnings and of the risks involved when one export commodity is a major source for foreign exchange. In this case, the volatility of world copper

[1] These points will be taken up more fully in the subsequent discussion of the copper and tea industries.

prices has been the significant factor. In 1955 and early 1956, copper was sold at record prices of more than £400 per ton. In 1957 and 1958, prevailing prices were generally less than half of this figure. Fluctuations in this one industry — which in the years of expansion accounted for nearly two-thirds of the Federation's export earnings and for more than one-third of the public revenues collected by all Central African governments — clearly have a formidable impact on the fortunes of the money economy.[1] Such disturbances have important effects, both directly and indirectly, on the national income aggregates.

Investment and the Growth of Money Income

Like foreign trade, investment from abroad has been one of the prime movers in the money economy's expansion. Without foreign capital, the achievements of the money economy to date would have been impossible. External investors have financed the establishment of the key export industries and — what is equally important — they have financed the overhead facilities required to bring the Central African territories into contact with international markets.

That capital imports have been the crucial component in capital formation in Central Africa there can be no doubt. Satisfactory measures of their importance are not readily obtainable. No systematic balance of payment accounts are available before the Second World War. The general trends, however, can be observed in the behaviour of the visible balance of trade. As might be expected, these data suggest that periods of rising export prices and improvements in foreign exchange earnings have usually been associated with heavier inflows of foreign investment.

This relationship is apparent from the visible trade returns of the Rhodesias.[2] In the late 1920s, for example, both Rhodesias enjoyed improvements in export earnings. At the same

---

[1] Based on statement by Sir Ronald Prain, Managing Director of Rhodesian Selection Trust, as reported in *East Africa and Rhodesia*, 13 November 1958.

[2] Methods of compiling trade statistics have not been uniform in Central Africa. Northern and Southern Rhodesian trade statistics have been collected by valuing exports at f.o.r.: imports have been valued, not on a c.i.f. basis, but either f.o.r. or f.o.b. Nyasaland has used the f.o.r. method for exports, but imports are shown at their c.i.f. value at the East African port of discharge. Reference to the 'visible' balance is made with these qualifications.

time, both territories generally showed deficits in their visible trade. Northern Rhodesia's deficit was particularly large with the Copperbelt in its development stages. The 1930s transformed the deficits into visible trade surpluses, although the absolute size of the export bill fell in Southern Rhodesia. Visible trade surpluses continued until the end of the Second World War. In the post-war decade, Southern Rhodesia once more sustained visible deficits. Northern Rhodesia, as a result of the influence of its copper industry, continued to earn a substantial surplus in its visible trade. Indeed its surpluses were large enough through 1956 to permit the Federation to show a visible trade surplus. With the decline in copper earnings, visible deficits emerged in 1957 and 1958.[1]

At best, trends in the visible balance of trade can serve only as a rough guide to movements of capital. With invisible expenditures omitted, an accurate assessment of the current and capital account position is precluded for much of Central African economic history. External freight and insurance charges are themselves sizeable items — in post-war Rhodesian experience, they have added from 12 to 18 per cent. to the f.o.b. or f.o.r. value of merchandise imports.[2] But these omissions are not the most serious ones for arriving at precise calculations of gross capital inflow. More significant are current transfers of profits, dividends, and interest. In economies whose export production has been largely organized by external capital, these transfers can make a substantial claim on foreign exchange earnings.

For recent years, an indication of the volume of external transfers may be gleaned from the balance of payments estimates available for the Rhodesias. In Northern Rhodesia, payments abroad of interest, dividends, and profits since the war have occasionally amounted to more than half of the total

[1] From 1953 to 1956, the Federation showed a substantial surplus in its visible trade. Calculations for the 'Federal area' have been made for the years 1949–52 by excluding all inter-territorial trade from the individual trade statements of the three territories. These results indicate surpluses in the visible trade of the 'Federal area' for 1950 and 1952 and deficits in 1949 and 1951. See *Monthly Digests of Statistics, Federation of Rhodesia and Nyasaland.*

[2] Based on calculations recorded in *The Balance of Payments of Southern Rhodesia, 1946–1952*, Central African Statistical Office, and *The National Income and Social Accounts of Northern Rhodesia, 1945–1953*, Central African Statistical Office, Tables XIII–XV, pp. 34–37.

export earnings. The bulk of these transfers has been made by the large mining companies. Interpretation of these results is complicated by the statistical treatment of the profits of the mining companies. Before 1951, the large mining organizations in the territory were registered abroad. For balance of payments purposes, their entire profits, whether distributed in dividends or retained, were treated as current transfers. If reinvestment was undertaken from these profits, they appeared again in the balance of payments accounts as an inflow of external capital.

TABLE VI

NORTHERN RHODESIA, TRANSFERS OF INTEREST, DIVIDENDS, AND PROFITS COMPARED
WITH THE VALUE OF DOMESTIC EXPORTS

	(1) Value of domestic exports, f.o.r. (£000,000s)	(2) Total transfers of income (including undistributed profits of mining cos.) (£000,000s)	(3) (2) as % of (1)	(4) Total transfers of income (excluding undistributed profits of mining cos.) (£000,000s)	(5) (4) as % of (1)
1945	11·5	2·4	21	1·5	13
1946	12·8	4·0	31	3·3	26
1947	21·0	10·5	50	9·0	43
1948	28·3	11·8	42	8·9	31
1949	32·9	13·8	42	9·8	30
1950	49·4	22·2	45	16·5	33
1951	66·4	38·3	58	25·0	38
1952	81·7	31·6	39	23·1	28
1953	93·7	32·7	35	24·9	27

Sources: Data on transfers are drawn from *The National Income and Social Accounts of Northern Rhodesia, 1945–1953,* Central African Statistical Office, Table XIII, p. 34.
  Adjustments for undistributed profits of mining companies are calculated from ibid., Table IV (b), p. 26; Table XII, p. 32; Table XXI, p. 41. The figures for the value of domestic exports are derived from the *Annual Statements of External Trade, Northern Rhodesia.*

Three of the large mining companies transferred their head-quarters to Central Africa in 1951 and the other two major companies followed in 1953. Since this change in residence, their undistributed profits have been treated as local savings and only dividend payments have appeared in the balance of payments accounts. When allowance has been made for profits retained in Northern Rhodesia during these years, the proportion of export income transferred abroad is still impressive. It has usually exceeded a quarter of the territory's export revenues and the percentage has frequently been higher.

Transfers of interest, dividends, and profits from Southern Rhodesia, where export activity is less concentrated, have taken a smaller proportion of total export receipts. Since 1939, these transfers have amounted to as much as 27 per cent. of the value of domestic exports and, to 1953, had never fallen below 14 per cent. These calculations include the undistributed profits

TABLE VII

SOUTHERN RHODESIA, TRANSFERS OF INTEREST, DIVIDENDS, AND PROFITS COMPARED WITH THE VALUE OF DOMESTIC EXPORTS

	(1) Value of domestic exports, f.o.r. (£000,000s)	(2) Total transfers of interest, dividends and profits (£000,000s)	(3) (2) as % of (1)
1939	10·2	2·8	27
1940	13·4	3·1	23
1941	13·5	3·3	24
1942	15·2	3·0	20
1943	13·9	2·9	21
1944	14·3	3·1	22
1945	15·8	3·0	19
1946	18·6	3·5	19
1947	20·8	4·6	22
1948	25·6	4·0	16
1949	29·6	4·7	16
1950	40·8	5·8	14
1951	42·0	7·0	17
1952	51·1	8·9	17
1953	54·0	10·3	19

Sources: Data on transfers are drawn from the *Economic and Statistical Bulletin, Southern Rhodesia*, 7 October 1948; *The Balance of Payments of Southern Rhodesia, 1946–1952*, Central African Statistical Office; and the *Annual Financial Statements, Southern Rhodesia*.

Statistics on the value of domestic exports are from the *Annual Statements of External Trade, Southern Rhodesia*.

of external firms. Expatriate firms in Southern Rhodesia are small compared with the Northern Rhodesian copper-mining groups but their contribution to the money economy has been substantial. In 1946, for example, it was estimated that firms registered abroad earned just under 45 per cent. of the taxable corporate income of the colony; in addition, an estimated 68 per cent. of the capital of companies registered in Southern

Rhodesia was held outside the colony.[1] While corporations have transferred a smaller share of the available foreign exchange in Southern than in Northern Rhodesia, interest payments abroad on the public debt have been much heavier in the former.

Since federation, income transfers abroad have continued to be heavy. From 1954 through 1959, they have claimed between a fifth and a quarter of Federal earnings from merchandise exports.

TABLE VIII

FEDERATION OF RHODESIA AND NYASALAND,
TRANSFERS OF INTEREST, DIVIDENDS, AND PROFITS
COMPARED WITH VALUE OF EXPORTS

	(1) Value of exports, f.o.r. (£000,000s)	*(2)* Total transfers of interest, dividends and profits (£000,000s)	*(3)* (2) as % of (1)
1954	153·4	35·1	23
1955	179·3	39·4	22
1956	188·1	46·9	25
1957	163·0	40·8	25
1958	142·6	30·6	21
1959	193·9	41·2	21

Sources: *Annual Economic Reports, Federation of Rhodesia and Nyasaland.*

These computations refer only to recent experience. But foreign enterprise has dominated export production throughout the life of the money economy and a share of the earnings has usually been repatriated. In the absence of fresh inflows of external capital or other means of international payment (e.g. grants or funds brought in by immigrants), this situation would normally produce a surplus in the merchandise trade. Deficits in the balance of merchandise trade (even if imports were measured c.i.f.) are thus an imperfect measure of the gross inflow of external capital. The gross sums received, in fact, are larger than the size of the net deficit would indicate.

In the post-war years, more refined measures of aggregate foreign investment are permitted by the officially prepared

[1] *Economic and Statistical Bulletin, Southern Rhodesia,* 7 October 1948, pp. 20–21. The former calculation was drawn from the records of the Commissioner of Taxes and excludes the income of the Rhodesia Railways.

capital accounts in the balance of payments estimates. But even these fail to convey the full impact of foreign investment on capital formation in Central Africa. A deficit in the capital account is a residual item representing the difference between capital inflows and outflows. In many years — particularly those in which money income has been rising — a part of domestic saving has flowed abroad. This has been the resultant of the combined operations of commercial banks, the monetary authority, and of governments. All of them have tended to accumulate reserves abroad. These holdings, of course, can be drawn down when required. But the effect of these factors is that

TABLE IX

NET INVESTMENT IN RELATION TO NET GEOGRAPHICAL INCOME AND SOURCES OF FINANCE, FEDERATION OF RHODESIA AND NYASALAND, 1950–59 (£000,000s)

	(1) *Net* *geographical* *income*	(2) *Net* *investment*	(3) *as a* % *of* (1)	(4) *Net* *domestic* *savings*	(5) *Net* *borrowing* *abroad*
1950	156·4	53·2	34	26·0	28·0
1951	191·4	83·7	44	34·8	49·1
1952	220·4	81·4	37	41·0	42·4
1953	248·9	70·6	28	46·1	23·9
1954	269·3	69·4	26	55·2	14·1
1955	314·6	93·4	30	77·3	16·1
1956	356·2	129·8	36	91·8	38·0
1957	345·8	134·0	39	59·5	74·5
1958	338·7	110·8	33	47·9	62·9
1959	395·9	101·1	26	82·1	18·9

Sources: *Monthly Digests of Statistics* and *Annual Economic Reports, Federation of Rhodesia and Nyasaland.*

the net deficit on capital account usually fails to represent accurately the actual volume of fresh investment from abroad.

Despite the deficiencies in the data, approximations of the volume of foreign investment in relation to aggregate domestic investment and of the relationship, in turn, of aggregate investment to expansion in money income can be made. These calculations for the Federal Area are shown in Table IX. From these data it is forcefully apparent that the ratio of net investment to net geographical product has been remarkably high since 1950. Such proportions (which far exceed the post-war performance of the American economy) would be noteworthy in an advanced economy. In an underdeveloped economy, they

are all the more impressive. Not all of the net investment undertaken, of course, has been supported from Central Africa's own
resources. Inflows of foreign capital have usually financed a
substantial share of the total. But this fact should not obscure
another which is equally striking: namely, the high ratio of net
savings to net geographical product which the Central African
territories have achieved on their own. This accomplishment
owes much to the rapid expansion in money income which the
Federal area has enjoyed and to the form which growth in
money income has taken. Two sources of saving — undis-

TABLE X

COMPONENTS OF NET DOMESTIC SAVINGS, FEDERATION OF RHODESIA AND NYASALAND,
1950–59 (£000,000s)

	Total	Personal saving	%	Government surpluses	%	Undistributed profits	%
1950	26·0	10·4	40	8·3	32	7·3	28
1951	34·8	5·7	16	11·4	33	17·7	51
1952	41·0	8·6	21	22·2	54	10·2	25
1953	46·1	11·0	24	21·9	47	13·2	29
1954	55·2	13·5	24	16·6	30	25·1	45
1955	77·3	20·7	27	25·6	33	31·1	40
1956	91·8	31·0	34	31·0	34	29·8	32
1957	59·5	29·1	49	33·7	57	−3·2	−5
1958	47·9	24·9	52	23·1	48	−0·1	—
1959	82·1	31·4	38	17·0	21	33·8	41

Notes: As in the Northern Rhodesian accounts, much of the rise in undistributed
profits is accounted for by the treatment of the large mining companies as local
firms. Calculation of undistributed profits includes the surpluses of statutory bodies.
    Government surpluses refer to the consolidated accounts of all echelons of
government: i.e. Federal, territorial, and local authorities. These surpluses are
defined to include all capital formation financed by governments out of revenue
appropriations as well as surpluses on current account which are transferred to the
capital accounts of governments.
Sources: *Annual Economic Reports* and *Monthly Digests of Statistics, Federation of
Rhodesia and Nyasaland.*

tributed corporate profits and government surpluses — have
made the overwhelming contribution to aggregate savings for
the Federal area. The volume of saving realized in both these
categories is closely tied to the fortunes of the copper industry.
The copper companies have been the major contributors to undistributed corporate profits. Their importance is indicated by
the sharp drop on the money economy's undistributed profits in
1957 and 1958 when the copper industry suffered setbacks in
earnings. Fluctuations in this industry, which is also the most
important taxpayer in the Federation, also affect the volume of

saving which can be realized by governments. This effect, how-ever, is lagged by the manner in which Central African fiscal practices have been designed. Taxes on the incomes of the copper companies are not paid until eighteen months after they have been earned. This procedure permits governments to estimate the revenue side of their budgets more accurately than would otherwise be possible.

General Observations on the Aggregative Performance of the Money Economy

The Central African territories are classic cases of 'export economies'. But external ties, which have provided their life-line, have not denied to them a rapid rate of economic expansion. It has often been argued that the growth process is dampened in territories which foreign investment has brought into the international trading network as exporters of primary products. Further, the case is frequently made that such arrangements are likely to work to the long-term disadvantage of the exporting economy. Three major lines of argument are offered in support of this interpretation.[1] First, it is held that leakages from the money income stream through repatriation of profits by expatriate enterprises have withdrawn from the underdeveloped country an important stimulus for sustained economic advance. Secondly, it is argued that the primary exporting countries are committed to economic instability be-cause the generation of money incomes locally is at the mercy of the terms of trade and the volume of overseas demand. Thirdly, the argument has been advanced that foreign invest-ment and the pattern of international specialization which it has created have made industrialization of the export economies more difficult; the energies of the underdeveloped countries have thus been directed into types of activity offering less scope for technical progress.

Central African experience to date does not bear out this pessimistic diagnosis. Leakages from the domestic income stream have occurred through transfers of profits and interest

[1] For example, see H. W. Singer, 'The Distribution of Gains between Investing and Borrowing Countries', *Papers and Proceedings of the American Economic Association* (May 1950), pp. 473–85, and Gunnar Myrdal, *Economic Theory and Under-Developed Regions* (Duckworth, London, 1957).

on imported capital but these have been more than offset by fresh inflows of foreign investment. The terms of trade have fluctuated — with serious temporary effects — but the overall experience of Central Africa in export markets has been favourable. Apart from the food industries, production for local as opposed to export markets is still limited. The growth in aggregate effective demand, however, has provided a base upon which manufacturing industries are now being built.

As the available aggregative data indicate, the money economy of the Central African territories has prospered. Money income has risen dramatically since the war. Adjustments of the money value of aggregate income to real income cannot yet be made with ideal precision in these territories. But the pace of the expansion which has taken place leaves no doubt that the first of the criteria for economic development has been satisfied in Central Africa.

CHAPTER VI

THE MONEY ECONOMY:
A SECTOR APPROACH

T HE results of the preceding survey of the aggregative variables in Central Africa's money economy provide an unmistakable demonstration of the rapid pace of its expansion. But an adequate understanding of the forces at work within the money economy cannot be obtained from analysis of these macro-economic categories alone. A micro-economic inspection of individual components of the money economy can offer further insights into the problems and prospects of development. For this purpose, the money economy may be subdivided into sectors. Each has its own peculiar properties. Nor are the various sectors uniform in their analytical significance. Developments in some sectors have initiated and shaped the overall pattern of expansion, while in others the level of activity has been more a by-product of the general process of expansion itself.

For the sake of convenience, four components of the money economy may be isolated for separate discussion: mining, agriculture, manufacturing, and the public sector. Lines of demarcation between these sectors cannot always be unambiguously drawn. This problem arises particularly with the public sector. In one fashion or another, public expenditures have influenced the performance of the mining, agricultural, and manufacturing industries. But public expenditure on social overhead capital — an important aspect of the development problem in itself — has made a major contribution to the growth of the money economy. Separate treatment of this type of activity will, therefore, be undertaken.

The Mining Industries

Mining has always been the mainstay of the money economy in the Rhodesias. Indeed the geological riches of the area provided the primary rationale for European enterprise and

I

settlement. Historically, mineral production has been directed almost entirely into export markets and this sector, in turn, has earned the bulk of the foreign exchange for both Rhodesias. But the economic importance of the different varieties of mineral output has altered appreciably over time. Changing economic conditions, both at home and abroad, have called for adjustments within the mining sector.

Notable adaptations have occurred in Southern Rhodesia. Originally, its mining activities were concentrated on gold. The early settlers entertained high expectations from this mineral. The Rhodesian fields, however, failed to yield deposits comparable to those in the Witwatersrand or, more recently, in the Orange Free State of the Union of South Africa. Deposits were scattered and the quality of ore was seldom high. Large-scale workings were thus precluded. A handful of medium-sized producers and often a large number of small workers have formed the backbone of the industry.

By its nature, the gold industry is, of course, unique. Prices of its output are not determined by market forces and need bear no relationship to other price trends.[1] In the 1930s gold mining prospered while other primary producers suffered setbacks. Immediately following the increased gold price brought by Britain's departure from the gold standard in 1931, output began to expand. In just over two years, Southern Rhodesian production increased by more than a quarter. The geological structure, permitting small workings, favoured a rapid growth in output. Almost all of the increase was attributable to small operators. Between 1931 and 1935, roughly 1300 new producers entered the industry and the share of small mines in the colony's output increased from 31 to 61 per cent. Some of the new propositions were worked by skilled labour transferring from other types of mining where employment was slack; but expansion was also supported by immigrants bringing capital as well as their technical and entrepreneurial skill.[2]

---

[1] Southern Rhodesia has attempted to escape from the inflexibility of the official price through the gold premium system. Under this arrangement, the output of the industry is pooled and sold collectively in the most favourable market for non-monetary gold.

[2] Immigration statistics of this period provide an indicator, although an imperfect one, of the occupations into which immigrants were drawn. Only those immigrants with a pre-arranged employment at the time of entry are included in

Since 1941, the number of producers in the industry has generally declined. By 1956, for example, the number of gold workings had fallen to 301; by contrast, 1,754 gold-mining propositions were at work in the peak year of 1935. Of the mines now remaining, only a dozen produce more than 10,000 ounces per annum. Yet this handful of medium-sized producers contributes nearly two-thirds of the territory's gold output. In the mid-1930s, this situation was reversed. Small workings thrived and contributed collectively nearly two-thirds of a territorial output which was then more than 50 per cent. greater than the annual production of the 1950s. This long-term decline in the gold industry has taken place despite the fact that the price per fine ounce has increased nearly threefold over the past three decades. In part, the decline can be attributed to deterioration in ore quality. But costs of production have also increased for other reasons and they have hit the small worker particularly hard. Governmental assistance to small workers through loans, subsidies, and the provision of an extraction plant for the processing of low grade ores have been unable to arrest the trend. Even the price rise accompanying the 1949 devaluation gave only a minor stimulus to the industry.

Asbestos, which has become Southern Rhodesia's most valuable mineral export, provides a more orthodox example of price and output relationships. Production has generally been dominated by two large mines, although some small workings have come and gone. When the market broke in the early 1930s, output was sharply curtailed. But production has been slower to respond to increases in price. Between 1935 and 1947, prices more than doubled, while output was virtually static in the range of 60,000 short tons per annum. The general upward trend in prices of the fibre, particularly after the war, attracted several new firms into the industry which began to swell the colony's output in 1949. The sharpest increase in prices came during the Korean War. By 1952, the average price realized by

the occupational classifications. These returns show that the flow of immigrants into mining increased from 54 in 1931 to more than 100 per year from 1934 to 1938 (*Economic and Statistical Bulletin, Southern Rhodesia*, 7 February 1934, pp. 3–4; ibid., 2 February 1935, p. 3; ibid., 7 March 1939, pp. 2–4). In this period, gold mining was the only Southern Rhodesian mining activity in which European employment showed any substantial increase.

the colony's producers was just under £80 per short ton —
roughly double the level prevailing in 1948.[1] Six new ventures
were incorporated for work in the territory in 1950 and 1951
alone, all of them largely financed by external capital. Two of
the new organizations, however, had suspended operations by
1954. Assisted by the contributions of the new entrants to the
industry, output has risen since 1950. By 1958, the volume of
production was approximately three times greater than it had
been in 1929. Prices in 1958, despite a drop from the 1952 peak,
were roughly 225 per cent. above the 1929 level.

The third of Southern Rhodesia's major mineral exports,
chrome ore, has been seriously affected by transport bottlenecks in the Rhodesian economy. As a high-bulk and low-value
commodity, chrome ore is low in the scale of the priorities set
by the Rhodesia Railways. This factor has often held output
well below potential capacity. Amounts of ore actually raised
have usually exceeded the tonnage for which rail allocation was
available and the excess has been stockpiled.[2] As well as the
internal transport difficulties, inadequate ore-loading facilities
at the port of Beira have further restricted exports. Relief has
been afforded in recent years through the expansion in the
capacity of the Rhodesia Railways, the construction of the
alternative rail link to Lourenço Marques, and the establishment of a local plant for the processing of ore into ferro-chrome.
In 1957 and 1958, the transport restrictions were also eased
considerably by the deceleration in the money economy's
activity. Demands on the railways were reduced and additional
service was made available to chrome producers.

In face of these obstacles, expansion in the chrome industry
has often been retarded. Production in 1955 was just over 50

[1] Asbestos prices have been calculated on the basis of the average price realized
from the annual mining reports. The pricing arrangements of the industry are
somewhat artificial. The output of the largest mines in the colony is controlled by
the Turner and Newall asbestos processing group in the United Kingdom and is
not sold on the market directly. The nominal value assigned by the group to its
output is shown in the export statistics and in the calculations of the gross value
of mineral production. Actual market value may be understated in the values
declared. This is apparent from the comparisons of prices received by independent
producers with those declared by the Turner and Newall group; see, for example,
the *Report of the Chief Government Mining Engineer, 1953*, pp. 22–24.

[2] In 1952 for example, the tonnage declared in stockpile represented more than a
normal year's output of the industry (*Report of the Chief Government Mining Engineer,
1952*).

per cent. greater than it had been in 1929, while the price was roughly twice as great and had reached higher levels in 1950–52.

TABLE I

SOUTHERN RHODESIA, QUANTITIES PRODUCED AND VALUES OF MAJOR MINERALS, 1925–59

	Gold		Chrome Ore		Asbestos	
	Quantity (*ooos fine ounces*)	*Value* (a) (*£ooos*)	*Quantity* (*ooos short tons*)	*Value* (*£ooos*)	*Quantity* (*ooos short tons*)	*Value* (*£ooos*)
1925	582	2,540	136	337	34	766
1926	593	2,509	181	420	33	727
1927	581	2,459	218	491	33	794
1928	576	2,438	219	472	40	970
1929	561	2,374	293	675	43	1,187
1930	548	2,317	227	520	38	1,071
1931	532	2,274	90	224	24	386
1932	574	3,366	17	34	16	197
1933	642	4,014	39	106	30	556
1934	691	4,696	79	241	32	403
1935	726	5,090	117	146	43	647
1936	797	6,041	202	251	56	836
1937	804	5,657	304	367	57	840
1938	814	5,821	205	242	59	1,021
1939	796	6,227	153	187	58	1,089
1940	826	6,942	273	449	56	1,107
1941	790	6,640	357	660	44	910
1942	760	6,384	384	667	56	1,488
1943	657	5,516	317	596	58	1,673
1944	593	4,979	305	609	58	1,674
1945	568	4,894	205	414	56	1,788
1946	545	4,698	167	330	56	1,677
1947	523	4,509	171	432	54	1,738
1948	514	4,437	254	825	69	2,600
1949	528	5,197	268	986	80	3,987
1950	511	6,345	321	1,220	72	4,615
1951	487	6,089	331	1,531	78	5,452
1952	497	6,520	862 (b)	4,279 (b)	85	6,652
1953	501	6,440	463	2,928	88	6,543
1954	536	6,687	443	2,493	80	5,923
1955	525	6,582	449	2,192	105	7,052
1956	535	6,725	449	2,671	119	8,525
1957	537	6,749	654	4,517	132	9,016
1958	555	6,950	619	3,977	127	8,594
1959	567	7,081	543	3,031	120	7,405

Notes: (a) The gold premium is included in the total value of gold production in all relevant years.

      (b) The 1952 figures for chrome ore production include stockpiles of 508,704 short tons, valued at £2,430,593.

Sources: *Annual Reports of the Chief Government Mining Engineer, Southern Rhodesia* and *Monthly Digests of Statistics, Federation of Rhodesia and Nyasaland.*

When railway services for the industry improved in 1957, marketings of chrome ore rose rapidly, with supplies coming both from increased current production and from stockpiles. In the depression years, the industry responded to price drops with even greater speed. Production of chrome ore has consistently been concentrated in two large firms although some smaller properties have been worked intermittently. Two new ventures were incorporated in 1950–51. Both were small firms and one suspended operations in 1953.

The shifts in emphasis which have characterized the Southern Rhodesian mineral exports have no parallel in Northern Rhodesia. On the contrary, specialization in copper has been consistently maintained since the Copperbelt was brought into production. Its mining operations completely overshadow those of Southern Rhodesia. Substantial mining development, however, was much later in coming to Northern Rhodesia. Before 1929, the principal minerals extracted were lead, zinc, and vanadium. All three were the product of one mine which had come into production in 1906. Copper working was undertaken after 1910, but the early mines, sited on ancient workings, were operated on a small scale. As late as the 1920s, professional opinion viewed sceptically the further mineral prospects of Northern Rhodesia. Discoveries in 1925 revolutionized the territory's economy. Extensive deposits of sulphide ore containing 3 to 5 per cent. copper were proved and the development of the present Copperbelt began soon after. Cobalt has recently been extracted as a by-product from the copper ores.

Before 1956, the total copper output of the territory came from four large mines controlled by two financial groups: the Anglo-American Corporation of South Africa and the Rhodesian Selection Trust. Each group controls two of the original large mines. The Anglo-American group also controls the only other sizeable mineral venture in the territory — the production of lead and zinc at Broken Hill. In addition, both groups operate refineries for the transformation of blister into electrolytic copper.[1]

---

[1] The Rhodesian Anglo-American Corporation, a subsidiary of the Anglo-American Corporation of South Africa, controls the Rhokana and Nchanga mines and the new Bancroft mine. Despite its name, the corporation has only insignificant support from American interests; its major shareholders are resident in the Union of South Africa or the United Kingdom. The Rhodesian Selection Trust group includes the Roan Antelope and Mufulira mines as well as new Chibuluma property. Controlling interest in the group is held by the American Metal Company

Copper production has generally increased throughout this period. Even through the slump years, the aggregate output of the industry expanded, although two of the new mines halted operations temporarily. The break in copper prices, of course, affected producers throughout the world, and attempts were made to check further deterioration in the price through an international restriction scheme. The Rhodesian companies were represented at the conference called to set quotas. Their support for these schemes was never enthusiastic. As low cost producers, their competitive position was stronger than that of many members of the scheme. Restrictive arrangements themselves soon broke down and their effect on the output of the Northern Rhodesian industry was temporary.[1] But the depression did shatter the atmosphere of optimism in which the Copperbelt was conceived. With further development work suspended, employment dropped and the European population of the territory fell by roughly a quarter in two years' time.[2]

The revival of international demand for copper during and immediately before the war raised total tonnage (blister and electrolytic combined) by 1943 to a level roughly two-thirds above that achieved in 1937. In the uncertainty about the state of post-war international demand, production was again cut back. But the boom accompanying and following the Korean War brought existing capacity back into full use. Yet, although the average prices received nearly tripled from 1948 to 1955, aggregate tonnage increased by little more than one-third.[3]

[1] For further details concerning the effect of quotas on the Copperbelt, see *Report of the Finance Committee, 1932, Northern Rhodesia*, esp. p. 6; and L. H. Gann, 'The Northern Rhodesian Copper Industry and the World of Copper, 1923–1952', *Rhodes-Livingstone Institute Journal*, vol. xviii (1955), pp. 1–18.

[2] For a discussion of the effects of depression on the Northern Rhodesian economy, see James A. Henry, 'Some Aspects of Economic Development of Northern Rhodesia', *South African Journal of Economics*, vol. xiv (1946), pp. 100–16.

[3] This calculation, which is based on the average prices received, takes into account the fixed price policy introduced by the Rhodesian Selection Trust group in 1955. R.S.T. then abandoned sales through the London Metal Exchange in favour of quoting fixed prices to its customers. The rationale of this policy was that a stabilized price would discourage the substitution of cheaper metals (particularly aluminium) for copper. This pricing policy has since been scrapped.

of New York. Shares of the Rhodesian Selection Trust and the Roan Antelope Copper Mines, Ltd., were listed on the New York Stock Exchange in 1955. They are the only African mining companies incorporated outside the U.S. with direct facilities in the United States securities' market.

In several recent years, output has been reduced by work stoppages caused by strikes of the European and African trade unions. But the basic factor underlying the inability of the industry to expand output more rapidly in the boom years was the time lag — a period of roughly five years — between the planning and the production stages of a large-scale copper mine. Stimulated by the upsurge in demand during the Korean War, each group undertook the development of one further mine. Neither property reached the production stage before the slump in copper prices had set in.

Several other factors have at times held back expansion in the four established mines. Shortages of fuel and power have been the major bottlenecks which, in turn, have been caused by the shortcomings in the Rhodesian transport system. To overcome this deficiency, the producing companies in combination formed the Rhodesia Congo Border Power Corporation, the function of which is to transmit hydro-electric power from the Belgian Congo. The transmission links were not completed until 1957. Power drawn from this source, however, was intended to provide only an interim solution to the long-term power requirements of the Copperbelt. With the commissioning of the Kariba hydro-electric project in 1960, the copper industry has become one of its major consumers. The copper companies in fact have underwritten a substantial share of the cost of the project by agreeing to provide £20,000,000 through medium-term loans and through surcharges on power when delivered.

Heavy capital sums have been invested in the industry from abroad. External finance in the amount of approximately £25,000,000 was made available up to 1936.[1] For later expansions in capacity and for the construction of refineries, the copper industry has turned more to ploughed-back profits than to fresh external capital. Compared with capital expenditure financed from profits, the volume of fresh external capital brought into the industry has been modest. For the Copperbelt's original mines, equity issues made since the initial development period have raised less than £8,000,000 (with receipts

---

[1] S. H. Frankel, *Capital Investment in Africa* (O.U.P., 1938), p. 249. This calculation includes only the sums raised through subscriptions to publicly listed securities. Reinvestments from earnings do not appear in this estimate.

from share premium sales included). The original Rhodesian Selection Trust mines obtained a further £1,700,000 in medium term loans and Rhokana (in the Anglo-American group) received a capital grant of £200,000 for the construction of a cobalt refinery. Through their combined efforts, the four mines of the Copperbelt borrowed £8,000,000 for the formation of the Rhodesia Congo Border Power Corporation. This sum was supplemented by £4,000,000 provided to the Corporation from the internal resources of the copper companies.[1]

Financing of the two new mines has also been partly accomplished from the internal resources of the established companies. All the initial equity capital — £1,000,000 — of the Chibuluma mine in the Rhodesian Selection Trust group was provided by one of the established companies. The additional resources required for initial development were raised through a medium term loan in the amount of £5,000,000. The Bancroft mine, the new property under the control of the Anglo-American group, was initiated with £6,000,000 in equity issues (including share premium receipts) and £8,000,000 in loan capital. Nearly half of the former was subscribed by the Rhokana Corporation, one of the original large companies. Reinvestment from profits has also financed the bulk of the capital expenditure on the new copper refinery constructed by the Rhodesian Selection Trust Group. Of the total capital requirement of £3,000,000, two-thirds was supplied from the reserves of the Roan Antelope mining corporation and the remainder by a copper processing firm in the United Kingdom.

It will be noted in the recent financing of the Copperbelt that loans have surpassed equity issues in volume. Moreover, the equity capital issued has largely been held within the groups. The preference of the established companies for these arrangements is readily comprehensible: in this manner, their control is retained. Their ability to acquire finance in this fashion has been enhanced by a unique combination of circumstances. The principal external source of loan funds to the Copperbelt has been the United States Government, which has provided £13,000,000 for its post-war expansion. Of this total, £8,000,000 have gone to the Rhodesia Congo Border Power Corporation and £5,000,000 for the development of the Chibuluma Copper

[1] Drawn from the *Annual Reports* of the Copperbelt mining companies.

mine. The terms of both loans called for the repayment of principal and interest in kind through the deliveries of metal to the strategic stockpiles of the American Government. Further, the United States Government provided the £200,000 grant to the Rhokana Corporation for the construction of its cobalt refinery. In return, the grantor received an option on its output. These activities by the United States Government were stimulated by the strategic materials requirements of the Korean War. Similar arrangements were made with mineral producers elsewhere in Africa. The Copperbelt directly, or indirectly through loans to the Rhodesia Railways which also called for repayment in strategic metals, received a larger share of this finance than did mineral producers in any other colonial African territory.[1] Official American lending, however, was related to specific stockpiling targets set by the government. As the stockpiling objectives have been approached, further finance for strategic minerals development has not been forthcoming.

Agriculture in the Money Economy

Unlike the mining industries (the output of which is directed almost entirely into export markets), agricultural production in the money economy is sold both at home and abroad. The division of energies between domestic and foreign markets has varied through time as have the commodities included in the productive pattern of Central African agriculture. These changes and their implications deserve closer inspection. Developments in the monetized agricultural sector are also of interest for another reason. Both European and African producers can participate in agricultural sales. The extent to which African real income has been advanced through this form of

---

[1] Two U.S. Government loans have been made to the Rhodesia Railways: one of $14,000,000 in 1951 and the other of $10,000,000 in 1954. These loans, plus the finance provided for the Rhodesia Congo Border Power Corporation, for the development of the Chibuluma mine and for the Rhokana cobalt refinery, have brought U.S. Government assistance to more than $60,000,000. Not all the loan funds were made available in dollar currency; the major share of this finance was in the form of sterling counterpart funds accumulated through Marshall Aid to the United Kingdom. See *Foreign Grants and Credits by the United States Government*, Department of Commerce, Washington, and the *Annual Reports of the Export-Import Bank*, Washington.

contact with the money economy bears on whether or not the second criterion of economic development has been fulfilled.

TABLE II

NORTHERN RHODESIA, QUANTITIES PRODUCED AND VALUES OF MAJOR MINERALS, 1925–58

| | Copper, blister | | Copper, electrolytic | | Zinc | | Lead | |
	Quantity (ooos long tons)	Value (£ooos)	Quantity (ooos long tons)	Value (£ooos)	Quantity (ooos long tons)	Value (£ooos)	Quantity (ooos long tons)	Value (£ooos)
1925	0·1	6	—	—	0·2	6	3·4	52
1926	0·7	27	—	—	0·7	2	3·8	231
1927	3	197	—	—	0·3	8	5·8	143
1928	6	383	—	—	13	331	4·7	99
1929	5	408	—	—	22	548	1·6	39
1930	6	344	—	—	20	340	(a)	(a)
1931	9	346	—	—	7	82	(a)	(a)
1932	68	2,095	—	—	(a)	(a)	(a)	(a)
1933	104	3,403	—	—	19	292	(a)	(a)
1934	137	4,147	0·6	19	19·5	266	0·2	2
1935	120	3,786	24	845	21	290	0·2	3
1936	114	4,464	28	1,205	21	309	0·3	5
1937	117	9,715	31	1,849	14	333	0·5	12
1938	182	7,445	31	1,441	10	142	0·3	4
1939	182	7,990	30	1,468	13	191	0·2	3
1940	236	11,249	27	1,430	13	353	0·3	6
1941	204	9,288	24	1,223	14	409	0·4	8
1942	202	9,089	45	2,287	13	472	1·1	47
1943	190	8,550	61	3,093	13	561	1·2	51
1944	159	7,172	62	3,124	14	611	1·0	39
1945	133	7,432	61	3,815	15	696	1·7	64
1946	129	8,470	54	3,856	17	870	8·2	486
1947	136	13,945	56	6,445	21	1,301	15·6	1,297
1948	152	18,161	61	7,695	22	1,700	13·0	1,243
1949	195	23,549	64	7,706	23	1,973	13·9	1,404
1950	199	30,678	78	12,732	23	3,127	13·7	1,538
1951	206	41,167	103	21,043	23	3,928	14·0	2,364
1952	201	45,969	112	26,415	23	2,859	12·6	1,582
1953	210	51,475	153	38,196	25	1,897	11·5	1,047
1954	204	48,008	174	43,136	27	2,075	15·0	1,446
1955	165	52,827	178	62,462	28	2,530	16·1	1,700
1956	157	47,271	226	73,730	29	2,828	15·4	1,768
1957	170	34,200	247	54,416	29	2,396	15·4	1,437
1958	133	23,192	242	46,659	30	1,995	13·4	949

Notes: (a) Negligible.

Sources: *Annual Blue Books, Northern Rhodesia,* and the *Monthly Digests of Statistics, Federation of Rhodesia and Nyasaland.*

As an export industry, agriculture has been an important contributor to foreign exchange receipts in two of the three territories — Southern Rhodesia and Nyasaland. In the latter, exports of agricultural crops have always dominated the export bill. Originally, the bulk of its export crops was produced on European estates. But the depression of the 1930s hit the European planters hard. Acreages cultivated by Europeans fell by roughly one-third between 1929 and 1935.[1] A change in commodity specialization was also undertaken. Land was withdrawn from the original export crops, tobacco and cotton, and put under tea. Although technically the Protectorate was committed to observe the regulations of the International Tea Agreements of the 1930s, its production was not large enough to be affected by these restrictions. Tea acreages steadily expanded throughout this period and since the late 1930s have generally absorbed nearly half the land cultivated by Europeans. The total acreage under plantation crops began to recover after 1936 and slow expansion has been continued since. Even so, the area under the plantation crops of Europeans was smaller in the late 1950s than it had been in the early 1920s. Since the war, much of the increased acreage has been planted to tung.[2]

With the shift in specialization of the European estates, the continued export of tobacco and cotton from Nyasaland has come largely from production by Africans. Cotton growing is now almost entirely in their hands. Since 1940, Africans have grown between a quarter and a half of the tobacco sold.[3] The share of African cultivators is difficult to establish precisely. Production of cash crops may be undertaken either by individual growers on Native Trust Land or by African tenant farmers on European estates. The sales of the former are conducted through government-sponsored marketing organizations, whereas the latter may escape record or be included in the output of European plantations. A shift of cotton and tobacco production from European to African growers, however, is unmistakable. In 1953, it was estimated that African sales of these crops from Native Trust Land alone were worth £2,400,000 —

---

[1] *Annual Reports of the Department of Agriculture, Protectorate of Nyasaland.*

[2] A substantial part of the tung planting has been done by the Colonial Development Corporation; see *Annual Reports of the Colonial Development Corporation.*

[3] Based on data contained in the *Annual Reports on Native Affairs, Protectorate of Nyasaland.* For a useful discussion of the African tobacco industry, see W. E. Haviland, 'The Rise of the African Tobacco Industry in Nyasaland and its Production Problems', *South African Journal of Economics,* vol. xxiii (1955), pp. 141–52.

approximately one-third of the total value of Nyasaland's exports during that year.[1]

All of Nyasaland's export commodities have enjoyed substantial improvements in prices during and since the war. But production has not expanded at the same pace. The average price realized from tea exports, for example, has risen roughly three times since 1940 while the quantity produced has changed little. The output of tobacco and cotton has been erratic with marked seasonal variations. Although the production of both crops has shown an upward trend, the expansion has been much slower than the rise in export prices.

Several special factors have dampened the responsiveness of Nyasaland's agricultural output to price improvements. Short-term increases in output cannot easily be accomplished through an extension of acreages. The area available has narrow limits and the most suitable land is already utilized. Plantation agriculture, however, has added to the value of its exports through local processing of its crops. Physical pressure on the land and governmental policy have combined to retard a further expansion in the production of export crops by Africans. Concerned with threatening food shortages, government has discouraged greater concentration on exports. In some cases, African producers have withdrawn from planting export crops in order to concentrate on food production for subsistence.

In Southern Rhodesia, some foreign exchange has always been earned through agricultural exports. Originally, the major crop produced by European farmers was maize. They viewed the provision of local consumption requirements as their first task, but in most years there was a surplus for export. During the depression, maize exports suffered severely and the European farming community sought shelter from government and from local price support schemes. But the factor which has reshaped European agriculture in Southern Rhodesia has been the development of the tobacco industry.

From an early date, some tobacco was produced in the colony. But neither in volume nor value was the industry important

---

[1] Estimates of the value of export crops produced by Africans are contained in the *Economic Reports, Federation of Rhodesia and Nyasaland* for the years since 1951. Estimates for the earlier years are available in the *Nyasaland Statistical Handbook, 1952* and in the *Annual Reports of the Department of Agriculture, Protectorate of Nyasaland*.

before the late 1920s. Initial efforts to establish tobacco growing reached a climax in 1928 when a crop of nearly 25,000,000 lb. was reaped. But the quality was poor — so poor that most was unmarketable. In the years immediately following, output dropped sharply. The subsequent recovery of the tobacco industry owes much to the sterling area connexions of Southern Rhodesia. After the establishment of the Imperial Preference system, the industry's output again increased. The most important expansion has come since the war when the industry has been a beneficiary of the sterling area's dollar exchange controls.[1]

Since 1934, the average export price received for tobacco has generally risen and by the mid-1950s was nearly four times greater than it had been in the early 1930s. Part of the increase in receipts reflects improvements in quality, although the Southern Rhodesian product is still not of sufficiently high grade to command the highest prices in world markets.[2] Tobacco producers have responded to the upward movement in prices with a steady increase in output and in acreages. Output, which in 1929 was less than 7,000,000 lb., exceeded 153,000,000 lb. in 1958. The major expansion in production has come since the war. Before 1945, production had never exceeded 50,000,000 lb. and in the 1930s, had usually been in the range of 25,000,000 lb. Acreage under tobacco has altered correspondingly. In the 1957/8 season, more than 190,000 acres were under tobacco. Acreages in the 1930s, although increasing, never exceeded 70,000.[3]

Two factors have combined to produce the expansion in tobacco outputs: the substitution of tobacco for maize on the established European farms, and the expansion in acreage

[1] For discussions of the history of the Southern Rhodesian tobacco industry, see H. W. Roberts, 'The Development of the Southern Rhodesian Tobacco Industry', *South African Journal of Economics*, vol. xix (1951), pp. 177–88; and W. E. Haviland, 'Tobacco Farm Organization, Costs and Land Use in Southern Rhodesia', *South African Journal of Economics*, vol. xxi (1953), pp. 367–80.

[2] The quality of the Southern Rhodesian leaf, although it has improved markedly in recent years, is still such that the bulk of it is suitable only for blending with higher grade tobaccos. Efforts on the part of the Southern Rhodesian Tobacco Association to persuade tobacco firms in the United Kingdom to increase the Southern Rhodesian content of their blends are continuous.

[3] Drawn from the *Annual Reports on Agricultural and Pastoral Production, Southern Rhodesia*. A small quantity of tobacco grown in the north-eastern section of Northern Rhodesia (but marketed in Southern Rhodesia) is included in 1958 data on output.

under cultivation with an increase in the number of farming units. In the 1930s, the former was the more important. Tobacco acreage expanded at the expense of maize. This shift was encouraged by the collapse in maize prices and the shrinkage of its export market. Continued production of maize, however, was made somewhat less unattractive through the price support and control schemes introduced by the farming community. But the post-war expansion in production has been largely accomplished through an increase in the number of producers. Total acreage under summer crops by 1954 was nearly double what it had been in 1929 and nearly 55 per cent. greater than in 1945. Acreage planted to tobacco has more than doubled in the post-war years. Meanwhile the number of producers has risen from just over 1,000 in 1945 to 2,669 in 1958. The bulk of the increase was accounted for by immigrants, most of whom were supported by capital which they brought with them.

With the rise of the tobacco industry, the gross value of European agricultural production has expanded impressively. Before 1939, the aggregate value of European output changed little, but it increased more than sixteenfold between 1939 and 1957 (see Table III). Tobacco has been responsible for the bulk of this expansion. It has become Southern Rhodesia's most important single export commodity and has contributed, on the average, more than a third of the colony's export receipts in the post-war period. For the Federation, tobacco — roughly three quarters of which is grown in Southern Rhodesia — is second only to copper as a foreign exchange earner.

Agricultural exports have clearly assumed added importance in the post-war years. But the further question arising from this phenomenon concerns its effect on the ability of home production to meet local food requirements. Southern Rhodesia provides an interesting illustration of this problem. A general impression of the position may be obtained by comparing the values of European agricultural production retained in the territory with trends in the imports of foodstuffs.[1] The sum of these calculations, it must be emphasized, does not represent the volume of consumer expenditure on foodstuffs. The import

[1] Because the collection of territorial trade statistics was discontinued with federation, this comparison cannot be carried beyond 1953.

data, expressed at f.o.b. or f.o.r. values, obviously do not measure the cost of these items to the consumer. A comparison of these magnitudes is, however, useful in illustrating the degree

TABLE III

SOUTHERN RHODESIA, ESTIMATED GROSS VALUE OF EUROPEAN AGRICULTURAL OUTPUT, 1925–57 (£000s)

	Field husbandry	Animal husbandry and dairying	Total
1925	970	1,010	1,980
1926	1,520	1,240	2,760
1927	2,140	1,250	3,390
1928	1,830	1,500	3,330
1929	1,590	1,560	3,150
1930	1,470	1,500	2,970
1931	1,270	870	2,140
1932	1,630	780	2,410
1933	1,250	1,030	2,280
1934	2,110	1,190	3,300
1935	1,700	1,160	2,860
1936	1,990	1,280	3,270
1937	2,180	1,470	3,650
1938	2,280	1,490	3,770
1939	2,080	1,480	3,560
1940	3,120	1,770	4,890
1941	3,570	1,760	5,330
1942	4,460	1,900	6,360
1943	4,550	2,140	6,690
1944	5,610	2,450	8,060
1945	7,170	2,600	9,770
1946	9,160	2,680	11,840
1947	10,080	3,000	13,080
1948	15,220	3,400	18,590
1949	15,250	3,800	19,050
1950	22,620	4,490	27,110
1951	18,490	5,870	24,360
1952	26,980	7,030	34,010
1953	26,010	8,210	34,220
1954	28,490	9,120	37,610
1955	29,414	9,044	38,458
1956	33,465	9,668	43,133
1957	33,912	11,174	45,086

Notes: These calculations refer to the farming season ending 30 September in the years shown.

Sources: *Annual Reports on Agricultural and Pastoral Production, Southern Rhodesia and Federation of Rhodesia and Nyasaland.*

to which the Southern Rhodesian economy is and has been self-sufficient in foodstuffs.

As indicated in Table IV, food imports have risen in relation to the local sales of European agriculture. This is particularly striking in the post-war years. In the 1930s, the value of retained imports (f.o.r. or f.o.b.) ran, on the average, at just over one-third the value of retained output of European agriculture. From 1947 to 1953, this ratio was generally in the range of three-quarters or more. In two years, food imports (f.o.b. or f.o.r.) have exceeded the value of European output sold locally. One of these years — 1951 — was exceptional in that traders were encouraged by the government to stockpile imports. The drop in food imports in 1953 is largely accounted for by the subsequent reduction in inventories.

These calculations are not intended as precise measures, but they do suggest that domestic food production has not kept pace with expanded home demand. Of course, the colony's agricultural resources are not suited to produce all varieties of foodstuffs sought by European consumers. The long-period comparisons indicate, however, that European production has not succeeded to the extent that it did in the 1930s in satisfying the requirements which were within its capabilities. This has clearly been the case in maize, the crop which was originally the main source of export incomes to the European farmers. Since 1940, Southern Rhodesia has often been a net importer of maize; in exceptionally good seasons surpluses for export have still been produced. A similar change has occurred in Northern Rhodesia where, since 1938, it has sometimes been necessary to import maize.

This short-fall in home-grown foodstuffs has caused concern in both Rhodesias. Subsidies have been offered to encourage the production of food crops and in Southern Rhodesia income tax rebates have been made to European food producers. But the official attitude has been ambivalent. The encouragement of a European population with roots in the land has always been a primary aim of policy and the prospects of high incomes from tobacco growing have served this objective. Additional European settlers have been attracted — immigrants who might not have been prepared to come if only the lower returns from food production were obtainable.[1] The government has maintained

[1] In recent years, gross income per acre from tobacco has been four to five times greater than from maize. This calculation is based on average yields shown in the *Annual Reports on Agricultural and Pastoral Production, Southern Rhodesia* and on price data shown in the *Annual Reports of the Maize Control Board* and in the foreign trade returns.

that there is no incompatibility between expansion of food production on European farms and an increase in the number of Europeans engaged in tobacco growing. It is argued that tobacco prosperity has created conditions in which the heavy initial costs of turning bush under the plough can be overcome. The capital outlays required in this process are high[1] and profits from tobacco undoubtedly facilitate the expansion in acreage cultivated by Europeans.

But whether the deficit in local food production can be reduced simultaneously is less certain. The official argument holds that, because tobacco ground must be rested periodically, food crops can be fitted into the rotational pattern. While this may occur, it does not necessarily follow that marketings of food crops increase. In the case of maize, a sizeable proportion of the total output is retained on the farm. In the 1930s, roughly one-third of the maize grown by European producers in Southern Rhodesia was not marketed. Since the war, this proportion — although fluctuating with the season — has tended to be closer to one-half. Ration requirements for African employees have claimed the major share of this retained production — generally about 75 per cent. in the post-war years — with livestock feed and seed accounting for the remainder.[2]

These circumstances, it might be thought, would be favourable for the marketing of surpluses by the indigenous economy. Sales by Africans — particularly of maize — have increased and the restrictions which characterized the marketing policies of the depression have been removed. Quantities sold by African growers have fluctuated sharply, depending on the season, but the average volume since 1950 has been much higher than in any earlier period. Simultaneously, the share of African pro-

[1] The results of a survey of European farming propositions in Northern Rhodesia indicate that costs for clearing and stumping virgin land amounted, on the average, to £6 per acre. A. M. Morgan Rees, 'Some Financial Aspects of European Farming in Northern Rhodesia', published as Appendix G, to the *Report of a Commission of Inquiry into the Future of the European Farming Industry of Northern Rhodesia (The Troup Report)*, (Government Printer, Lusaka, 1954), pp. 65–67. The main body of the report further notes (p. 35): 'The heavy cost of clearing and stumping land in the areas to be used for maize and mixed farming from Lusaka to the north of the line of rail . . . reaches a peak of from £20 to £30 an acre in the Copperbelt.'

[2] Drawn from the *Annual Reports on Agricultural and Pastoral Production, Southern Rhodesia, passim.*

TABLE IV

COMPARISON OF THE GROSS VALUE OF RETAINED
OUTPUT FROM EUROPEAN AGRICULTURE WITH
THE F.O.B. OR F.O.R. VALUE OF RETAINED FOOD
IMPORTS, SOUTHERN RHODESIA, 1930–53
(£000,000s)

	Gross value of European agricultural production (net of agricultural exports)	Value of retained imports of foodstuffs, f.o.r. or f.o.b.	(2) as a per cent. of (1)
1930	1,457	542	37
1931	1,017	532	52
1932	1,218	383	31
1933	1,346	373	28
1934	1,858	428	23
1935	1,620	474	29
1936	1,665	471	28
1937	1,319	535	41
1938	1,599	649	41
1939	1,801	680	38
1940	1,833	676	37
1941	1,802	1,067	59
1942	2,024	1,431	71
1943	2,921	1,157	40
1944	3,561	1,153	32
1945	3,833	1,409	37
1946	3,362	1,812	54
1947	2,998	5,071	170
1948	5,065	4,127	81
1949	4,682	4,397	94
1950	6,492	5,006	77
1951	5,797	8,816	152
1952	9,874	8,164	83
1953	11,595	6,736	58

Notes and Sources: Calculation of the retained value of European agricultural production is made by deducting the f.o.r. values of agricultural exports from the estimated gross value of European agricultural production. The value of retained imports is calculated from the f.o.r. or f.o.b. value of food imports with the value of re-exports deducted. The f.o.b. or f.o.r. values of retained imports is inevitably slightly understated in this method of calculation as re-exports are recorded at their f.o.r. value within Southern Rhodesia. Data are drawn from the *Annual Reports on Agricultural and Pastoral Production* and from the *Annual Statements on External Trade, Southern Rhodesia.*

ducers in total sales in both Rhodesias has tended to rise. This may be noted in the quantitative comparisons shown in Table V. These returns, however, conceal qualitative differences. In general, the quality of African output has been lower than that produced by European growers; only a small fraction of the African-grown crop has been graded in the highest quality

TABLE V

MAIZE MARKETING IN NORTHERN AND SOUTHERN RHODESIA BY EUROPEAN AND AFRICAN PRODUCERS (000S OF 200 LB. BAGS)

Marketing year	Southern Rhodesia			Northern Rhodesia		
	(1) European	*(2)* African	*(3)* *(2) as a % of (1)*	*(1)* European	*(2)* African	*(3)* *(2) as a % of (1)*
1933/4	794	107	13			
1934/5	1,150	236	21			
1935/6	806	204	25			
1936/7	1,409	442	31	274	235	86
1937/8	1,491	592	40	242	200	83
1938/9	952	309	32	158	130	82
1939/40	740	325	44	154	73	47
1940/1	1,065	395	38	203	127	63
1941/2	684	137	20	121	39	32
1942/3	689	210	31	149	46	31
1943/4	907	328	36	148	70	47
1944/5	962	457	47	219	130	59
1945/6	867	475	55	274	230	84
1946/7	797	307	38	318	173	54
1947/8	395	206	52	149	66	44
1948/9	1,161	679	58	344	362	105
1949/50	696	391	56	282	62	22
1950/1	979	848	87	448	373	83
1951/2	464	203	44	398	321	81
1952/3	1,402	692	49	390	179	46
1953/4	1,735	890	51	664	658	100
1954/5	1,780	706	40	606	433	71
1955/6	2,419	1,396	58	900	746	83
1956/7	2,546	929	36	1,190	710	60
1957/8 (a)	2,433	484	20	544	56	10

Notes: (a) 1957/8 figures are for nine months of the marketing year only.

Sources: *Annual Reports of the Maize Control Board* and the *Grain Marketing Board, Southern Rhodesia; Annual Reports of the Maize Control Board, Northern Rhodesia; Monthly Digests of Statistics, Federation of Rhodesia and Nyasaland.*

classification. But, even with the larger sales by Africans, a gap between the Rhodesian maize consumption and local supplies remains a threat.

In their concern about local food supplies, governments in the Rhodesian territories have taken a more active interest in African agriculture. The scale of their efforts has thus far been limited. Expenditure on the improvement of African agriculture is only a small fraction of that devoted to the exclusive benefit of the European farming community. But governments have expanded extension services for African farmers, and have made more energetic efforts to introduce new techniques. Governmental marketing organizations have encouraged the sale of surpluses and have stimulated the production of crops for which there is a demand in the money economy. But one basic obstacle continues to block an extensive entry of indigenous agriculture into the money economy — the remoteness of most of the reserves from the urban centres and the inadequate transport system with which they are served. These factors have effectively restricted marketing opportunities to those areas with proximity to European markets.

But not all of the farming lands within reach of the transport system are, in fact, utilized. This situation arises from the artificial restrictions which the Rhodesian social system imposes on economic behaviour. The crowded conditions in the Native Reserves are hardly favourable for producing large surpluses; even if production problems were solved, the difficulties in physical access to markets would impede their sale. Meanwhile only some 3 per cent. of the European farming area in Southern Rhodesia is cultivated and only a small fraction of the remainder is used for grazing. As was brought out in a 1949 report:

Large tracts of useful land in European areas [are] lying idle because of the large size of the farms or through being held for speculative purposes. The present owners of a very considerable number of farms are not even known or cannot be traced.[1]

This land remains unutilized because it is reserved for European occupation. In Northern Rhodesia, a similar situation obtains — less than 5 per cent. of the European-owned farm land is tilled. Yet, on the ground that land should be held by those who use it productively, it was argued in the report of a Northern Rhodesian committee of inquiry in 1946 that Native Trust Land should be made available to European farmers.[2]

The rigid division of land ownership and use imposed by the

---

[1] *Development Co-ordinating Commission, Southern Rhodesia, Second Interim Report*, C.S.R. 3, 1949, p. 38.
[2] *Report of the Committee Appointed to Enquire into the Development of the European Farming Industry in Northern Rhodesia* (Government Printer, Lusaka, 1946), p. 36.

land apportionment policies means that the Rhodesian territories are oriented all the more forcefully towards the attraction of European settlers into farming. Given the existing arrangements, only Europeans are eligible to employ these idle resources. Thus, 'development' plans for the expansion of agricultural output tend to concentrate on this alternative alone. The report of 1954 Commission in Northern Rhodesia illustrates this point of view:

The forecast of population and food consumption trends . . . indicates that the volume of imported food will increase steadily at any rate for the next ten years, and that the position of self-sufficiency will worsen, unless production within the Territory is increased by means of an active and vigorous development plan. The area alienated for European agriculture, although it will be seen to be limited in extent, nevertheless represents a considerable proportion of the usable agricultural land within reach of communications in Northern Rhodesia. In addition, it is apparent that the reasonable development of the existing area will certainly occupy the next decade, and therefore the question of its extension . . . need not be considered now.[1]

The point omitted from such surveys as the above is that the desired increase in output might be achieved by opening the unemployed land areas to African cultivators. This alternative, of course, is in direct conflict with the *status quo* in land apportionment. So long as the *status quo* in land distribution is maintained and effective measures to increase the productivity of African farmers are not taken, the case for further European settlement can be supported by another argument. Professor Sir Frank Engledow anticipated this situation in his 1950 report, observing that 'it is . . . an inescapable conclusion that in the near future European agriculture must raise more and more food to feed the country's native population'.[2]

Non-economic aspects of the Rhodesian scene have thus barred an expansion of local agricultural production which might otherwise have been stimulated by the growth of demand in the money economy. And, in particular, they have stood in the way of cash sales by the indigenous economy. Whether, in

---

[1] *The Troup Report*, p. 32.
[2] Professor Sir Frank Engledow, *Report on the Agricultural Development of Southern Rhodesia*, C.S.R. 23, 1950, p. 19.

the absence of these artificial restrictions, African production of surpluses for market would have been sufficient in quantity or quality to satisfy all consumption requirements cannot be ascertained. In all likelihood, technical assistance and guidance would have been necessary to accomplish a major improvement in productivity. But one thing is clear: that in the established system of the Rhodesias the effective opportunities for African farmers to take advantage of the growth in local demand accompanying the money economy's expansion have been circumscribed.

The Manufacturing Industries

The response of manufacturing industries to the expansion of the money economy is less inhibited by non-economic factors than is the case in agriculture. But manufacturers do not escape entirely from the influence of the value system around which Rhodesian economic life is organized. For the system, with its bias towards the attraction of European immigrants, may not create the most favourable climate for the marketing of local manufactures. The emergence of manufacturing industries, of course, confronts problems more complex than those found in agriculture. In part, the difficulties in Central Africa are similar to those encountered elsewhere in the underdeveloped world. The local market is small in the early stages of expansion — often too small to warrant production on any scale. But in the Rhodesias, prospective manufacturers also face other obstacles. The internal transport system is not tailored for their needs and freight rates are high. Capital from local sources is difficult to obtain; and further, local shortages of skill may inhibit efficient operations. In combination, these factors have not made the Central African territories the most attractive sites for industrial activity.

It requires only a brief inspection of the industrial structure of Central Africa to establish that Southern Rhodesia is the only territory in which manufacturing industry has made any considerable strides. In Northern Rhodesia, only 107 'secondary' establishments were recorded in the first census of industrial production taken in 1947. 'Secondary' industry was defined broadly and taken to include some activities (e.g. repair of transport equipment and provision of electricity and water supplies) which might be treated as services in other classifications. By far the most important contributor to the total was the output of the refineries of the Copperbelt. With services and copper refining excluded, the gross value of 'secondary' output in the territory was then less than £4,000,000.[1] Most of this production was in the light industrial category — the processing of foods and beverages, the manufacture of wearing apparel and furniture. Not all these activities served the local market. One of the first industrial enterprises in the territory, the Zambesi Sawmills, has produced timber for export as well as for the local mining industry. By 1954, 284 'factories' were reported in operation.[2] The only establishment of size created in the interim was a cement factory financed jointly by the Colonial Development Corporation and the Northern Rhodesian Government.[3] The remainder were small organizations, some of them financed through the Industrial Loans Board created by the government in 1951.[4]

Manufacturing industry in Nyasaland operates on an even smaller scale. Its few industrial activities are dominated by the processing of agricultural exports. One of the few exceptions is a small soap factory which produces for the home market.

Industrialization has gone much further in Southern Rhodesia than in the other Central African territories. When the first census of manufacturing was taken in 1938, 299 establishments were recorded with a gross output of slightly more than £5,000,000. By 1953, the number of firms had risen to more than 700 and their gross output was valued at nearly £62,000,000.[5] As in the Northern Rhodesian classifications, the

[1] *First Report on the Census of Industrial Production, Northern Rhodesia, 1947*, Central African Statistical Office.

[2] Budget address of the Financial Secretary, contained in the *Estimates of Revenue and Expenditure, 1955–6*, p. 219.

[3] *Annual Reports of the Colonial Development Corporation*. C.D.C., while initiating the project, has subsequently liquidated its share capital in the cement works through sale to a private organization.

[4] The advisability of government lending for the encouragement of secondary industries was one of the points considered by W. J. Busschau in his *Report on the Development of Secondary Industries in Northern Rhodesia*, prepared at the request of the Northern Rhodesian Government in 1945. His views on this subject were negative, although one of his recommendations was that an Advisory Committee on Industrial Development should be established.

[5] *Thirteenth Annual Report on the Census of Industrial Production, 1938–1953, Southern Rhodesia*, Central African Statistical Office.

definitions of manufacturing applied in Southern Rhodesia were broad and included such activities as printing and publishing and the repair of transport equipment.

At first inspection, this rate of expansion in Southern Rhodesian manufacturing industry appears impressive. But a closer examination of these results reveals that the processing of local food production accounts for a large share of this total. In the years for which Southern Rhodesian data are available, the food-processing industries have claimed roughly a third of the gross value of manufacturing output. Only limited progress has been made in the production of consumer goods of non-homogeneous character. Manufacturing in the non-food lines has focused largely on two types of activity: the production of investment goods and of low-quality consumer goods for sale to Africans. Investment goods, primarily building and construction materials, have generally accounted for roughly a quarter of the gross value of manufacturing output (when the service industries counted in the official aggregate have been excluded). These heavy goods have found a local market in the building boom which has accompanied the growth of the European population; the bulkiness of these materials affords a natural advantage to their production locally. The major component of manufacturing for trade with the African is low-quality textiles. But it must be noted that a substantial share of Southern Rhodesian's output of textiles and wearing apparel has been exported. Indeed, roughly one-fifth of the gross value of secondary production was exported between 1938 and 1953, and textiles have generally been the largest single contributor.

The failure of manufacturing industry to expand further might be explained, in part, by the absence of tariffs to protect infant industries. In view of the other factors deterring industrial development in Central Africa, the efficacy of tariffs in stimulating local industries may be questioned. Until recently, Northern Rhodesia and Nyasaland were debarred from erecting protective tariff walls. All of Nyasaland and part of Northern Rhodesia were within the Congo Basin area which, by a convention of 1888, was to remain a free trade area.[1] Southern

---

[1] In 1957, the Federal Government negotiated the abrogation of the Congo Basin Treaty; formerly a uniform tariff for the whole of the Federal area had not been possible.

Rhodesia had a freer hand. But official opinion there generally subscribed to free trade principles. At least as far as private manufacturing industry was concerned, government viewed sceptically the prospects of encouraging local industries through protection. This position was reflected in the report of a committee investigating the tariff question in 1946:

If the people of Southern Rhodesia are to maintain or raise their standard of living, then we must guard against so called 'remedies' applied internally which might hamper the necessary stimulus of income which arises from our export trade. Any assistance given to a particular industry in Southern Rhodesia must be judged in the light of its effects upon the cost structure of those industries producing for export, and cannot on economic grounds be justified if it results in an increase in this cost structure which is likely to prove of a permanent nature.[1]

Consistent with this theme, the committee discouraged the general adoption of protection. This negative view was slightly qualified, however, in the observation that protection might be granted for a limited and specified period but that 'to ensure . . . competitive conditions, assistance shall not be granted unless the market available is estimated to justify at least two competing manufacturing concerns . . .'.[2] Subsequent Southern Rhodesian commissions have been more sympathetic. The Development Co-ordinating Commission, appointed shortly after, was enthusiastic about the prospects of industrial expansion. While temporizing on the tariff issue, it emphasized the 'natural' protection which distance and transport charges could afford to local industry.[3]

---

[1] *Report of the Committee of Enquiry into the Protection of Secondary Industries in Southern Rhodesia (the Margolis Report), 1946*, p. 10. An earlier expression of the same theme was made in 1934: 'Opinions have been expressed that it would be better for the colony to assist secondary industries rather than agricultural industry, and rely on the native population to supply the raw materials and staple foods. Your committee does not agree because:
(a) we would have to rely mainly on our own market, which is limited, to absorb manufactures produced at a price which will tend to send up the cost of living;
(b) it will not be possible, having regard to our geographical position to compete against highly industrialized countries' (*Report of the Committee of Enquiry into the Economic Position of the Agricultural Industry of Southern Rhodesia, 1934*, pp. 1–2).
[2] *The Margolis Report*, p. 56.
[3] Cf. *Interim Reports of the Development Co-ordinating Commission, Southern Rhodesia*.

With this free trade mentality, the Southern Rhodesian Government preferred to enter trade agreements with its stronger southern neighbour. The legal instruments governing trading relationships between Southern Rhodesia and the Union of South Africa have altered from time to time, but up to 1955 these agreements effectively tied Southern Rhodesia's customs duties to those of the Union. Each party received preferential treatment in the markets of the other and enjoyed advantages not accorded to other trading partners. Although these arrangements brought some benefits to Southern Rhodesian exporters, they effectively precluded the extensive use of tariffs to protect local industry.

Indirectly, however, Southern Rhodesia's special trade relations with the Union have fostered several industries. This effect became apparent soon after India acquired independence. Traditionally, India had been the major supplier of low-quality piece goods used by textile manufacturers in the Union. When diplomatic relations grew tense between the two countries, an embargo was imposed on their commerce. Southern Rhodesia was the beneficiary of this situation. Whereas India cut off its exports to the Union, there was nothing to prevent the rerouting of this trade through Southern Rhodesia. In 1950 alone, the number of textile and wearing apparel firms in Southern Rhodesia increased by nearly 50 per cent., most of them processing piece goods of Indian origin for re-export to South Africa.[1] The same motive inspired the establishment of a plant for the processing of Indian jute into hessian.

Federation has brought a change in the atmosphere. A new agreement with South Africa was concluded in 1955 which has permitted greater autonomy to the Federal Government in its tariff policy.[2] But one of its conditions was that preferential access to the Union market was restricted to products with at least a 75 per cent. Federal 'content'. This clause effectively blocked much of the traffic in rerouted Indian materials. The industries brought into being by these special circumstances spoke loudly

[1] *Census of Manufacturing, 1953*, p. 23.

[2] In 1959, the Federal Government announced its intention to terminate this agreement with the Union of South Africa in 1960 and its determination to insist on still greater autonomy if a formal trade agreement were to be re-negotiated. This agreement was re-negotiated in 1960 with provisions affording the Federal Government further autonomy in its tariff policy.

in protest against these terms. Several of the industries affected have since been granted protection.

Before federation, the Southern Rhodesian Government was not completely consistent in its approach to manufacturing industries. While reluctant to protect private manufacturers, it initiated several industries of its own and sheltered them fully. Officially, the Southern Rhodesian Government maintained that it was opposed in principle to nationalized industries but prepared in practice to sponsor certain activities if private enterprise failed to take the initiative.[1] As private industrialists avoided numerous fields, this policy led public enterprise into several ventures.

The two largest industrial undertakings in the colony have been financed and organized by government. Their record has been mixed. One venture — a cotton-spinning mill — has been successful. It has gone through several stages of expansion and has generally shown a nominal profit. The rationale for the inception of this enterprise lay, in part, in the view that a substantial local textile industry could flourish, once this raw material base had been provided.[2] These expectations have not been fully realized. Until recently, the capacity of the local weaving industry was too small to utilize the full production of the spinning mill and a share of its output has often been exported. Meanwhile, the textile industries which have emerged have relied heavily on imported piece goods.

The most ambitious industrial venture of government has been a small-scale iron and steel works established in 1942. The results have not been entirely satisfactory. More than £5,000,000 of government funds were provided on loan to the enterprise. And, although the capital indebtedness of the Iron and Steel Commission was written down and much of the interest due to the government written off, the enterprise accumulated substantial operating losses. These continued even though the industry was sheltered by a variety of devices. Government subsidized the sale of its output in the local market (the subsidy reached £5 per ton in 1954) and regulations on exchange

---

[1] Cf. Policy statements on industrial development contained in the *Interim Reports of the Development Co-ordinating Commission*. The Federal Government has since subscribed to these views.

[2] In 1960, this enterprise — the Cotton Industries Board — was sold to private interests by the Federal Government.

control and import licensing were administered to shield it from foreign competitors. Local marketing of the Commission's products was also arranged to defend it from the competition of South African producers.[1] But all of these measures in combination failed to make the undertaking profitable.

In part, the troubles of the Iron and Steel Commission have been those to be expected in the infancy of industrial enterprises in underdeveloped territories. With only a limited local market to serve, the plant was designed on a small scale — too small to achieve the economies realized by large-scale firms abroad. But the industry suffered from a further handicap — the dearth of managerial and technical talent. A Commission of Inquiry put the point in muted phrases: 'Many [initial difficulties] could have been more readily surmounted or even avoided by better and more experienced management'.[2] The shortage of skill locally would, of course, have plagued the enterprise regardless of the manner in which it had been organized. But its status as a governmental enterprise in the Rhodesian setting compounded the difficulty. As a public undertaking, political pressure for the appointment of local people, whose training was not fully adequate for the task, was irresistible. In 1957, the Southern Rhodesian Government negotiated the sale of the property to a private consortium which has operational responsibility although the government has retained a financial interest.

From this summary sketch of the industrial scene in the Rhodesias, it is apparent that manufacturing activity has grown, particularly in Southern Rhodesia. For the Federation as a whole, 1,253 manufacturing establishments were recorded in the 1957/8 census of industrial production.[3] Special circumstances, however, have accounted for much of this expansion. Apart from the food-processing industries, only a small proportion of the output of local manufacturers is consumed by

[1] Internal distribution was placed exclusively in the hands of an organization known as the Rhodesia Steel Sales Co., a branch of a steel sales company in South Africa. This monopoly was granted on the understanding that the company was 'not allowed to sell in Rhodesia, South African steel which falls within Riscom's [Rhodesian Iron and Steel Commission] range of products unless Riscom is unable to supply', *Report of the Commission Appointed to Inquire into the Iron and Steel Industry of Southern Rhodesia, June 1954*, C.S.R. 29, p. 15.

[2] Ibid., pp. 18–19.

[3] *Census of Industrial Production, Federation of Rhodesia and Nyasaland, 1957/8.*

Europeans — and it is they who control the bulk of consumer purchasing power. Manufacturing industries have looked more to building and construction, to the export market, and to the African consumer for outlets for their products. These markets, nevertheless, have succeeded in earning a considerable status for manufacturing in Southern Rhodesia especially. By 1950, the contribution of manufacturing to the net geographical income of the territory was second only to that of European agriculture among the various sectors of its money economy[1] and the relative importance of manufacturing has since continued to increase. Moreover, manufacturing and the building trades have provided an important share of the employment opportunities for the heavy post-war influx of European immigrants.

The Public Sector

Potentially, governments may play a crucial role in the expansion process of export economies. By taxing the earnings of expatriate export producers, they may check part of the leakage from the domestic income stream and retain a larger volume of resources for local use than would otherwise have been available. Moreover, by taxing their own citizens, government may produce savings which would not otherwise have been realized. But governments also have a unique position as spending authorities. Many of the factors which inhibit growth of the money economy can most readily be counteracted through public action. Most of the basic services required for economic expansion are normally public responsibilities.

These problems are common to most underdeveloped economies. In the dualistic situation of Central Africa, the economic role of government must also be considered from another point of view. The fiscal programme of government affects both economies within the dualistic system. The activities of this sector may, therefore, have a formidable influence on the pattern of change both in the money economy and in the indigenous economy.

Only a brief inspection of the volume of public expenditure is necessary to indicate the magnitude of its impact upon the money income stream (see Table VI). In recent years, public

[1] *National Income and Social Accounts of Southern Rhodesia, 1946–51*, Table 17, p. 21.

expenditure has represented between 22 and 31 per cent. of gross geographical income in the Federal area. This calculation is derived by consolidating the expenditures on goods and services made by the Federal, territorial and local governments with the capital expenditures of statutory bodies which draw financial support from the public purse.

The public sector has always had at its command a high proportion of the money economy's resources throughout Central African economic experience. The absolute sums at its disposal have expanded enormously in the post-war years. In part, the growth in the absolute size of the public sector is a by-product

TABLE VI

PUBLIC EXPENDITURE IN RELATION TO GROSS GEOGRAPHICAL PRODUCT IN THE MONEY
ECONOMY, FEDERATION OF RHODESIA AND NYASALAND (£000,000s)

	(1) Gross geographical product	(2) Government current expenditure on goods and services	(3) Government capital formation	(4) Gross capital formation by statutory bodies and railways	(5) Total public expenditure	(6) (5) as a % of (1)
1954	290.3	28.2	24.9	13.8	66.9	23
1955	339·7	32·3	27·6	14·4	74·3	22
1956	384·6	38·6	30·7	20·6	89·9	23
1957	375·1	43·4	37·2	34·2	114·8	31
1958	368·6	46·8	35·1	22·4	104·3	28
1959	428·6	51·1	27·7	16·6	95·4	22

Notes: Expenditures on goods and services by the Federal, territorial, and local governments are consolidated in the accounts.

Sources: *Annual Economic Reports* and *Monthly Digests of Statistics, Federation of Rhodesia and Nyasaland.*

of expansion in the money economy itself. The revenues of all echelons of government have swollen as the yields from all forms of taxation have moved in sympathy with the money economy's activity. Taxes on corporate profits (particularly from the Copperbelt) make the major contribution to public revenues for the Federal area. With prosperity, this category of revenue has increased impressively. Receipts from personal income taxes and from indirect taxes on goods and services have also grown. The fortunes of the money economy have also affected receipts from direct taxes levied on the African population. The expected yield from poll and hut taxes is governed by two factors: the size of the population and the rates of assessment. Changes in the money economy, however, determine whether or not the budgeted yield can actually be collected.[1]

Receipts from local taxation, although greatly expanded, have not supported all of the growth in public expenditure. External financing has always been important in the fiscal pattern of Central African governments. Loans from overseas financed the early development works in all three territories and each raised substantial sums abroad after the war. With federation, the individual territories waived their powers to negotiate external loans and transferred them to the Federal Government. This administrative change has not diminished the importance of foreign borrowings by governments for the area as a whole. Between 1954 and mid-1959, official borrowing abroad raised £101,000,000.[2]

Another form of external support to public expenditures — grants from the Colonial Development Fund in the 1930s and later from Colonial Development and Welfare appropriations — has made substantial contributions to the sums available for development purposes in the two northern territories. As a self-governing colony, Southern Rhodesia was never eligible for this assistance. Unlike the other two territories, however, Southern Rhodesia borrowed considerable sums through the issue of stocks locally. Not all the sums raised in this fashion were in fact subscribed from domestic sources. Between 1947 and 1953, for example, it has been estimated that roughly one-fifth of the gross amount raised was subscribed by expatriate firms operating within the colony or by investors abroad.[3]

In an analysis of the economic impact of public expenditure, primary attention must be focused on the allocations to which public funds are put. In any society, part of the revenues available to governments must be spent on the maintenance of law and order and for administrative housekeeping. If resources

---

[1] All three territorial governments learned this during the slump years of the 1930s. Despite penal sanctions, not all of the tax levied on the native could be then collected. With the decline in wage employment opportunities and in the possibilities for acquiring cash through agricultural sales, it was impossible for all the males who were liable to tax to discharge their obligations in full.

[2] Statement of the Federal Minister of Finance, reported in *Federation of Rhodesia and Nyasaland Newsletter* (Washington), 8 May 1959.

[3] Calculated from *Financial Statements, 1953, Southern Rhodesia*, Table IV, p. 31.

remain at their command after these functions have been efficiently discharged, governments can allocate them to purposes which make a more direct contribution to economic advance. 'Surpluses' in this sense may be turned in a variety of directions. Depending on which combination of priorities is chosen, the effects of public expenditure on the character of economic development may differ substantially even when the same aggregate sum is spent.

Two categories of public expenditure are of particular interest in Rhodesia and Nyasaland for their impact on the course of economic growth. Governments have financed substantial outlays on their own account. In fact, capital expenditures made directly by governments have represented between 20 and 30 per cent. of the gross capital formation in the money economy in the post-Federal years through 1958. This computation does not include a second type of capital expenditure supported by public resources: gross capital formation by statutory bodies. When this is included, the public sector's share of gross capital formation ranged from one-third to nearly one-half of the aggregate for the money economy from 1954 to 1958.[1]

In most years the basic requirements of transport and communications have claimed the largest shares of direct public capital expenditure. Before Federation, each of the territorial governments allocated a high proportion of available capital resources to the construction of roads, bridges, and airfields and to the provision of postal and telegraphic services. In addition, the Southern Rhodesian Government assumed primary responsibility for financing the Rhodesia Railways. It found the funds to purchase the system in 1947 and subsequently channelled considerable sums into the network. Northern Rhodesia, on the other hand, was less directly committed to financing of railways. It nevertheless assisted their investment programme by transferring the proceeds of two external loans to the system. In Nyasaland, the railways are still privately managed. Government, however, is the major shareholder in the system and has undertaken to finance most of its post-war development.

---

[1] See Supplement to the *Monthly Digest of Statistics* (vol. vi, no. 3), esp. Table XIII, p. 9. Statutory bodies include the Rhodesia Railways, Federal Power Board, Electricity Supply Commissions, the Cotton Industries Board, Central African Airways, the Cold Storage Commission, the Sugar Industries Board, Maize and Grain Marketing Boards, and the Roasting Plant.

L

Since 1953, the Federal Government has taken over the responsibility for the major transport and communications networks although the territorial governments are still empowered to construct local roads on their own account. Heavy capital expenditures have continued to flow into these projects. The importance of their claim on the public capital budget can be indicated by the allocations assigned to them in the Federal development plans. In the first plan, scheduled for the years 1955–59, an expenditure of £63,300,000 was projected, not including the costs of Kariba. More than 40 per cent. of this total was alloted to the improvement of the Rhodesia Railways alone. In mid-1957, the Federal development plan was revised to call for an expenditure of £138,000,000 in the financial years 1957–61, including an assignment of £54,000,000 to the Kariba project. A further revision was made in mid-1958 when the drop in receipts from taxes on the copper industry dictated a reassessment of resources likely to be available. Planned expenditures were then cut back by £16,000,000. Allotments to road, rail and air transportation and to the telecommunications system, however, continued to command the bulk of the budgeted capital expenditure which was not assigned to the Kariba undertaking.[1]

Administratively, the Kariba project is treated as an autonomous statutory commission. Its detailed expenditures are not, therefore, included in the budgets of governments. But the Federal Government is responsible for finding finance for all of its capital requirements and has borrowed heavily for this purpose. The first stage of this project, completed in 1960, cost £80,000,000. A major share of the external borrowings raised since federation have been earmarked for it.

In addition to its indirect assistance to the money economy through the provision of basic services, governments in the Rhodesias have also given direct support to selected industries. Several devices have been used for this purpose. In Southern Rhodesia, the government has been an active lender. In this role, it has assumed two postures. In one, it has acted as the financier of the statutory boards and commissions. Through this device, new industries such as the steel works and the cotton-spinning mill were created. The railways and the electricity

[1] See *Development Plans, Federation of Rhodesia and Nyasaland.*

supply commission were financed in the same fashion. While statutory bodies have accounted for the largest share of governmental lending, the Southern Rhodesian Government has also acted as a financier of private undertakings. Two industries have been especially favoured in this respect: European agriculture and small-scale mining. Farmers have been able to obtain loans both through the Land and Agricultural Bank (a statutory organization with capital entirely subscribed by the government), and from loans provided directly from the budget. Small miners have been financed from a special fund and have also received loans on an *ad hoc* basis. In addition, small gold workers have been assisted by a statutory commission organized to extract gold from low grade ores.

In Northern Rhodesia, mining operations have been able to stand on their own feet without assistance from government. European agriculture, however, has been assisted there. Formal facilities for agricultural finance emerged only recently. A Land and Agricultural Bank was not actually formed in Northern Rhodesia until 1951. But a Land Board, which performed much the same function, began operations in 1947.

Apart from the public funds which have gone into statutory enterprises, manufacturing industries have not historically enjoyed the same privileges as European agriculture and small-scale mining. Governmental credit facilities to industrial undertakings were non-existent in the Rhodesias until after the Second World War. An Industrial Loans Board was dismantled after a short post-war life in Southern Rhodesia; borrowing facilities for industrial establishments were brought back into being in 1958 with the formation of an Industrial Development Fund by the Southern Rhodesian Government. In Northern Rhodesia, a similar organization has functioned since 1951. The Federal Government has recently entered this field by sponsoring an Industrial Development Corporation which began operations in 1960. The initial capital was subscribed by the Central Bank and by the Commonwealth Development Finance Corporation.

But credit facilities are by no means the only way in which the public purse has been used to foster favoured economic activities. In both Rhodesias, European agriculture has benefited greatly from the budgeted departmental expenditures of government. The benefits have been especially large in Southern Rhodesia where research and extension facilities for European agriculture have been segregated administratively from those for Africans. In addition, agricultural products required for local consumption have been heavily subsidized to encourage production. To some extent, African sellers also benefit from these payments. But by far the largest share of the subsidy payments has accrued to European producers.[1] Government has also assisted European farmers by bearing part of the cost of such capital improvements as dams, boreholes, and irrigation works. At times, government has also subsidized the cost of recruited African labour. This form of subsidy has also been available to operators of small mines.

These benefits to European producers in the money economy have not been matched by corresponding governmental aid to the indigenous economy. African agriculture has received, until recently, a very low priority in public expenditure. Before the war, expenditure on agricultural services for Africans in the Rhodesias was small indeed. Since the Second World War — and especially since enactment of the Native Land Husbandry Act in 1951 — much more has been spent on African agriculture in Southern Rhodesia. A Department of Native Agriculture was created within the Native Affairs Department in 1945/6 and a production and marketing branch was organized to encourage and facilitate the marketing of cash crops by African farmers. This branch also acts as custodian of the Native Development Fund which accumulates the sums deducted from sales to the statutory marketing boards. These deductions, in effect, are a forced saving levied on producers of cash crops. But, unlike the statutory marketing boards in some British African colonies, withholdings are not intended for the purpose of price stabilization. Instead, they are earmarked for development expenditure which will further benefit African agriculture.

---

[1] Subsidy payments on maize — the crop to which the heaviest volume of payments has been applied — were substantially reduced in 1958. The burden of this change, however, did not then fall on European farmers in whose interest the subsidy scheme had originally been devised. The price of maize to consumers was allowed to rise, but the government continued to guarantee an artificially high price to producers. Reductions in the government's buying price were scheduled for later years. It is intended, however, that the government's support price will continue to be based on calculations of production costs on European farms.

The 1950s witnessed a striking expansion in Southern Rhodesia's expenditure on African agriculture. Total outlays for Native Agriculture and Native Land Husbandry amounted to more than £17,000,000 from 1952 to 1960. Not all of these funds, however, were appropriated from public revenues. More than a third of the total was provided by the Native Development Fund from its own resources, accumulated primarily from levies on African crop sales. Nor can all of this high level of expenditure be regarded as providing a net improvement to African agriculture. A substantial part of the sums shown have been spent on the resettlement of Africans from European areas. One informed estimate attributes roughly half of the expenditure charged to Native agriculture since 1950 to this purpose.[1]

Despite the marked rise in public expenditure on African agriculture in recent years, these outlays have continued to fall far short of those spent on European agriculture.[2] Apart from indirect participation in the subsidies provided for home-grown foodstuffs, African producers have seldom been eligible for the other forms of governmental assistance to European farmers. Subsidization of capital improvements has been available only to Europeans. Nor have Africans had the facilities of the Land and Agricultural Bank at their disposal. Most of them have been automatically debarred by their inability to offer land titles as security for mortgages.[3] Technically, African farmers in the Native Purchase areas could meet this requirement. But even they have had little success in obtaining loans from governmental institutions.

In Northern Rhodesia and Nyasaland, both the European and African agricultural communities have traditionally been

[1] M. Yudelman and S. M. Makings, 'A Note on the Economics of African Development in Southern Rhodesia with Special Reference to Agriculture' (mimeographed), February 1960.

[2] Drawn from the *Annual Reports of the Auditor and Comptroller-General, Southern Rhodesia*.

[3] To overcome this handicap, the Southern Rhodesian Department of Native Agriculture has recently initiated a revolving fund to supply short- and medium-term credits to African farmers. This scheme, inaugurated in 1958, has been financed by an appropriation of £14,000 from the Native Development Fund and by a grant of £66,000 from the United States International Co-operation Administration. Northern Rhodesia has also made similar facilities available, although on a modest scale, through its African Farming Improvement Fund and Peasant Farming Scheme.

served by joint administrative departments. A precise determination of the priorities received by African agriculture cannot, therefore, be made from the public accounts. But it is apparent from the small size of the aggregate sums spent on agricultural services that little was devoted to the improvement of the indigenous economy. In Northern Rhodesia, departmental expenditure on agricultural and veterinary services (including game and tsetse control) did not exceed £200,000 before 1948.[1] This figure was not surpassed in Nyasaland until 1950.[2] In the 1930s, the expenditure on agricultural subjects was, with the exception of two years in Northern Rhodesia, consistently short of £50,000 per annum in both territories.

One of the results of federation was the segregation of agricultural services for Europeans and Africans in Northern Rhodesia in 1956. Formerly, this had been the case only in Southern Rhodesia. Since then, expenditures on agriculture by the Federal Government (which has jurisdiction over European agriculture in the two Rhodesias) have been far in excess of the combined expenditures charged to agricultural votes by the two territorial governments (which are responsible only for African agriculture).

The allocation of public finance to the direct benefit of selected enterprises has clearly favoured European producers over the indigenous economy. This scale of priorities has also characterized the direction of expenditures on the transport and communications network. The heavy volume of capital expenditure has unquestionably improved the capacity of the existing transport network and has facilitated the recent growth of the money economy. But two features in this record are striking: the narrow geographical base of the money economy has been widened little and the transport network in the African areas has received little substantial improvement. The case of Southern Rhodesia before federation illustrates the point. The bulk of its expenditure on road construction was administered by a department with jurisdiction only in the European areas of the colony. Most of its post-war effort was concentrated on

---

[1] *Annual Financial Statements, Northern Rhodesia*; some supplementary expenditure on these subjects was financed by Colonial Development and Welfare grants to both Northern territories.

[2] *Reports on the Accounts, Protectorate of Nyasaland.*

improving the capacity of the existing road network as opposed to the construction of extensions. Road construction in the African areas was administered by the Department of Native Affairs and the sums available to it were small. In the peak pre-Federal year, 1952/3, £80,000 was recorded for roads in the Native areas — less than 1 per cent. of the capital expenditure on roads in the European areas.[1] In earlier years, expenditure was even lower. In fact, it is questionable whether the inadequate roads in the reserves were even maintained.

The main thrust of post-federation capital outlays for the transport network have been similar in design. The big spender has been the Federal Government and its jurisdiction is restricted to the major inter-territorial arteries. Expenditures by the territories on roads which have the most direct effect on the African population have increased but they still command only a small share of the total. The heavy volume of resources which has been poured into these subjects in the post-war years has yet to break through the isolation of most of the African areas.

The Performance of the Various Sectors and Dualism

All sectors of the Central African money economy have been caught up in its post-war prosperity. But this fact should not obscure another — that the role of the various sectors has not been identical. Some activities — e.g. mining and the export specialties in agriculture — have provided the spring-board for general advance. Priority in the causal sequence belongs to them. Activity in other sectors has been largely derivative in character, and expansion within them owes much to the growth in primary export incomes. This category includes the manufacturing industries and that segment of agriculture which serves domestic demand.

The general growth in the money economy has created new opportunities for the indigenous population to enter the money economy as wage employees. It has also swollen the demand for foodstuffs and thereby enhanced possibilities that the indigenous population may advance its real income through the sale of agricultural surpluses. But the obstacles which have traditionally checked a high rate of monetization of the indigenous

[1] Drawn from the *Report of the Auditor and Comptroller-General, Southern Rhodesia, 1952–53.*

economy's output have not yet been overcome. A dualistic cleavage between the money and the indigenous economies has thus remained.

Potentially, the public sector might have made deep inroads into the barriers which have perpetuated dualism. Despite the large volume of resources at its disposal, it has not in fact done so. In the Rhodesias, the priorities established for public expenditure have been those which would satisfy the first of the two definitions of development: i.e. an expanding money economy, combined with a growing European population. In the post-war years, impressive strides have been taken towards overcoming deficiencies in basic services which might impede expansion in the money economy. The significance of these achievements, both for the expansion which has already occurred and for that which may come later, should not be minimized. But within the bounds of the money economy, certain items of social overhead capital have been neglected. Foremost among the omissions is the investment in housing for African wage-earners in the urban areas. At prevailing wage levels for African employees, support from the public sector for this part of the capital cost of expansion is essential. Governments, however, have continued to assign low priorities to this urgent problem. The Urban African Affairs Commission emphasized this shortcoming of policy for Southern Rhodesia as follows in its 1958 report:

There can be little doubt . . . that the ability to provide aid to meet the housing requirements of the lowest income groups among the Africans who lived in the urban areas did in fact exist. But the aid was not forthcoming. We make this point not solely on the basis of humanitarian sentiment, but also from the point of view of industrial efficiency and the future growth of urban development. In our opinion the present arrangements which govern urban development in African areas are not conducive to the growth of a healthy and efficient labour force; nor are they such as to enable the African to make his fullest contribution to the expansion of the country's economy.[1]

This deficiency in the investment allocations within the money economy has implications which reach beyond the

[1] *Report of the Urban African Affairs Commission* (the Plewman Report), (Government Printer, Salisbury, 1958), p. 87.

standards of efficiency achieved by the African wage labour force. It also affects the perpetuation of dualism on the traditional lines. Under existing conditions, much of the African wage labour force cannot make a permanent commitment to wage employment. If settled family life in the urban areas is precluded for the majority of African workers, they must continue to divide their energies and their loyalties.

CHAPTER VII

INCOME DISTRIBUTION AND THE EXPANSION OF THE MONEY ECONOMY

In the preceding discussions of the money economy, many aspects of income distribution have been touched upon. This subject now deserves separate attention. Like most of the important variables with which economists are concerned, income distribution can be viewed from a variety of perspectives. Two issues are of particular interest in the dualistic situation of Rhodesia and Nyasaland. One concerns the effects of the distribution of income on the process of expansion in the money economy. In this connexion, it is relevant to examine the manner in which the allocation of money income affects saving and investment, on the one hand, and aggregate demand for output on the other. In addition, the effects of expansion in the money economy on the distribution of incomes must also be examined. This point is pertinent to judgements on whether or not expansion in the money economy produces improvement in real income for the indigenous population. These two problems are analytically distinct. In empirical measurements, however, they can seldom be effectively isolated from one another.

Significant Features of the Distributive Pattern in Central Africa

To students of industrialized economies, several features of the post-war distribution of money income in Central Africa are noteworthy. None of them is surprising in light of what has already been said about the major properties of the money economy. In contrast with more advanced economic systems, the share of net geographical income paid out as wages and salaries is surprisingly low. By the same token, the share accruing in forms of corporate profits claims an unusually high proportion of the total.

A brief comparison of results recorded in Central Africa with those for the American economy in the same period is illuminating on this point. Since 1950, wage and salary payments have usually represented in the range of half of the net geographical income in the Federal area (see Table I). The relative stability of this relationship, however, was upset only in 1957–8 when the setbacks experienced by base metal exporters brought a reduction in aggregate money income. In the United States, by contrast, the wage and salary share of national income since the war has consistently been in the range of 68 to 70 per cent. The precise proportion has varied with changes in the level of economic activity, but the normal allocation to this distributive share of income has been much higher than in Rhodesia and Nyasaland.

TABLE I

NET GEOGRAPHICAL INCOME BY DISTRIBUTIVE SHARES, FEDERATION OF RHODESIA AND NYASALAND (£000,000S)

	Net geographical income	Wages and salaries	Income from unincorporated enterprise	Net profits of corporations and statutory bodies	Government income from property	Personal income from property
1950	156·4	77·2 (49)	26·6 (17)	48·9 (31)	2·3 (1)	1·4 (1)
1951	191·4	95·1 (50)	21·7 (11)	70·2 (37)	2·7 (1)	1·7 (1)
1952	220·4	114·1 (52)	29·8 (14)	71·0 (32)	3·3 (1)	2·2 (1)
1953	248·9	134·9 (54)	30·5 (12)	76·8 (31)	4·2 (2)	2·5 (1)
1954	269·3	141·5 (53)	34·6 (11)	82·3 (31)	6·5 (2)	4·4 (2)
1955	314·6	163·7 (52)	36·7 (11)	101·6 (32)	7·5 (2)	5·1 (2)
1956	356·2	186·4 (52)	41·1 (12)	113·8 (32)	9·4 (3)	5·4 (2)
1957	345·8	210·1 (61)	42·5 (12)	78·1 (23)	9·8 (3)	5·5 (2)
1958	338·7	220·6 (65)	40·6 (12)	61·4 (18)	10·1 (3)	6·0 (2)
1959	395·9	231·7 (58)	43·9 (11)	102·0 (26)	12·0 (3)	6·3 (2)

Notes: Percentages of each share to net geographical income are noted in parentheses. Percentages have been rounded.

Sources: *Monthly Digests of Statistics* and *Annual Economic Reports, Federation of Rhodesia and Nyasaland*.

With the share accruing to wage and salary earners proportionately lower, the share of corporate profits has been correspondingly higher in Central Africa than in the United States. Whereas the post-war corporate profits have normally claimed from 10 to 12 per cent. of the American national income, this distributive share received in the range of one-third of Central Africa's net geographical income from 1950 through 1956. In 1957 and 1958, corporate profits acutely felt the impact of the copper slump. Absolute profits fell sharply from their 1956 peak and their proportion of net geographical income also dropped markedly.

The divergence between the allocations to the various distributive shares in the Federation and in the United States is not difficult to comprehend. It reflects the quite different economic environments of the two economic systems under comparison. With resource endowments which are far from uniform, it should not be expected that the relative shares received by the owners of the several factors of production would be similar. The Central African case is also distinguished by the overwhelming impact of fluctuations in one industry on the allocations of money income. In a larger and more advanced economy, no single activity plays such a dominant role. But the process of income distribution in Central Africa is further differentiated from that in the United States through the influence of dualism in its wage structure. This effect can be viewed most readily through an inspection of the distribution of personal money incomes.

In the Central African money economy, the largest share by far of incomes paid out in wages and salaries or accruing to individuals from unincorporated enterprises (which includes farming) has gone to a small group, primarily composed of Europeans. The official statistics bracket the income of Asiatics and persons of mixed race with those of Europeans. The numbers of Asiatics and Coloureds are not large;[1] these minorities occupy an interemdiate position in the social scale, but their income level is closer to that of Europeans than Africans and they tend to emulate European habits of consumption. Europeans, Asiatics, and Coloureds collectively have never comprised more than 15 per cent. (and usually the proportion has been lower) of the working population in the money economy. Their share of personal incomes, however, has been 60 per cent. or more of the totals for the Federal area (see Table II). The more advanced skills possessed by the European make his individual contribution to production in the money economy more valuable than that of the African. But there is reason to doubt that all of the differential between European and African wage rates measures differences in their con-

[1] At the time of the 1956 census, Asiatics and Coloureds in Southern Rhodesia numbered just over 13,000 compared with 178,000 Europeans. Members of 'other races' in Northern Rhodesia numbered 7,100 while the European population totalled 66,000. In Nyasaland, the European population totalled 6,800 compared with 9,800 members of 'other races'.

tributions to production. In any case, it is clear that the African share of total 'personal incomes' in the money economy has been relatively low.

Not all of the sums shown in the official estimates as money income received by Africans represent cash which they may allocate at their discretion. In conventional practice, the employer is expected to see that his African employees are fed and housed at a minimum standard. He may provide rations and accommodation directly or pay equivalent sums in cash to his employees for this purpose. When the worker receives income in kind, its imputed value is included in the official cal-

TABLE II

DISTRIBUTION OF MONEY INCOME FROM WAGES, SALARIES, AND UNINCORPORATED ENTERPRISE BY ETHNIC GROUPS, FEDERATION OF RHODESIA AND NYASALAND ($£$000,000s)

	Total	European, Asiatic and Coloured	%	African
1950	103.8	70.1	68	33.7
1951	117.0	77.6	66	39.4
1952	143.9	97.3	68	46.6
1953	165.4	107.6	65	57.8
1954	176.0	113.3	64	62.7
1955	200.5	129.9	65	70.6
1956	227.7	145.2	64	82.5
1957	252.6	159.3	63	93.3
1958	261.1	168.8	65	92.3
1959	275.6	174.5	63	101.1

Sources: *Monthly Digests of Statistics, Federation of Rhodesia and Nyasaland.*

culations of the money wage. Nor does all of the wage actually paid in cash to the African contribute to effective demand in the territory in which it was earned. A high percentage of the African labour force, particularly in Southern Rhodesia, is of extraterritorial origin, and a portion of the migrant workers' cash earnings is transferred to the territory of residence. This arrangement has been encouraged by the governments of labour-supplying territories. The larger employers in Southern Rhodesia are permitted to draw labour from Nyasaland, for example, on the understanding that a sum is withheld from the migrant's cash wage and transferred, via the administrative officer in his home district, to await him on his return.

While the disposable income of the African is overstated in these estimates, that of the European is understated. The effective demand of Europeans may be supplemented through the receipt of interest or dividends (items which were not included in the classifications discussed above) or through funds brought in by immigrants. Some European income may also be remitted abroad. In recent Rhodesian experience, however, the inward flow of personal transfers has considerably exceeded the outward flow.

Income Distribution, Saving, and Investment

In most economic systems in the recent past, the major contributors to the national savings aggregate have been corporations and governments. Central Africa is no exception. Among the underdeveloped territories the Rhodesias have been strikingly successful in achieving high rates of saving during their post-war expansion. The nature of their institutional structure explains much of this accomplishment.

As has already been noted, the distribution of aggregate money income has been weighted relatively heavily in favour of corporate profits and, in turn, the fate of aggregate corporate profits is largely governed by the fortunes of the copper industry. This industry, directly and indirectly, has had a formidable influence on aggregate saving. Retained earnings within the industry have themselves been large. But perhaps more important for the money economy as a whole is its contribution to public revenues. Taxes on corporate incomes have succeeded in trapping locally resources which might otherwise have been transferred abroad. Moreover, the ability of governments to accumulate savings for capital formation out of tax receipts is closely tied to trends in this dominant industry.

Savings out of personal incomes, although usually a minor component of the total for the Federal area, have also been influenced by the pattern of income distribution. But trends in personal savings cannot be adequately explained with a Keynesian theory of income and savings relationships. It might be expected that the unequal distribution of personal money incomes and their concentration in the hands of Europeans would favour savings. Indeed the African in the Rhodesias is frequently admonished to emulate European habits of thrift. A review of the available data on personal savings fails, however,

TABLE III

CONSUMPTION EXPENDITURE AND SAVING FROM PERSONAL DISPOSABLE INCOME, FEDERATION OF RHODESIA AND NYASALAND (£000,000s)

	Personal disposable income	Consumption expenditure	%	Saving	%
1950	111.3	97.2	87	10.4	9
1951	124.6	115.2	93	5.7	5
1952	151.9	138.8	91	8.6	6
1953	175.4	158.8	90	11.0	6
1954	186.7	167.5	90	13.5	7
1955	211.4	185.4	88	20.7	10
1956	242.7	208.1	86	31.0	13
1957	267.9	231.4	85	29.1	11
1958	276.0	241.9	88	24.9	9
1959	293.6	252.3	86	31.4	11

Notes: Personal disposable income is defined as total personal income (including transfers from government and transfers from abroad) net of taxes and fines collected by government. For these purposes, disposable income includes the value of income in kind received by African wage-earners. The difference between the sum of consumption expenditure and saving and the figure shown for total disposable income represents transfers abroad.

Sources: *Monthly Digests of Statistics* and *Annual Economic Reports, Federation of Rhodesia and Nyasaland.*

to indicate a consistent pattern. Disposable income has steadily grown since the war, but personal savings have behaved

TABLE IV

CONSUMPTION EXPENDITURE AND SAVING FROM PERSONAL DISPOSABLE INCOME, SOUTHERN RHODESIA, 1946–53 (£000,000s)

	Personal disposable income	Consumption expenditure	%	Saving	%
1946	40.2	33.7	84	5.5	14
1947	48.9	43.2	88	4.7	10
1948	58.8	49.8	85	7.5	13
1949	63.9	59.2	93	2.7	4
1950	78.3	69.2	88	6.2	8
1951	83.8	80.0	95	0.9	1
1952	97.3	89.6	92	4.2	4
1953	106.9	95.9	90	6.1	6

Notes: Definitions are those discussed in notes to Table III.

Sources: *The National Income and Social Accounts of Southern Rhodesia, 1946–1951,* Table VI, p. 13, and the *Annual Financial Statements.*

erratically. The general pattern is indicated in Tables III–V. Admittedly, these data are imperfect. They refer to the whole of the money economy, not just to Europeans. Even if it is assumed that Africans, who receive roughly one-third of personal money incomes, do not save at all (an assumption which is not entirely correct), it would still not appear that Europeans have saved a notably high percentage of their incomes.

It is not adequate, of course, to draw conclusions about personal savings solely from absolute levels of money income. The Rhodesian economic scene is hardly one in which Keynesian hypotheses should be expected to apply. A modified version of Duesenberry's reformulation of the consumption function might better fit its environment. As Duesenberry noted in his interpretation, consumption and saving may be influenced as

TABLE V

CONSUMPTION EXPENDITURE AND SAVING FROM PERSONAL DISPOSABLE
INCOME, NORTHERN RHODESIA, 1945–53 (£000,000s)

	Personal disposable income	Consumption expenditure	%	Saving	%
1945	9.8	8.7	89	0.8	8
1946	10.9	9.9	91	0.7	6
1947	13.3	12.5	94	0.5	4
1948	16.7	15.3	92	0.8	5
1949	20.2	19.1	95	0.7	3
1950	24.9	22.6	91	1.4	6
1951	32.1	29.7	93	1.4	4
1952	39.4	26.1	92	2.1	5
1953	52.7	49.6	94	1.8	3

Notes and Sources: The definitions are the same as those discussed in the notes to Table III. Calculations are drawn from *The National Income and Social Accounts of Northern Rhodesia, 1945–1953*, Table VII, pp. 28–29.

much by the social class with which the individual identifies himself as by the absolute level of his money income.[1] But it is more than a class distinction which bears on these issues in the Rhodesias. The social system is fundamentally race-conscious. It is organized to afford a privileged status to the European and, by the same token, it expects him to maintain a standard of living which sharply differentiates him from the African.

At the same time, there is considerable variation in incomes within the European community. Those at the lower end of the scale often attempt to live at a higher standard than warranted

[1] Cf. James Duesenberry, *Income, Savings, and The Theory of Consumer Behavior* (Harvard University Press, 1950).

by their means. The findings of a Southern Rhodesian survey in 1950/1 illustrate the situation. This study, which was limited to European families with incomes of £90 per month or less, revealed that average monthly expenditure was slightly greater than average monthly income.[1] A Northern Rhodesian study, conducted on rather different lines, was made in 1951. It was designed as a sample of the urban European families of the territory; no upper limit to family income was set.[2] Nevertheless, the declared expenditure of more than a quarter of the families outside the Copperbelt mining towns exceeded their income. Moreover, those families reporting positive savings had earmarked a large share for holidays and leave periods abroad. But in both territories, European farm families have tended to save more than urban ones. In fact, the wide variation in the ratios of savings to income from year to year stems primarily from fluctuations in the profits of farmers.

Little evidence is available on the savings habits of Africans in the money economy. Intuitively, one would expect their saving to be negligible. Their real income is too low to permit much margin above consumption requirements. But some African saving out of money income does occur. For 1954, it was officially stated that nearly half of the accounts in the Federal Post Office Savings Bank were held by Africans.[3] These deposits may well represent the bulk of the money savings of the African population.[4] The Post Office Savings Bank is one of the few institutional channels to which they have unrestricted access. The commercial banks have not always welcomed accounts by Africans. The earlier reluctance of the commercial banks to accept African accounts is now, however, breaking down.

While the general pattern of income distribution has permitted a remarkably high ratio of saving to be realized for the

[1] *Report on Southern Rhodesian Family Expenditure Survey, 1950–1951*, Central African Statistical Office (Salisbury, 1952), esp. p. 7.

[2] *Report on Northern Rhodesian Family Expenditure Survey, 1951*, Central African Statistical Office (Salisbury, 1953), esp. p. 13.

[3] See *Annual Report of the Post Office Savings Bank, Federation of Rhodesia and Nyasaland, 1954*. The share of African holders in the total value of deposits could not then be ascertained.

[4] Either by preference or through the lack of an alternative outlet for his surplus cash, the African may save in kind. In the Copperbelt mining towns, for example, it is reported that African wage-earners often stockpile clothing.

M

money economy as a whole, it does not necessarily follow that these savings will always be channelled into productive capital formation locally. Rigidities in the local capital market are common to most underdeveloped economies. The Rhodesias can claim greater success than many such territories in utilizing domestic savings. Governments have sponsored lending institutions which have reallocated public savings to assist expansion of certain activities. In addition, the copper-mining groups have supported the foundation of investment banking houses with a portion of their retained earnings.

A substantial part of domestic savings held in the form of bank balances, however, has usually been exported. The commercial banks in Central Africa have consistently accumulated substantial excess reserves which have been held externally as balances with the head offices. The behaviour of the banking system and the ratios of local earning assets to its total assets have varied through time and with the state of the balance of payments. Southern Rhodesian banking, for example, has passed through several phases since 1936 when statistics were first collected. In the late 1930s, the ratio of local earning assets to total assets was just under 50 per cent. During the war years, the ratio fell considerably. Export revenues were rising sharply with the higher prices for primary products, but shipping shortages then restrained expansion in import volume. After the war, the visible balance of trade became adverse, and the ratio rose considerably. In 1951 and 1952, local earning assets accounted for more than three-quarters of the total assets of Southern Rhodesian commercial banks. The bulk of this expansion represented the short-term borrowings of importers who had been officially encouraged to stockpile imported goods in the Korean War period. These high ratios were abnormal and were associated with the unusual circumstances of the import trade. Since federation, local earning assets held by commercial banks in the Federal area have been in the range of 50 per cent. of their total assets.[1]

The practice of other private financial institutions serving the Central African territories has been similar. External com-

---

[1] Southern Rhodesian banking statistics are contained in the *Economic and Statistical Bulletins*; summaries of post-federation banking data have been published in the *Monthly Digests of Statistics*.

panies transact the bulk of the insurance business. The pattern of their financial operations has also been one of accumulating liabilities internally and holding the major share of their assets externally. Before federation, savings mobilized through the Post Office Savings Banks were also largely invested abroad.

The freedom of action of these institutions in the disposition of funds received from local sources has been circumscribed both by the conventions governing their behaviour and by the general state of the money economy of Central Africa. The lending policies of these organizations have been oriented towards short-term, liquid, and low risk assets. Loans for fixed capital formation, the type of financial service most required in under-developed economies, have been precluded. As a result, opportunities for local lending have been restricted largely to the financing of foreign trade and, to a lesser extent, the financing of governments.

Some first steps have also been taken towards creating machinery for channelling medium- to long-term finance into the business community. In their normal operations, the commercial banks, of course, are debarred from entering this field by the orthodox canons of the British banking tradition. One of the commercial banks, however, has set up a Central African branch of its development corporation. By 1958, the Barclays Overseas Development Corporation had invested more than £11,000,000 in the Federation in some eighty-two under-takings.[1] Most of its loans were in sums between £100,000 and £500,000. The terms have varied but the repayment period has generally been between six and twelve years. In some cases the corporation has been prepared to subscribe to local equity issues. Long-term finance in smaller sums has been made available through the African Finance Corporation. This organization, largely supported by the former shareholders of Cable and Wireless in the United Kingdom, has taken equities in smaller firms. The most recent entrants to this field have been the copper-mining groups. Both Rhodesian Anglo-American and the Rhodesian Selection Trust have sponsored 'development corporations'.

While the scale of their operations is still small, these new

[1] *Basic Information for the Potential Investor* (Office for Rhodesia and Nyasaland Affairs, Washington, 1959), p. 41.

institutions have introduced greater flexibility into the financial structure. Only the government had formerly been prepared to extend loans for illiquid investments, and its policies had been oriented towards assisting favoured activities.

Income Distribution, Effective Demand, and the Expansion of the Money Economy

The growth of aggregate money incomes in Central Africa has stimulated expansion of output in a variety of lines to serve the enlarging domestic market. The shape which this induced growth has taken cannot be understood without attention to the distribution of money incomes. The structure of the manufacturing industries is a case in point. The bulk of their activity has been concentrated on two types of output: low-quality consumer goods and heavy construction materials.

Many factors have influenced the course of the manufacturing sector's expansion. On the cost side, a wide range of industrial activities would be automatically ruled out because the market is still too limited to justify units of an economic size. But the pattern of income distribution has also had significant effects upon the character of industrial development. Thus, the fact that the public sector has had large sums at its disposal for capital outlays has provided a substantial market for building and construction materials. Similarly, the distribution of personal incomes between the racial groups has been a fundamental determinant of the character of consumer goods production.

Effective consumer demand has always been heavily concentrated with the European population. And this distribution of purchasing power has not been overwhelmingly favourable to expansion of local manufacturing industry. By and large, the consumption habits of Europeans are biased towards a preference for imports. Recent immigrants form a high proportion of the white population. The tastes to which they have been educated are those of Britain or the Union of South Africa and they bring an instinctive loyalty to the manufactured products of those countries. This natural preference for imported manufactured articles is supported by another aspect of Rhodesian society. Imports have a prestige value to which heightened importance is given by a social environment in which luxury consumption is regarded as 'setting an example of civilized standards before backward peoples'. A major fraction of the consumption expenditures of European families may still, however, accrue to local factors of production. Even though a high percentage of their purchases of manufactured goods may be on imports, their expenditures on services — e.g. medical care, entertainment, domestic servants and private education — are heavy and most of the outlays for services are made locally.

Potentially, African consumers — not European ones — offer the soundest base for the nascent manufacturing sector. Most of the soft-goods industries which have emerged thus far have been designed primarily for the African market. The aggregate money income of the indigenous population has risen markedly in recent years. At first inspection, this phenomenon would appear to indicate that the prospects for further expansion in manufactures would be bright.

In this connexion, a closer inspection of African money income and its disposition is appropriate. The bulk of the increase in African money income in recent years has been accounted for by the growth in wage employment. African sales of agricultural products have also expanded substantially, but their share of aggregate money income received by Africans has always been small and has continued to be so. This can be observed clearly in the national income accounts available since 1946 for the two Rhodesias (see Table VI). The official estimates identify two categories of African money income: wage-earning and income from unincorporated enterprises. The latter refers almost entirely to agricultural sales by the indigenous economy. The incomes of a few African traders and entrepreneurs are also included among the unincorporated enterprises, but their contribution to the aggregate is negligible.

Data on the disposition of African money income are less adequate than the estimates of aggregate money income. Surveys which have been undertaken thus far refer entirely to urban African families. Budgets of Africans employed by Europeans in the rural areas have not been investigated nor has the allocation of money income received by African agriculturalists been given comprehensive study. The results of budget surveys made in the main towns of Southern Rhodesia between 1957 and 1959 and in Northern Rhodesia in 1953/4 are nevertheless instructive. These findings are not typical, however, of African wage-earners in general because the areas surveyed include the most highly paid members of the African wage labour force.

Apart from income, many factors obviously influence the expenditure patterns of African wage-earners. The most important, of course, is family size. Variations in numbers of dependants cause considerable divergences in expenditure allocations between families receiving the same money income. But differing

TABLE VI

AFRICAN MONEY INCOMES BY SOURCE, SOUTHERN AND NORTHERN RHODESIA (£000,000s)

	Southern Rhodesia		Northern Rhodesia	
	Wage employment	Unincorporated enterprise	Wage employment	Unincorporated enterprise
1946	9.7	1.7	3.4	0.2
1947	11.0	1.9	4.0	0.2
1948	12.6	2.4	4.8	0.6
1949	15.4	2.3	6.2	0.4
1950	18.6	2.8	7.6	0.8
1951	21.7	2.3	10.6	0.8
1952	25.0	3.0	13.2	1.1
1953	26.8	3.5	20.7	1.4
1954	31.0	5.1	18.1	2.1
1955	34.4	5.6	22.1	2.0
1956	38.8	8.3	24.5	2.9
1957	45.6	5.7	27.6	3.7
1958	47.2	4.6	26.3	2.4
1959	50.5	5.4	28.2	3.6

Sources: *National Income Accounts, Southern Rhodesia; The National Income and Social Accounts, Northern Rhodesia; Monthly Digests of Statistics.*

terms of employment — e.g. whether rents and rations are provided directly by the employer or whether the employee is expected to procure all necessities on his own — also affect the interpretation of the survey results.

Despite substantial differences in the circumstances of individual families, the findings of these investigations of African budgets reveal a notable uniformity. In each of the groups surveyed, foodstuffs are by far the largest item of expenditure. This is hardly surprising in view of the prevailing wage rates, although the percentage of income allocated to food purchases has tended to decline as income has risen. In the Northern Rhodesian study, the proportion of total expenditure devoted to food purchases was found to be 53 per cent. for the survey group as a whole.[1] Results for the main towns in Southern Rhodesia for 1958/9 indicate that expenditures on foodstuffs accounted for roughly 46 per cent. of the cash outlays of Africans in Salisbury and Bulawayo and for approximately 50 per cent. in Umtali and Gwelo.[2] These calculations refer to cash expenditures only and do not differentiate between rationed and un-rationed individuals and families. For many unrationed families, the share of food purchases in total expenditure is considerably higher than these computations indicate.

These results may be contrasted with the findings of budget surveys of European families in the two Rhodesias. In both territories, food expenditures claimed approximately 25 per cent. of consumption expenditure.[3] The qualitative content of the food budget in European and African households is, of course, totally different. The African consumption pattern is dominated by the cheapest foodstuffs: mealie meal (ground maize), low quality meat, dried and fresh fish, bread, and sugar, account for roughly 80 per cent. of the food outlays of African families. But only in a minority of cases is food expenditure sufficient to maintain desirable standards of nutrition. An analysis accompanying the 1958 Report of the Urban African Affairs Commission brought out this point by constructing a 'minimum needs budget' (designated as the Poverty Datum Line) for families of different size and by comparing it with the actual circumstances of Salisbury's African population. This analysis concluded that the 'sample of households had 57·1 per cent. with incomes in the category "extremely impoverished", i.e. with incomes more than 35 per cent. below the P.D.L. level of income. Only 23·5 per cent had incomes within or above the limits of "P.D.L. latitude" . . . The overall picture is one of poverty in all but a few households composed of childless couples or with one or two children. The majority of children in the

[1] Central African Statistical Office, 'The African Consumer Prices Index, a Statement dealing with African Family Expenditure in the Urban Areas of Northern Rhodesia', Salisbury, 1959.

[2] *Monthly Digest of Statistics* (January 1960), pp. iii–v.

[3] Central African Statistical Office, *Report on Northern Rhodesia Family Expenditure Survey, 1951*, and *Report on Southern Rhodesia Family Expenditure Survey, 1950–1951*.

sample are being brought up under conditions of extreme poverty and in want of the essentials of life.'[1]

It would appear from this finding that money income of the majority of African urban families — despite improvements in wage rates in recent years — is still insufficient to maintain socially desirable levels of living. Potentially, this group may provide a formidable stimulus to the expansion of manufacturing industries if substantial gains in its real purchasing power continue. But at present income levels, effective demand of Africans is still heavily concentrated on food purchases. This pattern of effective demand has enlarged the market opportunities of local food producers. To date, however, indigenous agriculture has supplied only a minor fraction of the food requirements of Africans employed for wages.

[1] D. G. Bettison, Appendix N, *Report of the Urban African Affairs Commission*, p. 193.

CHAPTER VIII

THE INTERACTION BETWEEN THE MONEY AND THE INDIGENOUS ECONOMIES: A THEORETICAL INTERPRETATION

FROM the discussion this far, it would appear that the first of the two conditions for economic development — or at least the interpretation placed upon it by the governing minority of the Rhodesias — has been satisfied. Real income in the money economy has expanded through time and the European population has grown. But has the second definition of economic development also been satisfied? For an affirmative answer, it would be necessary to demonstrate that the monetization of the indigenous economy has proceeded at a rate exceeding the growth of its population. Unfortunately, the statistical evidence bearing on these points is imperfect. It may, therefore, be instructive to consider this problem initially from a different point of view: i.e. by inspecting the mechanics of the economic system to ascertain whether any features within it might tend either to abet or to block the participation of the indigenous population in the money economy.

Without any deeper probing into the nature of the system, two reasons might be advanced to account for a lack of economic advance by the African community. It could be argued — and frequently has been in some quarters — that the basic explanation for any failure of the indigenous peoples to enjoy more fully the fruits of the money economy's expansion lies in their reluctance to seize new opportunities. This argument cannot be dismissed lightly. Any social system is likely to resist rapid change threatening its cohesion. Adjustment to new circumstances is inevitably slow and often painful. But while the African has displayed some inertia in his reaction to a novel economic environment, two further observations should be made on this point in the Rhodesias. The policy of the governing minority has encouraged the preservation of traditional institutions. This has been implicit in its approach to the

administration of Africans, although its policies have been enforced only half-heartedly. Nevertheless, new economic
incentives have been dampened. But another factor is more
significant: the response which the African has made to the
money economy despite these restraints. The evidence available, which was examined in Chapter IV, suggests that he has
tended to order his contacts with the money economy to
maximize the real income of his family. At least in the recent
past, he has taken advantage of the limited opportunities open
to him. When allowance has been made for the non-economic
pressures which condition his actions, it would appear that his
economic behaviour has been rational.

A second general explanation might be advanced to account
for a failure of the indigenous population to be absorbed more
completely into the money economy as it has expanded. In
conformity with the value premises of the governing group
in the Rhodesias, the most attractive positions in the money
economy have been closed to Africans. As a result, the forms
which the African's response could assume have been limited
and directed into particular channels. His ability to improve
his real income as a wage employee has been circumscribed by
a colour bar which has tended to exclude him from skilled
positions. Nor has he had complete freedom of opportunity
to earn cash by selling his agricultural products. The land
distribution policies and the lack of transport services in his
own areas have placed major obstacles in his path. If the
participation of the African in the money economy has not been
more thorough, the restrictions imposed by the doctrine of
settler supremacy in the Rhodesias may be partially responsible. It cannot, of course, be demonstrated that the economic
response of the indigenous peoples would have been perfect,
even in the absence of these factors. But it is at least clear that
they have not had the advantage of unrestricted access to the
opportunities created by growth in the money economy.

A treatment resting on these observations alone would be far
from adequate. Once the influence of the value premises of the
governing group has been recognized, investigation of more
basic relationships can begin and abstract economic reasoning
can profitably be brought into play. Its use, however, is subject
to the limitations inherent in any formal argument. At best,

the abstract categories employed by the economist can claim to be no more than simplifications of the real world. Much of its complexity, of necessity, cannot be drawn into account. But abstract discussion is not thereby robbed of utility. When properly employed, the tools of formal analysis can perform a valuable function in illuminating the fundamental relationships within an economic system — relationships which may easily be obscured in an exclusive preoccupation with its superficial characteristics.

For the study of the interaction between the money and the indigenous economies, the analytical tools of the neo-classical and Keynesian traditions have limited usefulness. These methodological tools have been constructed in the more advanced economies and their categories are those which conveniently fit their conditions. They can not be uncritically transplanted to the underdeveloped world. The realities of economic life in areas such as Central Africa are fundamentally at variance with some of the presuppositions of Western economic thought. A unity which underlies the economic structure in the industrialized countries does not exist. The market is not ubiquitous. The taste and habit patterns of populations within the same territory differ widely — and these patterns may not be sufficiently stable to permit even short-term economic change to be analysed at the margin. Moreover, the problems of economic development are essentially different in character from those to which the post-Marshallian tradition has addressed itself. Development implies change through time. The method of static equilibrium analysis is not best suited to deal with it.[1] A more satisfactory conceptual apparatus must be equipped to deal with long-term adjustments. And it must bring to the foreground the peculiar property of underdeveloped economies such as Central Africa: the dual structure of the economic system, containing two economies within it.

[1] In this connexion, it is interesting to note that, while economic literature has made little contribution of late to the broader questions of the development process in Africa, economists have embraced with disproportionate enthusiasm one of the few aspects of economic relationships in African territories which can be interpreted in static equilibrium terms: namely, the price policies of the statutory marketing boards. The literature on this subject is voluminous. For a representative illustration, see the exchanges between P. T. Bauer, F. W. Paish, M. Friedman, and B. M. Niculescu in the *Economic Journal*, vol. lxiv (1954).

Within the main stream of formal economic thought, the literature of the earlier classical tradition has relevance to the problems of economic development. Analogies with the issues of current concern may be found, for example, in the works of Smith, Malthus, Ricardo, and Marx. Many recent commentators have turned to this literature for inspiration when dealing with the contemporary problems of economic development. One in particular — W. A. Lewis — has devised a modified 'classical' growth model which can provide a useful springboard for the examination of the Central African economic system. His argument has the advantage of drawing to the centre of the stage two of the unique problems confronting analysts of the underdeveloped territories: the fact that the scope of the money economy is not all-embracing and that economic development must be analysed as a long-term process through time.[1]

The Major Properties of Lewis's Modified Classical Growth Model

Lewis begins his analysis by dividing the underdeveloped economy into two components: the capitalist sector and the subsistence sector. The former is defined as 'that part of the economy which uses reproducible capital and pays capitalists for the use thereof'.[2] The subsistence sector, on the other hand, embraces the traditional economic activities of the indigenous peoples whose production is concentrated in agriculture. With backward techniques, the standard of *per capita* real income generated within the subsistence sector is low and often not much above the minimum required for survival. The problem of poverty in this sector may be further complicated by persistent population pressures — pressures so intense that, with the available techniques, the marginal product of labour in agricultural production may be zero or negative. This is the most widely discussed case of disguised unemployment.[3]

[1] W. A. Lewis, 'Economic Development with Unlimited Supplies of Labour', *The Manchester School*, vol. xxii (1954), pp. 139-91, and 'Unlimited Labour'. Further Notes', *The Manchester School*, vol. xxvi (1958), pp. 1-32. The same argument is restated in his book, *The Theory of Economic Growth*.

[2] Op. cit., *The Manchester School*, 1954, p. 146.

[3] Lewis works with this assumption of disguised unemployment. It is not, however, essential to his argument. The crucial condition is that the economic structure is dualistic and that average income in one of its components is low.

Lewis then offers an account of the connecting links between the two sectors within the dualistic economic structure. The expansive force in the system is generated from the capitalist sector. As it grows, labour is withdrawn from the subsistence sector and enters capitalist employment. Lewis postulates that the real wage necessary to induce a voluntary movement of labour into the capitalist sector will be based on the average product in the subsistence sector. It is important to note that the floor to the capitalist wage is set by the average, not the marginal, product of labour in subsistence production. Even though labour's marginal product may be zero or negative, subsistence workers nevertheless receive a positive return. This is possible because the total product is shared among the members of the family or kinship group. To compete with the subsistence sector for labour, the capitalist employer must, therefore, offer a wage which exceeds the average product by a sufficient margin to make movement attractive. The size of this margin cannot be precisely stated and will vary with local circumstances. In his 1954 statement, Lewis estimated that a gap of 30 per cent. or more between subsistence earnings and capitalist wages would be required; this estimate was increased to a 50 per cent. differential in the 1958 article.[1] The size of the margin, however, is less important than the analytical relationship involved: that the capitalist wage is a function of the average subsistence product.

These considerations permit Lewis to maintain that the supply of labour available to the capitalist economy will be perfectly elastic at a low real wage in the initial stage of economic expansion.[2] The capitalist sector can thus expand by drawing cheap labour into its ranks and, because this wage rate will be determined by the real income alternative offered by traditional agriculture, profits accruing to the capitalist will be high. Lewis further assumes that capital accumulation is

---

[1] Op. cit., *The Manchester School*, 1954, p. 150; 1958, p. 20.

[2] The classical overtones of this line of reasoning are obvious. Like Malthus and Ricardo, Lewis assumes that the long-period supply function for labour is horizontal. But the explanation offered for this conclusion is different in the two cases. The classical argument was based on Malthusian postulates concerning the relationship between real wages and population (i.e. long-period labour supply). Lewis's model is based on the low-income level of the subsistence sector with which the capitalist sector must compete for workers.

sustained through reinvestment of profits, leading to a further
withdrawal of labour from the subsistence sector.[1]

But the capitalist sector may not be confronted with a labour
supply which is always perfectly elastic at a low real wage. As
the sector grows, its demand for labour swells. Ultimately, the
subsistence sector will be completely absorbed into capitalist
production. Lewis recognizes, however, that several forces
might produce higher real wages before this physical limit has
been reached. For example, if the productivity of subsistence
agriculture increased substantially — and, in particular, if
marketable surpluses could be produced which would enable
the traditional agricultural sector to acquire cash income —
then the economic alternative to wage employment would
become more attractive. The capitalist would be obliged to
raise the real wage even though the reservoir of labour from the
subsistence sector had not been completely drained. Lewis
minimizes the importance of this possibility, partly on the
grounds that capitalists will have no enthusiasm for reform in
peasant agriculture. (It should be noted that Lewis's choice of
the label 'subsistence' to identify the indigenous agricultural
sector is not ideal in this context. If the production of marketable surpluses is entertained as a real possibility, it would no
longer be appropriate to regard traditional agriculture as
always remaining at the subsistence level.)

Another potential disturbance to the initial level of real
wages is implicit in Lewis's assumption of disguised unemployment. If the total product does not fall as labour is withdrawn,
the average product received by those remaining in subsistence
agriculture will rise. After a time, this improvement in real
income may become noticeable and workers might insist upon a
higher capitalist wage before offering themselves for employment. The impact of this effect may also be exaggerated. Two
considerations might be introduced (although Lewis does not
advance them) to support the original case for a perfectly
elastic labour supply. First, if the initial margin between the
average product in the subsistence sector and the real wage paid
by the capitalist is large, it may be possible to compress this
margin through time and thus to forestall improvement in real

---

[1] Throughout this portion of his analysis, Lewis makes the tacit assumption that
investment will not be limited by deficiency in aggregate demand.

wages, despite the higher average product from subsistence production. In the initial stages of capitalist recruiting, the margin may, in fact, have been abnormally high in order to overcome the reluctance of the indigenous peoples to enter an unfamiliar environment. Later, when their tastes have become conditioned to the novel assortment of goods obtainable only with cash, the attractiveness of wage employment may be enhanced. The positive satisfactions offered by a money income may thus be intensified relative to the disutilities of employment. Further, in those cases in which the subsistence agricultural community is cut off from opportunities to exchange agricultural surpluses for cash, another factor may counteract upward pressures on the capitalist real wage as the average subsistence product increases. Higher average product in the subsistence sector will permit consumption there to rise. But if agricultural output (even though abysmally low by the standards of external observers) was still initially sufficient to satisfy the modest tastes of the indigenous peoples, it does not necessarily follow that an increased availability of foodstuffs will expand commensurately the economic satisfactions of the indigenous community. In more technical language, the demand for foodstuffs may be relatively inelastic, even in communities which are primarily self-sufficient.

The real wage may still rise for reasons which are largely non-economic. Employers, for example, may be moved by humanitarian considerations to increase the real wage although economic forces alone might not oblige them to do so. Alternatively, governments may introduce minimum wage legislation or encourage the formation of trade unions and support their wage bargaining efforts. Improvements in the real wage may therefore occur, even though workers from the subsistence sector might still be prepared to accept employment on the original terms.

Despite these qualifications, Lewis is disposed to interpret the economic expansion process as falling into two separate and distinct phases. In the first, the supply of labour to the capital sector expands by progressively absorbing the subsistence sector. The second stage emerges when the absorption has been completed; the supply function for labour then becomes highly inelastic. The importance of these polar cases to his analysis is indicated by the following passage from his 1958 article.

When capital catches up with labour supply, an economy enters upon the second stage of development. Classical economics ceases to apply; we are in a world of neo-classical economics, where all factors of production are scarce, in the sense that their supply is inelastic. Wages are no longer constant as accumulation proceeds; the benefits of improved technology do not all accrue to profits; and the profit margin does not necessarily increase all the time.[1]

Revisions in a Modified 'Classical' Model Appropriate to the Central African Case

Lewis's formulation has the recommendation of highlighting features of dualism which are analytically useful. But his categories fail to come completely to grips with the realities of the Central African economic environment. In the first place, his division between the 'capitalist' and 'subsistence' sectors fails to fit well in this situation. Distinctions between the money and the indigenous economies — which emphasize the contrasting modes of economic organization prevailing in the dualistic components of the economic system — are more closely in touch with its circumstances.

The Central African situation also calls for amendments in Lewis's assumption of disguised unemployment. Indigenous economic organization there, it will be recalled, has certain peculiar properties which must now be drawn into account. The family is the basic productive unit. Given the traditional division of labour, individual members of its labour force are not homogeneous factors of production which are perfectly substitutable for one another.[2] Instead, they have specialized and well-defined tasks to perform. This phenomenon has important consequences for the conditions of contact between the two economies. The adult male — the one member of the family team for whose services the money economy initially creates a demand — is responsible for tasks which do not require his

---

[1] Op. cit., *The Manchester School*, 1958, p. 26.

[2] Even in cases in which the traditional sexual division of labour has broken down, the indigenous economy may not be able to tolerate a drain of more than half of its adult man-power. See, for example, Watson's findings cited in Chapter IV.

energies for substantial periods of time. It would be incorrect, however, to regard his marginal product as zero, even though his absence would not be felt in a reduction in output for a considerable period. Under the *chitemene* system, his contribution to production, although intermittent, is still indispensable. A form of disguised unemployment prevails in such circumstances. But it is quite different from the usual types. It is much more than seasonal underemployment and it is also distinct from the case Lewis postulates when assuming that the marginal product of labour is zero or negative. Lewis's case may be termed 'general' disguised unemployment: it arises when population pressure has become so intense that additional labour (which in the traditional system is absorbed on the land because it has nowhere else to go) makes no addition to output. Thus, with fixed land resources and with constant techniques, aggregate output of agricultural commodities ceases to rise and may actually fall. To avoid confusion with 'general' disguised unemployment, the form of disguised unemployment typical of traditional agriculture in Central Africa may be termed 'periodic'. It exists when individual members of the family productive unit can be withdrawn for at least a full annual cycle without any sacrifice in indigenous agricultural production.

A further structural modification in Lewis's model is also required in Central Africa. The essential portion of Lewis's argument is developed around assumptions of closed conditions.[1] Foreign trade, foreign investment, and international migrations of labour are discussed only as peripheral matters. But in Central Africa — and in other underdeveloped economies also — openness is a basic characteristic. Assumptions of closed conditions have little meaning, even when used as a first approximation and later relaxed. Openness, however, is an ambiguous term. The obvious cases are those in which an economy is open to foreign trade and to foreign investment. But of considerable importance in the Central African case is the openness of the money economy to labour movements. Settler supremacy in the Rhodesias has promoted this type of openness in order to

---

[1] A section of Lewis's 1954 article in the *Manchester School*, is labelled as dealing with the case of the open economy. This part of the discussion, however, is largely concerned with a reinterpretation of the classical doctrine of comparative costs. The essential properties of his model are developed around assumptions of closed conditions.

increase the European population. But the system has also been receptive to the importation of unskilled African labour.

With these amendments, it is now possible to reformulate the problem of interaction between the two economies in Central Africa. In the first statement of the relationships between them, it will be assumed that fresh supplies of land are still available to the indigenous population. The money economy is the dynamic force in the system. Production in the money economy has been initiated by the inflow of capital, skill, and entrepreneurship from abroad. In setting up its production process, the money economy combined the capital which it provides with labour drawn from the indigenous economy. The two economies, from the outset, were thus brought into contact with one another.

On what terms will indigenous labour be prepared to accept employment in such a dualistic system? Lewis's reply was that the real wage must exceed the average subsistence product by an incentive margin. The alternative concepts (outlined above) permit a different answer: namely, that the indigenous male will accept wage employment when it serves to maximize the real income of his family group.[1]

In this dualistic system, the real income of the indigenous family may be drawn from two sources: from production within the indigenous economy itself and from wage-earning in the money economy by its adult male members. When allocating his labour time, the adult male must weigh the gains in real income from one source against the possible loss in real income which might follow in the other. When 'periodic' disguised unemployment exists, temporary wage employment by the adult male does not reduce the agricultural output of the indigenous family. The additional income obtainable from money wages earned by the absent member is a net gain for the family. In these circumstances, a low real wage may succeed

[1] In practice, this choice was not always completely free. Because of direct taxation, the African male was obliged to obtain cash by some device. This pressure might force him into wage employment, regardless of his inclination to enter it previously. But the negative incentive of taxation must be supplemented by some positive inducements, unless a government is prepared to enforce a regime of conscript labour. This is a rigorous expedient to which the Central African governments have not resorted. To afford a positive inducement, the wage rate must provide more than the means with which to discharge tax obligations; it must offer a higher real income than could otherwise be obtained.

in attracting workers into the labour force of the money economy. But should employers wish to draw off man-power beyond the limits of 'periodic' disguised unemployment, then the adult male would accept wage employment only on much improved terms — in fact, only on terms which would more than compensate for the loss in real income which his absence from the indigenous economy would entail.

Wage-earning, of course, is not the only channel through which members of the indigenous economy might increase their real income as the money economy expands. They may also acquire higher real incomes through the sale of agricultural surpluses in response to the growing money demand for food-stuffs. Periodic disguised unemployment would then be partially absorbed with adult males exerting themselves more continuously in agricultural production, thereby enabling surpluses to be produced for sale. To the extent that the indigenous population participates in the money economy in this fashion, an upward pressure on the original level of real wages in the money economy would be created.

Disturbances to the conventional level of real wages arising from this source have been minimized in the Rhodesias. Historically, little encouragement has been given to agricultural sales by Africans and a formidable deterrent to the marketing of the surpluses from the indigenous economy is built into the social structure.[1] Land apportionment policies have compressed the bulk of indigenous agriculturists into the least fertile areas and the ones most remote from the markets of the money economy. African farmers outside those reserves favoured by

[1] This is not to say that the European community has deliberately devised instruments to hold back the African farmer. With the exception of the marketing discrimination of the 1930s, when active steps were taken to impede the sale of African agricultural surpluses, the system has operated in another fashion. No conscious effort has been made to check African agricultural progress. A passive attitude, combined with the geographical segregation policies, has achieved this result. The land area served by the communications system has been reserved for European occupation; low priorities have been assigned to the development of road systems into the reserve areas; and little action has been taken to improve the physical productivity of African agriculture or to assist it in adapting production to the varieties demanded in the money economy. Not positive action, but the lack of it, has created a situation in which African farmers have had little opportunity to penetrate the market through the sale of agricultural surpluses. As a result, a factor which might produce an improvement in the African wage-earner's position has been contained.

geographical proximity to European centres have had little access to markets. Only a small proportion of the indigenous population has a genuine option between selling crops and selling labour as methods for achieving higher real incomes.

In these circumstances (as in the case assumed by Lewis), the supply of indigenous labour available to wage employers would initially be perfectly elastic. Further, as long as the volume of absenteeism of adult male workers did not alter the family's agricultural output, there would be no tendency for the supply of labour to lose its elasticity. This implies that migration between the two economies by the adult male is possible and that — after a period in wage employment — he can return to maintain the productivity of the land worked by the indigenous productive unit.

Migration in this form has advantages for both parties to the wage bargain. On the one hand, it offers opportunities for the indigenous family to increase its real income. At the same time, it frees the employer from the responsibility to pay a wage high enough to support both the worker and his family. Thus, in all probability, the money wage is lower than it would be if the indigenous family were completely dependent upon cash wages for their minimum requirements. But there are also pronounced economic disadvantages to this system. High turnover rates in the wage labour force are not conducive to improvements in efficiency and productivity. The employer has little incentive to invest in training a transient labour force and tends to organize his production on the premise that indigenous labour is cheap, abundant, and undifferentiated by skill.

In the Rhodesian system, the premises of settler supremacy also have an important influence on the supply of indigenous labour. One of its effects is achieved through the encouragement of the survival of the indigenous social system. The assumptions upon which the political structure of the community is built presuppose that the African in wage employment must retain an identity with his tribal community. Officially, it is held that only a 50 per cent. rate of absenteeism by adult males is consistent with the preservation of the indigenous social structure. While little direct action has been taken to check a higher rate of absenteeism, the other side of the policy has been maintained — namely, that Africans (with only a few exceptions) have not been permitted to grow permanent roots in the European areas.

A more important relationship between the policies of the governing group and the market for indigenous labour concerns the objective to expand both the money economy and the size of the European population. To achieve the latter, the money economy attempts to offer real incomes to Europeans which exceed those they can earn elsewhere. This is not to suggest that economic factors alone are responsible for all international migrations of labour. The flow of European immigrants into the Rhodesias has stemmed from a mixture of motives. Political considerations have accounted for part of this movement, particularly for some of the migration of English-speaking peoples from the Union of South Africa in the post-war years. But it remains the case that the ability of the Rhodesias to retain these immigrants depends largely upon their success in fitting them into economic life on terms competitive with, if not superior to, those previously enjoyed. The immigrant whose transfer of domicile has been motivated by non-economic reasons might appear to be an exception. He may be willing to accept a lower standard of living; but even he may set a mini-mum limit to the economic sacrifice which he is prepared to make if he is to remain.

To provide the economic conditions for attracting and re-taining European immigrants, the Rhodesian economic system is organized to afford higher real incomes to its European members than their skills or energies could obtain in other countries. It might be maintained that the higher price of European labour in these territories is purely the product of natural economic forces — i.e. that skills are scarce and can therefore command a higher price than in the more developed countries. Whether competitive forces would have produced this result or not, it is obvious that the European position is buttressed by artificial supports which the governing minority is reluctant to scrap. It must be noted also that a system in which the wages paid to the African labour force need not be based on marginal productivity criteria provides the possibili-ties for rewarding the European members of the labour force at rates exceeding the value of their contribution to the pro-ductive process. Formulation of the problem of racial income distribution in terms of marginal productivity, of course, defies empirical measurement. But the structural features of the system suggest that European incomes are inflated and that it is the intention of the governing minority to keep them so. One of the factors which permits this arrangement to flourish is the low wage required to obtain the services of African workers. The conditions under which the value premises of the governing group and the functioning of the economic system are most compatible are present, in other words, when the supply of African labour is perfectly elastic at a low level of money wages. Initially, the wage for the African is low because of the low level of income obtainable from indigenous agriculture. Employers in the money economy may attempt to preserve this initial pattern as the conventional norm. Through agreement among themselves, competition in the market for African labour may be repressed and the minimum wage necessary to attract African workers may tend to become the maximum which is paid.

Even though important influences may be present which tend to preserve the original situation of perfect elasticity in the supply function of indigenous labour, this condition may no longer obtain as the money economy continues to expand. Lewis recognized that the limit to the perfectly elastic supply function would be reached when his subsistence sector had been completely absorbed (or nearly so) by the capitalist sector. In the Rhodesian situation, the labour supply function may lose perfect elasticity long before this physical limit is reached and for quite different reasons.

As the money economy grows, its requirements for African labour may swell to the point that a further withdrawal of man-power from the indigenous economy cannot be accomplished without upsetting its traditional productive processes. If the assumption of the Native Administrators about the proportion of the adult males required to maintain the integrity of the indigenous economy is correct, then a withdrawal of more than 50 per cent. of its able-bodied males would lead to a sharp reduction in the agricultural output of the indigenous family. At this point, the supply of labour would cease to be perfectly elastic. To attract additional indigenous workers, a rise in the real wage would be required. The employer in the money economy would be obliged to offer a real wage which would offset the loss in the real income of the family in indigenous agriculture, and to provide a further increment to the real wage sufficient to induce the African worker to make this break with his accustomed way of life. An alteration in the labour supply function could, of course, be brought about even sooner if substantial earnings from the sale of agricultural surpluses were possible for the members of the indigenous economy.

When the supply of labour from the indigenous economy becomes less than perfectly elastic, a new set of conditions arises, with implications of major importance for the process of economic development. This stage in the evolution of contact between the indigenous and the money economies may be described as 'quasi-full employment'. The situation bears a superficial resemblance to the orthodox concept of full employment. The economic system cannot expand output in one direction without a sacrifice in output in another. An expansion of production in the money economy which requires the employment of additional indigenous labour would necessitate a fall in output in indigenous agriculture. But the analogy to the orthodox concept of full employment is far from exact. The capacity of the economic system as a whole has not been fully extended. The dual structure of the economic system has blocked the allocation of resources to their most productive uses and has kept some of its resources from being utilized at all. The total output of the economic system would be further increased if non-economic restrictions placed upon it did not impede the transfer of indigenous labour into employments where its productivity was higher than in the traditional agriculture, or if African farmers were permitted to bring unutilized land resources into production. Quasi-full employment implies that the economic circumstances in which the objectives of settler supremacy can most easily be pursued no longer prevail. Adjustments in the method of economic expansion or in the social structure itself may thus be required if growth of the money economy is to be sustained.

But the necessity of adjustments may be avoided, or at least mitigated, if the openness of the money economy assumes another form: openness to the import of unskilled labour. When the perfectly elastic portion of the supply curve for labour from the local indigenous economy approaches its limit, it may yet be possible to obtain African labour from outside without increasing the real wage rate. A break in the previous pattern of income distribution may thus be postponed. In this manner, the functioning of the system on its original terms may be perpetuated. Through an extension of the perfectly elastic portion of the supply curve for African labour, a rise in its real wage may be checked and the system could thereby continue to attract European immigrants by offering them artificially high real incomes.

This expedient would permit the money economy to function without major modifications by forestalling a rise in the real wage paid to African labour. In this sense, perfect elasticity in the supply of African labour could be maintained. But in another sense, the supply function for African labour would not be the same when labour has been imported as it had been when male workers were drawn from the indigenous economy. Although the real wage received by the African would be unchanged, wage costs to the employer would be somewhat higher when extraterritorial workers are engaged. In tapping new supplies, the employer may be obliged to hire professional recruiters and to pay the transport costs of his immigrant workers. Recruiting, however, may still be economic. Had the employer drawn more man-power from the local indigenous economy, his labour costs would have been inflated still more by the increase in the real wages which would have been required. But a substantial portion of the additional labour sought by the money economy may be acquired without incurring these costs if the money economy merely remains open to the migration of African workers. Extraterritorial labour may flow in voluntarily from adjacent territories where the money economy is less advanced and wage employment opportunities fewer.

The employment of extraterritorial workers to relieve the demands for labour from the local indigenous economy has been particularly popular in Southern Rhodesia. The practice is highly developed there. For some time, a major share of the African labour force of the colony has been drawn from outside the territory. As a result, adjustments which otherwise would have been required have been avoided or at least postponed.

Interaction of the Money and Indigenous Economies and its Implications for Fulfilment of the Second Criterion of Economic Development

The second of the two criteria of economic development required that the real income of the indigenous population should improve while the money economy in the same territory expanded. It has already been observed that the opportunities open to the indigenous peoples for acquiring money incomes through the sale of agricultural surpluses have been localized to particular areas. The only method of earning cash which is open to all members of the indigenous population is the sale of labour. But it can now be seen that the proponents of settler supremacy in the Rhodesias have a stake in restricting the proportion of males in the indigenous population employed for wages at any one time. It is to their advantage to prevent an upward pressure on the real wage of the African labour force. But if this is to be avoided after the expansion of the money economy has passed a certain stage, indigenous labour cannot be drawn forth in quantities sufficient to satisfy the full labour requirement of the money economy. Instead, the money economy must look beyond its own borders if it is to obtain labour on terms which do not force the real wage upward. Effectively, these circumstances mean that the money economy, once conditions of quasi-full employment have been approached, may attempt to limit its demands for labour from the indigenous economy to the normal increment to the male labour force made available by population growth. This would tend to prevent the second condition for economic development from being satisfied. The entry of the indigenous population into the money economy would not proceed at a rate exceeding the growth in its population. Instead, it would be geared to the population expansion and, if possible, would not be permitted to expand at a faster pace. By the same token, if the supply of African labour can no longer be maintained with perfect elasticity and the quasi-full employment position is in fact passed, then new opportunities for the economic development of the indigenous population may be opened up. Not only might the rate of growth in wage employment exceed the rate of population increases, but the real income of Africans in wage employment may then also begin to rise.

This turn of events would disturb the continued expansion of the money economy on the original terms. One of the features of the Rhodesian scene which has permitted the version of economic development sponsored by the governing group to thrive has been terms of contact with the indigenous economy under which the supply of African labour was perfectly elastic at a low real wage. If the conditions of contact between the two economies are changed and the money economy begins to employ indigenous labour in a volume which would require a rise in its real wage, an economic support to the value premises of the Rhodesian system has been dislodged. Circumstances may then be more favourable for a loosening in the restrictions which have characterized its economic life.

Adjustments may be made to keep the system from reaching quasi-full employment. Openness to the importation of African labour is a means towards this end. But, through time, this device may not be completely effective. Labour supplied from external sources is not fully within the control of the territory desiring to employ it and its continued availability is uncertain. It is possible that economic advance in the labour-supplying territories may diminish the attractiveness of emigration. Moreover, the governments of the labour-supplying territories may restrict the exodus of their man-power. While the capacity of governments to enforce such regulations with thoroughness is questionable in the African interior, the flow of migrant workers could be substantially reduced, if not completely cut off.

The continued growth of the money economy may ultimately result in quasi-full employment, despite delaying actions. But quasi-full employment is not a stable situation. Time may also bring changes in the productivity of indigenous agriculture. As its population grows and is confined on a restricted land area, a decline in *per capita* real income from indigenous agriculture becomes a real possibility. Should this occur, the perfectly elastic portion of the supply curve for indigenous labour would be extended. Indigenous labour would become available for wage employment in greater volume without a rise in its real wage. It would appear that population pressure of this intensity has already developed in Nyasaland. In the Rhodesias, it is still an unusual phenomenon, although some districts in Southern

Rhodesia appear to have reached this stage. In time, the position there may further deteriorate. Should this transpire, the original definitions of economic development would no longer apply. It would not then be possible to maintain that a monetization of the indigenous economy would be equivalent to an improvement in its real income. With real income *per capita* falling in the indigenous economy, labour might be forced into wage employment without a long-term improvement in its real income. Apart from this exception, the original criteria of economic development would hold.

From these observations, it would appear that the inter-action between the money and the indigenous economies might produce a situation in which their traditional terms of contact would be changed. A fresh set of conditions would be created. And a climate more favourable to the improvement in the real income of the indigenous population and to a relaxation in the impediments imposed by the value system of the Rhodesias might emerge. These effects could follow if the money economy continues to expand and calls for more indigenous man-power beyond quasi-full employment. But these consequences are not certain. A deterioration in indigenous agriculture would alter the result; and it may also be possible that adjustments within the money economy may neutralize the potential gains which might then flow to the indigenous population.

The following two chapters will return to empirical analysis. Their purpose is to assess the validity of the relationships between the indigenous and the money economy now formulated. Chapter IX deals with the market for African labour and attempts to establish the extent to which the Central African economic system has evolved towards quasi-full employment. Chapter X will reconsider events in the money economy in light of its contact with the indigenous economy.

THE INTERACTION BETWEEN THE INDIGENOUS AND THE MONEY ECONOMIES: THE LABOUR MARKET

In the preceding chapter, an hypothesis was advanced concerning the relationship between the indigenous and money economies. It was there argued on theoretical grounds that the indigenous economy might reshape the form of the expansion process through its role as a supplier of labour to the money economy. In the early stages of growth, this influence would be slight but, with the continued expansion of the money economy, it could become important. This stage would be reached when the supply of labour from the indigenous economy was no longer perfectly elastic: i.e. the situation which has been described as quasi-full employment. At that point — if the indigenous economy could still function along its traditional lines — a further withdrawal of male labour from its ranks could not be accomplished without a reduction in agricultural output. A readjustment in the former pattern of relationships between the money and the indigenous economies would then be required.

It is now appropriate to make an empirical investigation of the labour market in Central Africa to test the hypothesis which has been advanced and to establish whether or not the conditions necessary to satisfy the criteria of economic development have been fulfilled. Several variables are important for this analysis. First, the trends in the volume of employment of indigenous labour must be examined. The composition of the labour force must then be scrutinized to determine the areas from which workers are drawn. Further, an examination must be made of wage rates and their variation as the volume of employment has changed. It will be recalled that the theoretical discussion focused on the real wage as the significant factor in the determination of the quantity of wage labour which the indigenous economy would be prepared to offer. The analysis of the trends in wage rates must, therefore, be conducted in two stages. First, trends in money wages will be examined; then the conversion of these results into real wages will be attempted.

Non-economic Factors Affecting the Labour Market

In any economic system, an aggregative analysis of the structure of the labour market is beset by complexities which reveal the inadequacy of many of the economist's simplifications. Units of labour are not homogeneous and the market for labour is seldom a perfect one. Further, the allocation of an economy's labour resources is likely to be distorted by non-economic forces. Aggregative statistical analysis, at best, must be content with surveying the general uniformities. Generalizations can only be made with caution and, even when they are legitimate, it is inevitable that particular industries or particular localities will stand out as exceptions.

Relative to the labour market in more advanced countries, the market for indigenous employees in the Central African territories is at once more simple and more complex. African labour, as it has been traditionally employed, is more homogeneous than the labour force in highly developed economies. With but a few exceptions, Africans are engaged only for work requiring little or no skill. Some occupations, however, are more handsomely rewarded than others. The less attractive and more hazardous — mining, for example — have offered better wage terms than such employments as agriculture or domestic service. But the gap between the highest and the lowest paid African members of the labour force is considerably less pronounced than in the labour markets of more developed economies. Indeed the value system of Rhodesian society has tended to check the emergence of substantial differentials. Its influence on the African wage structure is brought out in the words of a Southern Rhodesian Committee appointed to advise on wage policy:

It is reasonable to assume that, when labour is scarce, the shortage will be most severely felt in the labourer class because so many of them, and usually the best, will be absorbed in better paid classes of work. It is therefore undesirable that the difference between the scales of pay of the labourer class and those of the worker class next above it should be unduly marked.[1]

But this element of simplicity in the labour market is the product of a variety of complex forces, many of which are unfamiliar in the more economically advanced communities. Some of them are clearly non-economic in character and others are reflections of the contrasts in material and cultural standards and in the historical experience of the races in Central Africa. The process of merging members of these differing societies into the productive apparatus of the money economy has demanded adjustments and adaptations. It would be idle to pretend that the adjustment is yet perfect. In general, neither race has adapted its contact with the other in a manner compatible with maximum realization of the economic potential of Central Africa.

Initially, the pains of adjustment fell most heavily on the African entering wage employment. The transition from his traditional society to the money economy placed him in an alien world. Within his experience, there was no precedent for the discipline of regular work. He was expected to master new methods and to respond to new incentives, often without the link of common language with his employer. Even if the psychological adjustment could be made, the African wage-earner was often physically handicapped in coping with his new environment. The dietary standards of his tribal community, by Western standards, were seldom adequate. Malnutrition was common and this, in turn, left the African vulnerable to disease. It is still the case that the majority of recruits to wage employment in the Central African territories are found to be suffering from some endemic disease.[2] European employers, in

---

[1] *Report of the National Native Labour Board, Southern Rhodesia,* 6 November 1948, p. 16.

[2] In Southern Rhodesia, medical examinations of Africans admitted to the Medical Ward of the Salisbury Hospital in the first half of 1944 illustrate the magnitude of the problem: 'About 3 natives in every 4 were suffering either from malnutrition or a disease such as bilharzia or hook-worm. It is considered by the Public Health Department that this sample reflects very fairly the incidence of malnutrition among natives in general. The natives were admitted to hospital suffering from pneumonia, tuberculosis, severe malaria and other complaints. There was hardly any instance of an admission for malnutrition, bilharzia, or even hook-worm' (*Report of the Social Security Officer, Southern Rhodesia, Part II: Social Services,* October, 1944, p. 17). Similar conclusions were put forward on the

their own interest, have tended to adopt a paternalistic attitude towards their African workers. Governments have generally required employers to provide minimum standards of food and shelter. But even without governmental intervention, it would still have been worth the employer's while, in the interests of efficiency, to assume direct responsibility for the provision of these necessities.[1]

To the employer, the problem of dealing with a primitive and alien labour force was perplexing. African labour hardly presented the most attractive raw material for wage employment. Not only was its physical capacity often unimpressive, but its behaviour was difficult to comprehend. The African worker was regarded as irresponsible and unreliable, lazy and inefficient. Whatever the explanation of these observed characteristics of African labour in the early stages of European contact with Central Africa, they have imprinted a set of stereotypes on the settlers' minds — stereotypes which still tend to dominate their thinking on the capabilities of the indigenous peoples. There are, however, exceptions. Some employers in the Rhodesias now speak highly of the efficiency of African personnel when properly trained. As the Development Co-ordinating Commission in Southern Rhodesia noted:

> Sufficient evidence is already forthcoming in the secondary industries that have been established around the main cities to show that, given proper equipment and adequate training, the native African possesses a high standard of manipulative dexterity. Moreover, he is not so greatly affected by the monotony factor as is his European counterpart.[2]

The results achieved by a minority of employers contradict the view that African workers are constitutionally incapable of achieving high standards of productivity. Nevertheless, it

---

[1] This is not to suggest that all employers have recognized the importance of these factors affecting productivity. A Southern Rhodesian report in 1944 expressed amazement at the apparent indifference of some employers towards the physical well-being of their African labour force. See *Report of the Committee to Investigate the Economic, Social and Health Conditions of Africans Employed in the Urban Areas, 1944* (Government Stationery Office, Salisbury).

[2] *First Interim Report of the Development Co-ordinating Commission, Southern Rhodesia, 1948*, p. 11.

---

incidence of disease among the African population by Dr. M. Gelfand, 'Medical Problems in the Native of Southern Rhodesia', *NADA*, 1944.

remains the case that the most commonly expressed judgement of the majority is the reverse. High rates of labour turnover and absenteeism are expected. It is, therefore, thought unprofitable to invest in imparting skills to a labour force which is only transient.[1] This assessment buttresses the view that skill should remain a monopoly of the European. The cycle of low productivity and low incomes on the part of the African employee thus becomes self-perpetuating. It may be noted that the thinking of the settler community in the Rhodesias is not entirely consistent on these matters. If it were genuinely true, as is sometimes alleged, that the African is incapable of acquiring and exercising skills, the bolstering of colour-bar practices through legislation and trade union contracts would be redundant.

Many aspects of the social and human problems of labour relations in Central Africa defy treatment within any analytical framework which begins from premises that human behaviour is completely rational. The transfer from tribal life to the money economy is neither easy nor frictionless. Unaccountable and unanticipated responses often are made by those caught up in the transition and the emotions, rather than reason, can become the primary stimulants to action. The recurrent labour difficulties on the Northern Rhodesian Copperbelt present these problems in bold relief. The issues there are complicated by the clash between a class of European artisans, defending an entrenched position, and a group of African workers, increasingly detribalized, with aspirations to fuller participation in the benefits of the money economy. In this supercharged atmosphere, apparently trivial incidents can spark trouble.[2] More fundamental issues of economic policy are frequently submerged

[1] On this point, the *National Native Labour Board of Southern Rhodesia* observed: 'Much of the labour at present in employment is used wastefully. Many employers have little or no regard for the welfare of their employees, are at no pains to instruct them in their work, or to increase their efficiency, and neglect to give proper supervision. These conditions encourage the creation and maintenance of a poor type of labourer with a low standard of work and output', loc. cit., p. 17.

[2] Among the contributory causes to the disturbances in the Copperbelt in 1956, for example, was the protest of the African Mine Workers' Union against the wearing of leg guards and the 'posting of discs' (a procedure in the time-keeping arrangements). The grievance in both cases stemmed from the feeling that these practices were discriminatory; they were applied to African but not to European miners. For a fuller discussion of these issues, see *Report of the Commission Appointed to Inquire into the Unrest in the Mining Industry in Northern Rhodesia in Recent Months* (*The Branigan Report*) (Government Printer, Lusaka, November 1956).

in the sensitivity of all parties on relatively minor matters.

In acute form, the labour relations problems of the Copper-belt illustrate the force of other non-economic factors distorting and simplifying the market for African labour. The situation may be best understood from its historical origins. When the copper-mining industry was established, it was necessary for the companies to import European labour for a wide range of jobs. In practice, however, many of these tasks did not require advanced training and could be performed by indigenous labour once it had acquired experience. These posts have come to be regarded as reserved for Europeans. Efforts on the part of the mining companies to fill them with qualified Africans were obstructed by the European Mine Workers' Union. The necessity for revision in the conditions of employment for the industry were officially recognized as early as 1940.[1] But a lag of fifteen years elapsed before agreement was reached.[2] In the interim, a further commission in 1948 recommended specific categories of jobs which should be taken over by Africans and a 1954 Board of Inquiry re-emphasized the urgency of a solution.[3] Agreement to release twenty-four categories of jobs to Africans was ultimately achieved between the European Union and the mining companies in September 1955.[4]

[1] In 1940, the Forster Commission recommended that 'the mine managements should consider with representatives of the Government and the Northern Rhodesia Mine Workers' Union to what positions, not now open to him, the African worker should be encouraged to advance', *Report of the Commission Appointed to Inquire into Disturbances in the Copperbelt, Northern Rhodesia, July, 1940* (Government Printer, Lusaka).

[2] One of the two large mining groups on the Copperbelt, the Rhodesian Selection Trust, would have preferred a settlement at a much earlier date and was prepared to risk a strike of its European employees to achieve it. They were dissuaded from undertaking serious negotiations earlier by government requests to maintain production, without interruption, because of strategic requirements during the war years and because of the dollar earnings of the industry in the immediate post-war years. This account of the group's policy is offered by its chairman, R. L. Prain, 'The Problem of African Advancement on the Copperbelt', *African Affairs*, vol. 53 (1954), pp. 91–103.

[3] *Report of the Commission Appointed to Consider African Advancement in the Copper Mining Industry, Northern Rhodesia (The Dalgleish Commission)* (Government Printer, Lusaka, 1948), and the *Forster Board of Inquiry*, 1954. These views were also supported by the Jack Board of Inquiry of 1950.

[4] It would be erroneous to suggest that the signing of the agreement itself dissolved many of the sources of friction. The European Mine Workers' Union has since been unco-operative in providing on-the-job training for the African employees moving into more responsible positions.

O

While social problems of this type create distortions in the labour market of the Rhodesian territories, it would be mistaken to regard these difficulties as fundamental. They place serious obstacles across the path of economic expansion. But these obstacles may not themselves be permanent features of the social environment; they can survive only as long as their economic cost is contained within tolerable bounds. An analysis of the forces underlying the labour market is therefore in order.

Trends in the Volume of Wage Employment

Since 1930, the employment of African labour in the Central African territories has expanded remarkably and with little

TABLE I

CENSUS RETURNS ON THE NUMBERS OF AFRICANS IN WAGE EMPLOYMENT IN THE CENTRAL AFRICAN TERRITORIES

	Southern Rhodesia	Northern Rhodesia	Nyasaland
1926	173,598	—	—
1931	180,158	79,813	—
1936	254,297	—	—
1941	303,279	—	—
1946	376,868	140,776	—
1951	530,203	228,676	—
1956	609,953	263,132	164,258

Notes and Sources: Data are drawn from the census returns of the several territories. No census of African employment was taken in Northern Rhodesia and Nyasaland in the years omitted.

interruption. The broad outlines of the changes in the volume of employment in the three territories may be observed in Table I.

The census figures are valuable as indicators of the major changes in African employment over the long period. But their method of preparation is not ideal for all purposes. They cover the number of Africans employed by Europeans on census day — normally this has been in early May. Measurements of the labour force on a particular day, however, may not typify the general situation. Labour is often employed for only a portion of the year and turnover rates are high. Generally, the timing of the census has coincided with a period of high seasonal activity in European agriculture. The returns may thus misrepresent the average volume of employment throughout the year. Where European agriculture is the predominant employer, as in Nyasaland, the tendency of the census returns to exaggerate the average employment position may be the most serious.

A further defect in the census calculations, although a less serious one, is the exclusive concentration on Africans employed in the European areas. The returns, in this respect, are probably quite comprehensive. But no measurement is made of the number of Africans who are the wage employees of other

TABLE II

ANNUAL ESTIMATES OF THE AVERAGE NUMBERS OF AFRICAN MALES IN WAGE EMPLOYMENT, SOUTHERN RHODESIA, 1929–45 (000s)

1929	161.7	1938	255.8
1930	156.7	1939	242.4
1931	164.3	1940	249.6
1932	157.2	1941	285.5
1933	176.5	1942	295.2
1934	184.1	1943	310.7
1935	204.6	1944	293.7
1936	221.4	1945	298.4
1937	243.7		

Sources: Derived from the annual estimates of the Department of Native Affairs, contained in the *Annual Reports of the Chief Native Commissioner, Southern Rhodesia.*

Africans. This component of total wage employment remains unknown, but it is unlikely that Africans in any appreciable number are employed for wages by other Africans.[1]

From the census results, the dominance of the Rhodesian territories (and of Southern Rhodesia in particular) in the labour market of Central Africa is apparent. This is hardly remarkable. In these territories, the money economy is the most advanced.

In Southern Rhodesia, the volume of African employment has increased steadily. Even during the period 1930–45, when

[1] One group of Africans who might potentially be employers — farmers in the Native Purchase Areas of Southern Rhodesia — do not appear to have engaged any substantial number of employees. A 1950 report commented on this matter: 'Few labourers seem to be employed by farmers in the [Native Purchase] Areas; frequently none, save casually, and rarely more than one or two. One alleged reason for this is unreasonably low wages, often not more than one-third of European farms nearby', Professor Sir Frank Engledow, *Report on the Agricultural Development of Southern Rhodesia*, C.S.R. 23, 1950, p. 23.

the pace of expansion in the money economy was slow, the volume of African employment increased with little interruption. Only in the early years of the depression and in the middle of the war was expansion arrested (see Table II).

These estimates differ from the census figures in that they attempt to show the average volume of employment throughout the year. For several of the more important industries in Southern Rhodesia, returns on the average number of Africans employed are submitted annually. But the coverage is not complete. The aggregate, therefore, combines some reasonably reliable data with indirect estimates of the volume of employment in the remainder of the economy. These estimates indicate that, in a period of slow growth in the money economy

TABLE III

AVERAGE NUMBERS OF AFRICAN MALES EMPLOYED IN MINING AND EUROPEAN AGRICULTURE, SOUTHERN RHODESIA, FOR SELECTED YEARS

	Mining (ooos)	% of total African employment	European agriculture (ooos)	% of total African employment
1929	47.0	29	69.7	43
1931	35.2	21	67.7	41
1939	83.8	34	93.6	38
1943	78.5	25	114.3	37
1945	71.7	24	130.6	44

Sources: Mining estimates are compiled from the *Annual Reports of the Chief Government Mining Engineer, Southern Rhodesia*. Estimates of African employment in European agriculture are drawn from *The Economic and Statistical Bulletin, Southern Rhodesia*, 21 July 1933, p. 5; and the *Report on Agricultural and Pastoral Production, Southern Rhodesia, 1946-47*, p. 3.

generally, the average volume of African employment increased by roughly 85 per cent.

Two activities — mining and European agriculture — have been the major employers of African labour in Southern Rhodesia. Between them, they have normally employed nearly two-thirds and often more of the African wage-earners (see Table III).

It may be noted that aggregate African employment in the mining industry passed through several phases during this period. In the early 1930s, it fell with the reduction in activity in asbestos and chrome mining. From 1932, employment expanded, led by the gold industry's revival. The expansion in aggregate employment reached its high water mark in 1937 when, on the average, 90,600 African males were employed. Of this total, nearly 80 per cent. were engaged in gold mining. A decline in the aggregate was continued from 1937 to 1945, the gold industry being responsible for this reduction in numbers.[1]

The remainder of the African labour force in Southern Rhodesia has been divided between manufacturing, construction, transportation, and domestic and other services. Only the manufacturing industries showed a consistent tendency to increase their relative importance as employers of African labour between 1930 and the end of the war. By 1945, more than 30,000 Africans on the average were employed in manufacturing, slightly more than 10 per cent. of the total African employment.[2]

In Northern Rhodesia, the pattern of expansion in African employment in the years 1930–45 was less consistent. The economy of the territory underwent a considerable shock with the collapse in the copper market and the check to the development of the industry which followed. This brought a sharp drop in all lines of employment. Building activity was largely suspended; railway employment fell. As the European population diminished, so also did the demand for African labour in domestic service and in agriculture. Not until 1938 did African employment recover the position it had reached in 1930. Expansion, however, was sustained through the war years. These changes are reflected in the estimates of the average numbers of Africans employed (see Table IV).

Estimates of the volume of African labour employed within Nyasaland are much less reliable than for the Rhodesias but, by any measure, the opportunities for wage employment are much more restricted there than elsewhere in Central Africa. The bulk of the wage labour force has traditionally been engaged by the European planters. One estimate of the average numbers of Africans employed in 1930 put the total at just over 80,000, of whom 70,000 were agricultural labourers.[3] Although no

---

[1] Based on data in the *Annual Reports of the Chief Government Mining Engineer, Southern Rhodesia, 1930–1945.*

[2] *Thirteenth Report of the Census of Industrial Production, Southern Rhodesia*, p. 7.

[3] This estimate, published in the *Blue Book, Nyasaland, 1930*, differs from the estimate prepared by the Native Affairs Department for August in the same year. The latter estimated the total numbers in wage employment at just over 60,000.

estimates were prepared for the early years of the 1930s, it is clear that the total volume of employment fell with the declining fortunes of the plantations. By 1936, the numbers employed for wages within the Protectorate was estimated at 49,000.[1] The official estimate of average wage employment had risen to over 55,000 in 1938; in that year, the total for European agriculture was placed at 39,000.[2] These aggregates had increased little by the end of the war. Even including seasonal labour on the plantations, the official estimate of African wage employment was only slightly more than 75,000 in 1946.[3]

TABLE IV

ESTIMATES OF AVERAGE NUMBERS OF AFRICANS EMPLOYED FOR WAGES IN NORTHERN RHODESIA FOR SELECTED YEARS COMPARED WITH NUMBERS EMPLOYED IN MINING AND EUROPEAN AGRICULTURE (000s)

	Total	Mining	%	European agriculture	%
1929	56.7	16.6	29	10.1	18
1930	70.5	21.8	31	10.9	15
1933	37.5	8.1	22	5.6	15
1936	53.5	15.1	28	9.2	17
1939	88.5	29.5	33	13.5	15
1945	100.3	33.0	33	15.0	15

Sources: *Report of the Commission Appointed to Enquire into the Financial and Economic Position of Northern Rhodesia (The Pim Report)*, Col. No. 145, p. 35, contains estimates for the years 1929–36. Subsequent estimates are drawn from the *Annual Blue Books, Northern Rhodesia.* For the earlier years, the Blue Book estimates and those shown in the Pim Report do not agree in all particulars. The latter are probably the more accurate.

Money Wage Rates, 1930–45

In the Rhodesian territories, the most reliable data on the course of money wages are obtainable on the principal export industry — mining. The absolute level of money wages in this industry is not typical of the rates prevailing elsewhere in the economy. Measured by their wage scales, African mine workers have traditionally formed the aristocracy of the African labour force. The other major employer, European agriculture, has typically paid a considerably lower wage.

In Southern Rhodesia, the average level of wages paid in the mining industry fell by approximately one-third in the early

[1] *Rhodesia-Nyasaland Royal Commission Report*, Cmd. 5949, p. 183.
[2] *Annual Blue Book, Protectorate of Nyasaland, 1938.*
[3] *Colonial Annual Report, Protectorate of Nyasaland, 1946*, p. 19.

1930s. In 1930, average cash wages were roughly 31s. per month. Up to 1935, the average money wage fell steadily and, in that year reached its lowest point at 21s. per month. From 1936 to 1945, a gradual upward movement developed. But even in 1945, the average cash wage had not been restored to its 1930 level. At the close of the war, the mining industry, on the average, was paying less than 29s. per month in cash to its African employees.[1]

The mining industry of Northern Rhodesia passed through similar experiences in the 1930s. The Forster Commission, examining the structure of African wages on the Copperbelt in 1940, reached the conclusion that:

On the evidence submitted, it appears that the existing basic minimum rates for both sections of workers [i.e. surface and underground] were at the commencement of the strike actually lower than they were when the serious development of the Copperbelt was in progress. The reason given by the representatives of the mine owners was that in the development days of the Copperbelt, labour was more difficult to obtain. Since the slump in 1931–32, more labour was available and consequently the mine owners felt justified in paying a lower rate, even though the prosperity of the mines during the years immediately before the strike showed remarkable strides. No improvements in wages had occurred since the reductions immediately subsequent to the slump.[2]

In 1940, average wages paid to Africans in the Northern Rhodesian mining industry were comparable to those prevailing in mining in Southern Rhodesia. From 1941 onwards, wage scales for African miners in the two Rhodesias steadily diverged. The cash wage paid in the Northern Rhodesian industry expanded at a faster rate than in Southern Rhodesia. One of the major factors responsible for this more rapid rate of increase was official intervention in the wage-fixing process in Northern Rhodesia. One of the recommendations of the Forster Commission in 1940 was that the basic rate of pay should be increased by 2s. 6d. per month. This recommendation was accepted by the mining companies. In addition, they agreed to the

---

[1] See *Reports of the Chief Government Mining Engineer, Southern Rhodesia*, and the *Economic and Statistical Bulletin, Southern Rhodesia*, 21 July 1938, pp. 1–2; 21 May 1946, pp. 4-5.

[2] *Forster Commission*, p. 29.

principle of a cost-of-living bonus.[1] These factors, in combination with the prosperity of the Northern Rhodesian industry during the war, produced a wage level higher than that paid by the Southern Rhodesian industry.[2]

Data on wage rates in agriculture are less reliable. Only general approximations on the level of wages in this industry are possible. One point, however, is clear — the standard rate of cash remuneration in European agriculture has generally been considerably below that obtainable in other industries. In part, this discrepancy is offset by the greater income in kind received by African farm workers. It is a common practice in the Rhodesias for European farmers to provide space for gardening to their African employees. An estimate of the average cash wage paid by Southern Rhodesian farmers in 1932 was less than 14s. per month, roughly half the average wage in mining.[3] The Chief Native Commissioner of Southern Rhodesia reported in 1934 that the cash wage in European agriculture was tending to fall to 8s. per month in some areas.[4] The standard rate in Northern Rhodesian agriculture was generally lower. One set of estimates indicates that the basic rate was 7s. 6d. per month in 1929; by 1932, this had fallen to 6s. 6d., and fell further the following year to 5s. per month.[5]

Approximations of the Course of Real Wages, 1930–45

Broadly speaking, it is doubtful if the money wage received by Africans was on the average much higher in 1945 than it had been in 1930. Even in those industries in which the money wage

[1] The Forster Commission recommended that a cost-of-living bonus in the amount of 2s. 6d. per month be paid to African miners. The bonus was subsequently increased to 5s. in July 1942, and to 7s. 6d. in November 1945. For details see the *Final Report of the Commission of Enquiry into the Cost of Living, Northern Rhodesia* (Government Printer, Lusaka, 1950), p. 41.

[2] A cost-of-living bonus was not generally paid in Southern Rhodesia. Asbestos mines in the colony, however, introduced a cost-of-living allowance in 1943. *Report of the Chief Mining Engineer, Southern Rhodesia, 1953*, p. 12.

[3] This figure has been derived from the estimated cash wage bill paid to African labour by Southern Rhodesian farmers in 1932, *Economic and Statistical Bulletin, Southern Rhodesia*, 21 July 1933.

[4] *Annual Report of the Chief Native Commissioner, Southern Rhodesia, 1934*, p. 5.

[5] *The Pim Report*, p. 52. The Report notes further that 'although 5s. is given as the lowest figure reached, it is not uncommon for labourers to work at 3s.–4s. per month on the poorer class of farms'.

rose, it is not clear that there was any improvement in real wages. In the early 1930s with prices of consumer goods dropping, it is possible that the real wage received by the African deteriorated little as his money wage fell. This situation was reversed in the war years. All consumer prices were rising rapidly, including those items normally included in the African budget. In Northern Rhodesia, the Acting Commissioner of Labour estimated in 1940 that the prices of several of the principal commodities consumed by Africans (and to which, according to his estimates, a third of their cash expenditure was allocated) had risen by 25 per cent. in less than twelve months.[1] The Chief Native Commissioner of Southern Rhodesia observed in 1942 that, although there was some tendency for an increase in wages, 'it is doubtful whether this kept up with the rise in the cost of living'.[2] In 1943, he pointed out that prices of the major consumer goods purchased by Africans were more than double their pre-war figure.[3]

In the absence of more refined measures of price changes of goods consumed by African wage-earners, judgments on their real income can only be approximate. No price index based on an African budget was constructed in the Rhodesias at this time.[4] *Ad hoc* estimates of the price changes affecting the African mine worker in Northern Rhodesia were made, however, by the mining companies in co-operation with the Provincial Commissioners. This index was constructed on the basis of a hypothetical budget, without investigations to determine the manner in which African wage-earners actually allocated their cash expenditures. Food was excluded from the budget on

[1] Statement of Acting Labour Commissioner Howe before the *Forster Commission*, p. 14.

[2] *Annual Report of the Chief Native Commissioner, Southern Rhodesia*, 1942, p. 53.

[3] Ibid., p. 121.

[4] In Northern Rhodesia, preparation of a consumer price index for Africans in urban areas was begun in 1955. Before that, the official indices (maintained in Southern Rhodesia since 1929 and in Northern Rhodesia since 1939) referred exclusively to the budgets of European households. According to these calculations, the European cost of living rose by about 30 per cent. from 1939 to 1945. It is interesting to note that the wages of African domestic servants are included in the calculations of the European cost of living.

The failure of the official estimates to take account of changes in the African's cost of living was criticized by the Forster Commission. It recommended an inquiry into the subject for the purpose of determining the scale of bonus appropriate on the Copperbelt (*The Forster Commission*, p. 37).

the grounds that it was provided by the employer. The prices of the commodities selected as representative of African cash expenditure nearly doubled between 1939 and 1947.[1] The overall increase in the prices of goods actually purchased by the African may have been slightly less rapid. Investigations made in 1947 into the expenditure patterns of African wage-earners in Northern Rhodesia revealed that nearly one-third of their spending was on foodstuffs.[2] This survey hardly constituted a representative sample of the African labour force. It was conducted by written questionnaire and was therefore biased in favour of the literate (and higher wage) group of African workers; no agricultural labourers were included in the survey. The findings were still striking. Formerly, it had been assumed that changes in food prices could be ignored in estimating the African's cost of living.[3] As food prices tended to rise more slowly than the retail prices of imported manufactured commodities during this period, it is likely that the total rise in the prices affecting the African was somewhat less than the estimates based solely on specimen manufactured articles would indicate.

Similar conclusions were reached in Southern Rhodesia concerning the change in prices of goods consumed by the African wage-earners during the war and in the immediate post-war years. In evidence before the National Native Labour Board in 1948, the Government Statistician estimated that:

The worth to the African in April, 1948 of the 1939 pound was as follows:

(*a*) if the African received and does not pay for his
rations and accommodation   ...   . 8s.
(*b*) if the African buys his own rations and provides
his own accommodation...   ...   . 9s. 5d.[4]

---

[1] See the *Final Report of the Commission of Enquiry into the Cost of Living, Northern Rhodesia*, p. 41. These price changes served as the basis for the adjustment in the cost-of-living bonus paid to African mine workers on the Copperbelt.

[2] Ibid., p. 194.

[3] The danger of this omission had been pointed out by the Forster Commission. Although the African employee is provided with minimum rations and, on the Copperbelt, his wife and family are given a portion of their food requirements, it noted that the items of food most desired by the African might not be included in the rations. Further, it was necessary to purchase food to supplement the allowance made for wife and family. Cf. *Forster Commission*, pp. 36–37.

[4] *Report of the National Native Labour Board, 1948*, p. 23. The report notes that these calculations 'were disputed by Advocate Dendy Young on behalf of various

These estimates were based on the comparison of the 1939 and 1948 prices of certain commodities commonly bought by the African wage-earner. The conclusion of the Board was that 'the evidence indicates that the average present wage will not buy as much as the wage that was paid for similar work in 1939'.[1]

These calculations for the Rhodesian territories, even though crude, suggest that the real wage of the average African employee deteriorated during the war and early post-war years. Although there was a slight upward movement in the average money wage, it generally failed to keep pace with the increased prices of items consumed by Africans. The only significant exception to this generalization was among the African employees of the mining industry of Northern Rhodesia.

It may be asked why the African employee did not resist this lowering in standards which, by any measure, were not high initially. Part of the explanation must lie in the lack of bargaining strength of African workers and their general inability to make an organized defence of their position in the money economy. But it does not follow that the African employee was indifferent to or unaware of the change in his economic circumstances. Although no organized African trade union existed during these years, alternative forms of protest were made when the opportunities presented themselves. One such occasion was the African strike in the Copperbelt in 1940. This followed a strike action by the European Union which had secured a wage advance. With this evidence of success before them, African workers in several mines emulated the European example. Their organization was rudimentary and the statement of their case poorly presented. But their economic objective was to resist the decline in their real earnings.[2]

[1] Ibid., p. 23.

[2] On the reasons why a wage demand had not been made earlier, the Forster Commission reported (without qualifying comment) the explanation offered by an African witness. According to this account, the chiefs and the missionaries had explained the international situation to the African miners and had advised them to do their part in the war effort without asking for more money. No claim was therefore made until the European miners had gone on strike (*Forster Commission*, p. 30).

An earlier stoppage had been brought about by African miners on the Copper-

employers' organizations, who, however, did not call expert evidence to deny their accuracy. Later he and Advocate Lloyd, representing African organizations, agreed that the 1939 pound should be regarded as worth approximately 10s. in 1948'.

In Southern Rhodesia, the pattern of African wage employment lacked the industrial and geographical concentration of the Copperbelt. This situation was less favourable for effective economic protests in the absence of trade unions. Nevertheless, some sporadic action was taken. In 1945, African employees of the Railways went on strike and were followed by the workers at one of the colony's largest gold mines. The Chief Native Commissioner reported that 'one of the strikers' main grievances was the disparity between the pre-war value of cash wages and current commodity prices'.[1]

The Composition of the African Wage Labour Force

While real wages, apart from the Copperbelt, showed a tendency to decline in these years, the volume of African employment continued to expand. This apparently contradictory phenomenon must be examined more closely. Southern Rhodesia presents the most interesting case. Not only has it

---

[1] *Annual Report of the Chief Native Commissioner, Southern Rhodesia, 1945*, p. 207. A more general protest came later. In October 1947, African employees of the Bulawayo municipality presented a wage claim. The municipality's offer was rejected and the Africans requested the appointment of a National Labour Board to investigate their case. To this request, the government agreed. The events which followed provide an interesting illustration of the manner in which African workers with only rudimentary organization can, on occasion, make effective economic protest. Shortly after the government agreed to investigate, the Rhodesia Federated Chambers of Commerce met in special session. At the meeting a resolution was passed deprecating the action of the government and recommending minimum pay scales for Africans of 30s. per month in the urban areas and 25s. per month in the rural areas. The publication of these resolutions was immediately followed by a succession of strikes among African workers which, in ten days, spread to all of the major employment areas of the colony. On 16 April 1948, the government announced that it would appoint a board to 'inquire into the grievances of the many different categories of Africans concerned'. But no investigation would begin while the employees remained on strike. The final report of the board produced the recommendation that the basic minimum wage for adult males in the urban centres should be 35s. per month. Details are described in the *Report of the Commissioner of Native Labour, 1948*, p. 46, and the *Report of the National Native Labour Board*, esp. pp. 8–11.

---

belt in 1935. The immediate circumstance provoking the action was an increase in taxes on African males in the mining areas. The commission investigating these disturbances concluded that higher taxes, in themselves, had not produced the unrest. Rather, it was the injudicious manner in which the Africans were informed of the tax change that incited them. See *Report of the Commission Appointed to Enquire into the Disturbances in the Copperbelt, Northern Rhodesia (Alison Russell Report)*, Cmd. 5009, 1935.

been the major wage employer in Central Africa, but the bulk of the increase in the volume of African employment occurred there between 1930 and 1945.

The most striking characteristic of the position in Southern Rhodesia is the extent to which the colony has been supplied with African labour from outside its territorial boundaries. From 1930 to 1945, the number of immigrant labourers consistently exceeded the number of Southern Rhodesian Africans employed in the money economy. The contribution of each group to aggregate employment may be observed in Table V.

TABLE V

INDIGENOUS AND NON-INDIGENOUS AFRICAN MALES
EMPLOYED FOR WAGES IN SOUTHERN RHODESIA FOR
SELECTED YEARS (000S)

	Non-indigenous males employed (average numbers)	*% of total employment in Southern Rhodesia*	*Southern Rhodesian males employed (average numbers)*
1929	90.3	56	71.4
1932	84.7	54	72.5
1935	121.0	59	83.6
1939	146.9	60	95.5
1942	161.0	54	134.2
1945	174.2	58	124.2

Sources: These estimates have been derived from the *Annual Reports of the Chief Native Commissioner, Southern Rhodesia.* Census returns in the comparable years give slightly different absolute totals, but the proportions of indigenous to non-indigenous Africans in employment are consistent with the estimates based on the average numbers employed during the year.

Immigrant labour employed in Southern Rhodesia has been drawn from three principal sources: Nyasaland, Portuguese East Africa, and Northern Rhodesia. During this period, Nyasaland was consistently the most important supplier, providing more than 40 per cent. of the extraterritorial labour employed in the colony. Northern Rhodesia, with the development of wage employment opportunities locally, has declined considerably in relative importance. According to the census reports, Northern Rhodesia's contribution shrank to 22 per cent. of the total in 1946 from over 35 per cent. in 1931. By 1946, Portuguese East Africa had displaced it as the second most important contributor to the extraterritorial labour force employed in Southern Rhodesia.[1]

This pattern of labour immigration into Southern Rhodesia has been shaped by a variety of forces, not all of them purely economic in character. In broad outline, the movement of labour would appear consistent with the results of competitive economic choice — the flow of labour has been from the areas in which money income earning possibilities were less favourable (or non-existent) to those areas in which wage rates were more attractive. But, in practice, the allocation of labour in Central Africa has not been governed exclusively by freely operating market forces. Special factors have conditioned this pattern. Perhaps the most important has been the activities of labour recruiters. Their role has been to tap fresh supplies of African workers from the remoter areas and to draw them into wage employment. Recruiting, in some form, has been a common practice since the earliest days of the money economy in Central Africa.[2] Generally, the task has been performed by

---

[1] The Southern Rhodesian census returns classify the non-indigenous males employed by territory of origin, as follows:

	1931	1936	1941	1946	1951	1956
Nyasaland	49,487	70,362	71,505	80,480	86,287	123,025
Northern Rhodesia	35,542	46,884	48,163	45,413	48,514	39,580
Portuguese territories	14,896	25,215	45,970	72,120	101,618	105,406
Others	2,983	2,440	2,468	4,399	10,353	8,796

[2] The labour recruiting system, in uninhibited form, was subject to serious abuses. The African signing an employment contract often did so without knowledge of the prevailing wage rates or without fully comprehending the terms under which he was engaged. In addition, the governments of the labour-supplying territories have frequently expressed concern about the effects of large-scale migration of male workers on the social and political solidarity of the indigenous communities. The government of Nyasaland has chronically struggled with this problem. But its attitude has been ambivalent. Realizing that competitive employment opportunities were not available within the Protectorate, it has attempted to regulate rather than check the outward flow of migrants. Agreements were signed with the Rhodesian territories in 1936 and 1948 for the purpose of standardizing the conditions of service and ensuring that the migrant labourer returned to his home at least once in two years. A procedure for withholding a part of the migrant worker's pay until he had returned home was also arranged. Nyasaland has also attempted to contain the volume of emigration by requiring exit permits, but the effectiveness of this control is hardly complete. For details, see *Report of the Migrant Labour Committee, 1935*, and the *Migrant Labour Agreements, 1936* and *1948*.

The formation of policy towards professional recruiting by the governments of the labour-supplying territories has faced a dilemma. Undesirable features of the practice have been recognized; i.e. that the recruiter may take advantage of the African's ignorance. But formal recruiting has not been outlawed. The argument

professional labour agents or by employers directly. More recently, government in Southern Rhodesia has assumed a direct responsibility for engaging contract labour from adjacent territories. This step was taken with the formation of the Native Labour Supply Commission in 1946. The Southern Rhodesian Government has further facilitated the inward flow of labour through the operation of a bus service for the transport of migrant workers.

In economic terms, the effect of drawing in extraterritorial labour has been to enable the money economy of Southern Rhodesia to expand the volume of employment without a corresponding rise in the real wage rate. But employers of extraterritorial labour in Southern Rhodesia have at times ascribed their preference for immigrant workers to other considerations. African workers from outside the territory are often described as more dependable, more amenable to discipline, and less prone to absenteeism than their counterparts from Southern Rhodesia. Similar phenomena may be noted in each of the Central African territories. Even in Nyasaland, the major exporter of labour, European employers have depended upon alien workers for certain types of work. The Native Department of the Protectorate went so far as to remark in 1934 that the 'employment of alien labour is essential to the successful working of the agricultural estates of the Protectorate'.[1] It was noted that indigenous man-power could be obtained for the lighter tasks, but that the heavy manual work was performed by immigrants.

That sociological factors influence the composition of the labour force in Central Africa, as they do in any economic

[1] *Annual Native Affairs Report, Protectorate of Nyasaland, 1934*, p. 13.
In Northern Rhodesia, a special factor has influenced the employment of extraterritorial labour. The large mines of the Copperbelt, as a matter of deliberate policy, arrange their engagements of African workers to avoid a concentration of any one tribal grouping. Indirectly, this policy of tribal distribution has resulted in the employment of immigrants although indigenous men offered themselves for these jobs.

in its favour is that, for the African who desires to migrate in any case, the system may offer some compensations. It assures him of adequate food and shelter *en route* as well as providing free transportation. Further, no time is wasted in seeking employment after arrival in the employment centres. The advantages and disadvantages of the system are well discussed by G. St. J. Orde-Browne, *Labour Conditions in Northern Rhodesia*, Col. No. 150 (H.M.S.O., 1938), esp. pp. 15–19.

system, cannot be denied. When geographically detached from his customary environment, the African will accept tasks which he would decline when closer to his home. Similarly, physical separation from relatives may alter his attitude towards wage employment. Wage-earning may be more attractive when there is no necessity to share its rewards with his kinfolk. The extent to which this traditional practice continues to be a disincentive to wage employment may be exaggerated.[1]

African Male Labour and the Indigenous Economy

A full account of the reliance on immigrant labour for wage employment in Southern Rhodesia cannot rest on these sociological factors alone. It is worth considering whether a more fundamental explanation may not have its roots in the relationships between the money and the indigenous economies. In the preceding chapter, it was indicated that there might be strong economic reasons why the supply of indigenous labour for wage employment might be restricted unless a rise in the real wage rate occurred. This point turned on the productive contribution of male labour to the agricultural system. The quantity of male labour which could be spared, without a serious reduction in agricultural output, was limited. The numbers who might be absent could not be measured precisely. The rule of thumb ratio suggested by the Native Commissioners indicated that the tolerable limit of absenteeism at any one time was in the range of half of the able-bodied males. This calculation was only approximate. The proportion may change with time; it will vary with changes in the availability of fresh land and with alterations in productive techniques. But as a first approximation, this ratio may be tentatively used.

For the money economy, the important consequence of these productive relationships within the indigenous economy is that the supply of indigenous labour is kept from being infinitely elastic. If more labour were to be obtained voluntarily after

---

[1] As the African has increasingly emulated European codes of economic behaviour, such traditional practices have tended to break down. Audrey Richards, in her study of the Bemba in Northern Rhodesia in the mid-1930s, noted that even in famine years, a distinction was drawn between home-produced foods and those obtained with cash. Those possessing the latter were not expected to share with their less fortunate brethren. See *Land, Labour and Diet in Northern Rhodesia*, pp. 152–3.

quasi-full employment has been reached, a substantial rise in the real wage rate would be required to over-compensate the wage employee for the loss in real income which would follow his absence from indigenous agriculture.

It is now pertinent to examine the extent to which these relationships have influenced contact between the indigenous and money economies in Central Africa. Because of the limitations of the available data, only approximations are possible. Further, the analysis must be conducted in terms of long-period trends. In particular years, the volume of indigenous labour offering itself for wage employment may be influenced by seasonal variations in the harvest which are not typical of the general pattern.

An approximation of the allocation of the male labour supply of Southern Rhodesia during this period can be made by comparing the estimates of the average numbers of indigenous Africans employed with the number of African males on the tax registers of the colony. These ratios can provide a clue to the distribution of the local African labour force between indigenous agriculture and employment in the money economy. The crude results of this method, compared with the census returns on the employment of indigenous Africans, are shown in Table VI. It is reasonable to expect that the census calculations, which measure the volume of employment on one day of the year only should be higher than the estimates for the average numbers employed throughout the year.

These results suggest that wage employment in Southern Rhodesia generally occupied from just under 30 per cent. to approximately 40 per cent. of the adult male Africans indigenous to the territory. The 40 per cent. mark was temporarily passed in the mid-war years. But this coincided with a period of crop failures.[1]

These crude figures require further adjustment if the overall pattern is to be revealed. The tax registers, although reasonably accurate indices of the indigenous adult male population, fail to depict the total number of able-bodied males within the African population. With only a few exceptions, all adult males are subject to tax. But contained within their number are some

[1] The *Annual Report of the Chief Native Commissioner, 1942*, describes 1942 as a hunger year.

P

disqualified from employment in the money economy by age or disease. Those not considered 'able-bodied' by the standards of the money economy may still be capable of making a productive contribution to indigenous agriculture. No precise data are available on the numbers of taxpayers physically eligible for wage employment. Two estimates suggest that the proportion

TABLE VI

TOTAL INDIGENOUS ADULT MALES ON THE TAX REGISTER, SOUTHERN RHODESIA, COMPARED WITH THE AVERAGE NUMBERS OF INDIGENOUS MALES IN WAGE EMPLOYMENT FOR SELECTED YEARS

	Total adult males on the tax register (ooos)	*Average number of indigenous males in wage employment in Southern Rhodesia (ooos)*	*Percentage of total taxpayers in wage employment in Southern Rhodesia*
1929	244.4	71.4	29
1931	257.4	68.4 (76.2)	27 (30)
1934	261.2	79.1	30
1936	267.7	87.7 (107.6)	33 (40)
1939	282.3	95.5	34
1941	295.5	118.7 (131.4)	40 (44)
1942	303.4	134.2	44
1945	332.0	124.2	37

Sources: *Annual Reports of the Chief Native Commissioner, Southern Rhodesia,* and the *Census Reports, Southern Rhodesia.* Figures in parentheses indicate the census returns on the aggregate number of indigenous males employed on census day and their percentage of the taxpaying male population.

is in the region of 80 per cent. of those on the tax registers.[1] Eliminating roughly one-fifth of the indigenous tax-paying population, it would appear that wage employment in Southern Rhodesia had increased its claim on the able-bodied males from approximately a 35 per cent. share in 1930 to approximately 45 per cent. by 1945.

[1] A continuing estimate has not been prepared in Southern Rhodesia on the numbers of able-bodied males within the adult African population. Estimates prepared for the Bledisloe Commission (p. 182) indicated that able-bodied males numbered 218,000 in 1936 out of a tax-paying male population of nearly 268,000. In 1947, the Commissioner of Native Labour in Southern Rhodesia put the number of able-bodied males at 270,000. The tax registers in that year carried nearly 347,000 adult males (*Report of the Commissioner of Native Labour, Southern Rhodesia, 1947*, pp. 37–39).

The amount of male labour available to African agriculture was further reduced by two other forms of absenteeism — migration to wage employment outside Southern Rhodesia and the exodus of Africans into the money economy as self-employed traders and craftsmen. During this period, neither claimed a sizeable proportion of the labour supply. The number of self-employed Africans in the money economy was less than 900 in 1930; the figure had risen to over 3,500 by 1938. In 1946, their number was just in excess of 5,500.[1] The exodus to the Union of South Africa was quantitatively probably more significant, although technically this migration from Southern Rhodesia was illegal; effective enforcement, however, was impossible. No estimates are available during these years of the total number involved. For 1947, the Commissioner of Native Labour in Southern Rhodesia put the figure at 25,000, less than 15 per cent. of the average number of indigenous males employed inside Southern Rhodesia in that year.[2] In the earlier years, when differentials in money wages between Southern Rhodesia and the Union were greater, the proportion of the total number of wage-earners employed in the latter may have been somewhat higher.

These calculations, even though only approximate, suggest that at no point did the drain on the available supply of male labour from African agriculture pass the point at which the traditional productive relationships within it would be seriously disrupted. The average number of absentees was never in excess of half of the male labour force, with the possible exception of the drought period in the mid-1940s. No upward pressure on the real wage rate was therefore forthcoming from this source. Whether it would have been possible for employers in Southern Rhodesia to procure more indigenous labour than was actually employed in the early 1930s is a question to which no definitive answer can be given. In those years, the ratio of

[1] *Reports of the Chief Native Commissioner, Southern Rhodesia, 1931*, p. 7; *1938*, p. 7; *1946*, pp. 9–10. It may be noted that self-employed Africans plied their trades predominantly in the European areas. Only a few could earn a cash income in the Reserves.

[2] *Report of the Commissioner of Native Labour, Southern Rhodesia, 1947*, pp. 37–39. This estimate is consistent with the results of the sample survey taken a year later. It put the number of indigenous males over puberty who were outside Southern Rhodesia at 27,400. See *Report on the Demographic Sample Survey of the African Population of Southern Rhodesia*, p. 6.

able-bodied males in wage employment locally was lower than it has been later. But one point is clear: if employers had been obliged to attract the increment to labour force from local sources, the aggregate volume of employment could not have expanded as much as it actually did without sweeping adjustments in the indigenous economy. Employers would probably have had to pay for these adjustments in the form of higher real wages. The importation of African labour thus enabled aggregate employment to increase without a rise in real wage rates.

The post-war period in Southern Rhodesia has produced a different set of relationships. The share of indigenous labour in the aggregate wage labour force has increased. The census of 1951 revealed that, of the male labourers employed in the colony, just under half were of Southern Rhodesian origin. In absolute terms, the employment of both indigenous and non-indigenous labour has increased substantially since 1946. But the more rapid rate of increase has occurred in the employment of indigenous labour. Estimates of the size of the labour force for 1954, in average numbers employed, put the aggregate at 550,000. Of this total, 280,000 were believed to be of Southern Rhodesian origin.[1] Southern Rhodesia has remained open to immigrant labourers and has continued to welcome them.[2] But its ability to attract them from other territories has not matched the growth in demand for African workers.

The major trends in the aggregate employment of Africans since the war may be observed in Table VII.

As the number of indigenous males employed in Southern

[1] The average size of the labour force cited above, it should be noted, is not strictly comparable with the estimates prepared before the war. The latter referred only to the employment of male Africans. The exclusion of females was legitimate in those years because the number employed was negligible. Since the war, the employment of African women has become more important. The 1956 census indicated that roughly 45,000 were then working for wages — just over 7 per cent. of the wage labour force on census day.

[2] During the post-1957 recession Southern Rhodesia modified the nature of its welcome to extraterritorial workers. The Migrant Labour Bill of 1958 empowered the government to restrict the entry of extraterritorial workers into urban areas if a labour surplus existed. European agriculture and mining — the two fields of employment which have relied the most heavily on extraterritorial employees — were excluded from the provisions of the bill. Southern Rhodesia's longstanding interest in attracting extraterritorial workers was not diminished by this legislation. Its effect was not to reduce the aggregate inflow, but rather to give special powers over the allocation of extraterritorial workers to the government.

Rhodesia's money economy has grown, the average number of indigenous males in wage employment has surpassed the average number remaining in indigenous agriculture. The data are not sufficiently precise to permit an exact date to be assigned to this shift in the balance of indigenous male labour. But, by the mid-1950s, it is unmistakable that more indigenous males have been employed by Europeans than have remained in the indigenous economy. Between 1946 and 1954, for example, the numbers of males on the tax rolls increased by more than 100,000 — from 336,000 to 444,000. In the same

TABLE VII

ESTIMATES OF VOLUME OF AFRICAN EMPLOYMENT FOR WAGES IN THE POST-WAR YEARS, SOUTHERN RHODESIA.
(000s)

	Average numbers employed	Average numbers of males employed	Non-indigenous males employed
1946	368.3 (376.9)	363.0 (363.3)	(202.4)
1948	408.3	400.0	
1951	500.8 (530.2)	488.0 (488.5)	(246.8)
1954	550.0		270.0
1956	594.0 (610.0)	(565.0)	(297.7)
1958	617.0		

Notes and Sources: Figures in parentheses are census returns. The estimates for 1946–51 are drawn from *The National Income and Social Accounts of Southern Rhodesia, 1946–1951*, Table I, p. 10. These estimates are generally comparable with those prepared by the Native Affairs Department. The 1954 estimate is based on material obtained from interview with the Deputy Commissioner for Native Labour, Southern Rhodesia. Data for 1956 and 1958 are drawn from the *Monthly Digest of Statistics, Federation of Rhodesia and Nyasaland (Supplement)*, vol. vi, no. 3.

period, the employment of indigenous males expanded even more. The data, although imperfect, indicate that the average number of indigenous males employed in Southern Rhodesia, which never exceeded half of the taxable male population before 1946, had increased to well over 50 per cent. of the male taxpayers by 1954.

The results of this first method of approximation suggest a marked departure from the earlier pattern. But the emphasis on wage employment appears more striking when allowance is made for a portion of the adult male population which is not 'able-bodied'. If the taxable population is deflated by the same fraction as was applied in the earlier years, it appears that wage-earning has attracted considerably more than half of the male workers physically fit for employment in the money economy. Additional drains on the supply of male labour available to indigenous agriculture are little more important than in the earlier years. Self-employed Africans in the European areas still numbered less than 9,000 in 1951.[1] No precise information is available on the numbers of Southern Rhodesian Africans employed outside the colony; it appears unlikely, however, that the volume of this migration is notably heavier than it had been in 1947. Further support for the general conclusion that employment in the money economy has, in recent years, claimed the major share of the aggregate supply of indigenous male labour is provided by the sample surveys of the African population of 1948 and 1953. For each of the areas for which comparable data were prepared in both years, the ratio of male absentees to the total *de jure* population increased.[2]

Post-War Trends in Real and Money Wages, Southern Rhodesia

From the calculations above, it would appear (if the 50 per cent. ratio is valid) that the money economy in Southern Rhodesia has attracted more male labour than indigenous agriculture could spare, under the traditional productive relationships, without a reduction in its output. If the general hypothesis is valid, it should follow either that real wage rates for indigenous labour have increased in recent years; or, that changes in techniques or in the availability of land have altered the productive role of male labour to such an extent that a higher proportion of the adult males can be released than was formerly the case.

The course of wage rates in the money economy must first be examined. As was the case in the consideration of wage movements between 1930 and 1945, the data will warrant only general observations. But these are adequate for the purpose of

---

[1] *Report of the Chief Native Commissioner, Southern Rhodesia, 1951*, p. 126. By 1957, self-employed Africans recorded by the Chief Native Commissioner numbered just over 10,000. Ibid., *1957*, p. 26.

[2] Cf. *Reports on the Demographic Sample Surveys of the Indigenous African Population, 1948 and 1953*.

establishing the major trends. For the post-war years in Southern Rhodesia, an approximation of changes in average money wages can be obtained from the national income accounts which contain estimates of the African wage bill in the money economy. This form of calculation introduces a further complication. The estimate of African wage income includes both the cash payment to African employees and the value of income received in kind. The employer has been responsible for providing free rations, according to a minimum diet prescribed in government regulations and for the housing of his African employees. The value of these goods and services is included in the national income estimates of African income. The food component of this income in kind has increased in value in recent years with the substantial rises in food prices. This has inflated the aggregate estimate of African income considerably. An adjustment in the global wage bill is therefore required to exclude rations provided by the employers. Table VIII indicates, in general terms, the comparison between the wage bill (including income received in kind) and the adjusted results when the value of rations has been excluded.

The results of these calculations may now be further adjusted to reach a crude approximation of the movements in average income per African employee (excluding the value of rations). These results appear in Table IX.

It must be re-emphasized that these calculations afford only a rough guide to average wage movements. But the general pattern is consistent with the earlier conclusion that the African's money wage failed to advance and that his real income deteriorated during the war and early post-war years. Since 1949, the government has intervened in the wage-fixing process. The basic minimum cash wage was set at £21 per annum in 1949 and was revised to £30 per annum in 1954. In 1958, the minimum was again raised, but the new calculation referred, not to the wage paid in cash over and above provision for rations and accommodation, but to the total payment required if the African worker provided for food requirements on his own. On this basis, the minimum applicable in Salisbury and Bulawayo was £78 per annum. The rates were scaled downwards in other urban areas. All of these regulations applied only to Africans employed in the urban areas. Those

TABLE VIII

AGGREGATE AFRICAN WAGE BILL, SOUTHERN RHODESIA, FOR SELECTED YEARS (£000,000s)

	Aggregate wage bill (including income in kind)	Aggregate wage bill (adjusted to exclude value of rations)
1939	5.9	4.8
1945	9.7	6.4
1948	12.6	7.7
1951	21.7	13.1
1954	34.9	23.3
1958	47.2	31.2

Notes and Sources: Aggregate wage bill estimates (including income in kind) have been obtained from *The National Income and Social Accounts, 1946–1951*, Southern Rhodesia, Table XIX, p. 23, and Table V, p. 12; and from estimates published in the *Annual Financial Statements* and in the *Monthly Digest of Statistics*. The adjusted figures have been derived by multiplying the cost of the minimum ration by the estimates of the average numbers employed during the various years. The monthly cost of the basic ration has been estimated as follows: 1937: 7s. 6d.; 1945: 12s. 6d.; 1946: 15s.; 1948: 20s.; 1950: 25s.; 1951: 28s.; (*Economic and Statistical Bulletin, Southern Rhodesia*, 21 August 1938, p. 4; 21 June 1946, p. 8; 7 November 1947, p. 9; 21 September 1953, pp. 12–13). Government regulations since 1949 have allowed the employer the option of providing rations directly or paying a cash allowance in lieu of rations. The ration allowance was set at 25s. per month in 1949. This was raised to 35s. per month in 1954. The 1958 adjustment is based on the value of the ration received by African employees in Salisbury as calculated from a survey taken in July 1957; it was then estimated that the value of rations was approximately £2 3s. 3d. per month (see *Report of the Urban African Affairs Commission*, 1958, Appendix N, p. 181).

employed in European agriculture and on small mining propositions were specifically excluded from their provisions.[1]

The estimates shown in Table IX are not identical with the average disposable income received by Africans. No allowance has yet been made for the imputed value of housing which it is usually the employer's responsibility to provide. An assessment of the magnitude of this item is more hazardous than the estimation of the value of foodstuffs. While there is a reasonable degree of uniformity in standards of rationing, this is not the case with housing in Southern Rhodesia. The quality of

TABLE IX

APPROXIMATE AVERAGE INCOME (EXCLUDING RATIONS) OF AFRICAN WAGE-EARNERS IN SOUTHERN RHODESIA FOR SELECTED YEARS (£s PER ANNUM)

1939	19–20
1945	17–18
1948	18–19
1951	26–27
1954	42–43
1958	50–51

Notes: These calculations have been derived from the adjusted global estimates and the estimates of the average numbers employed during the year.

accommodation varies widely in different industries and in different parts of the colony. On the small mines, for example, it has been a common practice to provide the employee with the materials and to allow him several days, usually with pay, for the construction of a simple shelter. This procedure is often followed in European agriculture. The larger mines, on the other hand, have constructed well-appointed townships for their African employees. In the urban areas, standards also differ materially. Domestic servants frequently have rudimentary shelters in the back gardens of their employers. Most

[1] It should be noted that the decisions of the Native Labour Boards on minimum wages are based on assessments of the minimum requirements of 'single' labourers. Commenting on this procedure, the Report of the Urban African Affairs Commission observed that if 'comparisons show the inadequacy of the existing minimum rates for single adult males they must point to the even greater inadequacy of the rates when applied to married adult males' (p. 77).

other workers are housed in the municipal compounds, some at a considerably higher standard, with the rents paid by the employer. In the post-war period, there has been a tendency to improve housing conditions for African workers. This improvement must be regarded as a genuine advance in the levels of real income received by the African worker.

These movements in the level of average wages paid to the African employee have referred to the average for the entire colony. Wage rates, however, are not uniform in all lines of employment. It is not possible to measure, on an aggregative basis, the wage bills paid by all industries employing Africans.

TABLE X

ALLOCATION OF AFRICANS EMPLOYED FOR WAGES (IN AVERAGE NUMBERS EMPLOYED), BETWEEN THE PRINCIPAL ACTIVITIES, SOUTHERN RHODESIA, FOR SELECTED POST-WAR YEARS (000s)

	Mining (average numbers employed)	% of aggregate employment	European agriculture (average numbers employed)	% of aggregate employment	Secondary industries (average numbers employed)	% of aggregate employment
1946	70.6	19	135.8	37	57.0	15
1948	63.4	16	147.3	36	72.3	18
1951	60.7	12	181.4	36	98.5	20
1954	56.5	10	194.3	35	—	—
1956	55.8	9	203.3	34	138.7	23

Notes and Sources: Apart from the 1956 figure for secondary industries (which is a census return), these data refer to the average volume of African employment throughout the year and are drawn from the *Reports of the Chief Government Mining Engineer*, *Reports on Agricultural and Pastoral Production*, and the *Censuses of Industrial Production*. Secondary industries include manufacturing, construction, and the supply of water and electricity.

For the principal categories of employment, an approximation can be made for the more recent years. Broadly, the post-war allocation of African labour in European employment has assumed the pattern shown in Table X. It may be noted that the mining industry has declined both in relative and in absolute importance as an employer of African labour while employment in secondary industries has expanded. European agriculture, continuing the pre-war pattern, has remained the most important single employer of African labour.

A comparison of the average levels of wages in these industries must now be made. This can be done by calculating the aggregate wage bill (including cash and kind) of each industry, and adjusting it by the average numbers employed. The results of these calculations appear in Table XI.

While these calculations serve as only a rough guide to the relative position of the various industries, the divergence

TABLE XI

AGGREGATE WAGE BILLS (INCLUDING INCOME IN KIND) OF THE PRINCIPAL EMPLOYERS
OF AFRICAN LABOUR IN SOUTHERN RHODESIA AND APPROXIMATE AVERAGE WAGE IN
EACH FOR POST-WAR YEARS

| | Mining | | European agriculture | | Secondary industries | |
	Aggregate wage bill (cash and kind) (£ooos)	Average wage (cash and kind) (£s per annum)	Aggregate wage bill (cash and kind) (£ooos)	Average wage (cash and kind) (£s per annum)	Aggregate wage bill (cash and kind) (£ooos)	Average wage (cash and kind) (£s per annum)
1946	1,993	28.2	—	—	1,379	24.2
1948	2,220	35.0	—	—	2,533	35.1
1950	2,542	42.8	4,930	29.2	4,260	44.1
1951	3,000	49.4	5,518	30.4	5,300	53.9
1952	3,745	61.4	6,381	34.8	6,003	56.5
1953	3,746	63.0	7,000	37.3	—	—
1954	3,779	67.0	7,500	38.5	—	—
1956	—	—	8,700	42.8	9,880	71.2

Notes and Sources: Mining: Data from 1950 have been based on the wage bill (including cash and kind) published in the *Monthly Digest of Statistics, Federation of Rhodesia and Nyasaland*, April 1955, Table XV, p. xiv. The 1946 and 1948 calculations are derived from data on the cash wage bill of the industry reported in the *Economic and Statistical Bulletin, Southern Rhodesia*, 21 August 1947, p. 5, and 21 September 1951, pp. 7–16. These figures have been adjusted to include the gross value of income in kind; this calculation has been based on the estimated average value of rations and housing as shown in the *Economic and Statistical Bulletin, Southern Rhodesia*, 7 November 1947, p. 9, and 21 September 1951, p. 8. Estimates of the wage bill for 1956 are not available.

European agriculture: Comparable agricultural estimates are not available before 1950. Those shown are from the *Monthly Digest of Statistics*, and the *Reports on Agricultural and Pastoral Production*.

Secondary industries: Data through 1952 are drawn from the *Censuses of Industrial Production, Southern Rhodesia*. The 1956 Census of Industrial Production referred to the entire Federal area and did not report separately on employment and wages in each territory. The figures shown above for 1956 are, therefore, crude estimates. The Southern Rhodesian wage bill is derived from the Federal wage bill on the assumption that Southern Rhodesia's share in Federal wages is the same as its proportionate share of African employment in secondary industries (as shown in the Census of Population, 1956). This method of approximation probably understates average wages for Africans in Southern Rhodesia's secondary industries.

between the rates obtaining in European agriculture and in the other two industries is striking. The actual differential between the returns in agricultural and in the other forms of employment, however, may be slightly exaggerated in these comparisons. Because the bulk of the rations provided to agricultural workers are produced on the farm and do not pass through the market place, the cost of these rations to the European employer may be lower in agriculture than in mining or in secondary industries. Nevertheless, the margin between the various forms of employment is too great to be accounted for by this factor alone.

There is another factor responsible for part of this discrepancy. Thus far, the market for African labour has been discussed in aggregative terms, assuming that the units of labour can be regarded as undifferentiated. This assumption would clearly be unrealistic if applied to the more advanced economies. But, relatively speaking, a high degree of uniformity exists among the units of the African labour force. With only a few exceptions, its members are unskilled. This is, in part, the result of their lack of education; in part, the result of the colour bar which excludes the African employee from rising to more advanced positions; and, in part the product of a system which clings to a segregationist mentality, holding that only a few Africans can achieve security of tenure outside the native areas. In these circumstances, employers may be discouraged from spending money to train their African employees. While these characteristics are common to the Rhodesian economy at large, some differences in degree of skill have emerged in recent years. It is, therefore, only in broad terms that an inter-industry comparison can be drawn. The agricultural labour force is largely unskilled in the strictest sense and is engaged in manual labour for which no prior training is required. But in secondary industry, a few African workers have risen to semi-skilled positions with rates of pay well above the average. This is also true in a few of the large mines. The smaller mines — particularly the gold mines — have always called for little or no skill and have offered less favourable terms.

In absolute terms, the numbers of Africans who have achieved these advanced positions is small. And, compared with the unskilled workers who compose the bulk of the labour force in all industries, their numbers are of little significance. Nevertheless, the incomes received by this minority raise the average level of wages prevailing in the non-agricultural industries. Further, the fact that some members of the African labour force have risen above the unskilled status to more productive positions means that it cannot be assumed that African labour is perfectly substitutable between industries. Thus, the higher rates prevailing in large-scale mining and in secondary industrial employments than in European agriculture reflect, to some degree, qualitative differentials in the labour force. But these differences in skill affect only a small percentage of the total labour force employed in the industries in which the average wage rate is higher.

It is now of interest to determine whether this increase in money wages, particularly in the non-agricultural employments, has been accompanied by an improvement in real wages. As will be recalled from the consideration of real wage changes for the African in the war years, it was estimated that the purchasing power of the African's pound by 1948 was less than half its 1939 value. This estimate was rough, but it can serve as a general guide. If it is to be maintained that the African's real income has advanced in the post-war years, it will be necessary to show that the money wage has increased by more than twice the 1939 figure, plus a further increment to offset increases in prices which have occurred since 1948.

Measurements of the post-1948 price changes encounter the difficulty which has been met earlier. No price index based on African budgets in Southern Rhodesia was produced until 1960. The official calculations before that date referred only to the European cost of living. The European index is an imperfect indicator of price changes affecting Africans, but for the period in question it is the only one available. With adjustments, however, it may illustrate the approximate orders of magnitude. According to the official indices, prices of consumer goods in the budget of European households increased by approximately 28 per cent. between 1949 and 1954. The most rapid rate of increase occurred in the prices of foodstuffs. Food prices rose by approximately 50 per cent. in this period, whereas the prices of clothing and footwear expanded by less than 20 per cent.[1]

In part, the African wage-earner has been defended from the

[1] Based on the cost-of-living indices prepared by the Central African Statistical Office, and reported in the *Economic and Statistical Bulletins, Southern Rhodesia* and the *Monthly Digest of Statistics, Federation of Rhodesia and Nyasaland*. A price index for Africans in Southern Rhodesia first appeared in November 1960. The earliest computations then shown were for March 1958. See *Monthly Digest of Statistics*, vol. vii, no. 8.

full effect of increased food prices. Traditionally, he has usually received a basic ration (or its cash equivalent) from his employer. Allowance for this has been made in the calculation of the average African income net of the value of the minimum ration. But the African employee is still not completely protected from a deterioration in his real income as food prices rise. Part of his money income may be used to buy food items not included in the ration. And, as his money income is but a small fraction of that received by Europeans, it may well be that the supplementary foodstuffs purchased by the African are proportionately as significant in his cash expenditure as are purchases of foodstuffs in the budgets of European households.

For the purpose of a general assessment of the post-war changes in the real income of the African wage-earner, let it be assumed that money income received by the African (net of rations) must have expanded by at least two and a quarter times its 1939 level, to maintain the same real income in 1954. For the economy as a whole, it can be observed from Table IX that the average income (net of rations) has expanded by roughly this percentage over the 15-year period in question. This would suggest that, on the average, there has been little change in the real income received by the African wage-earner. But, for different industries, this generalization may not apply. The two industries which have offered more attractive rewards in the post-war period must be considered independently. The movements in average wages, net of the value of rations, for mining and secondary industries are shown in Table XII. The results of these comparisons indicate that the money wage has increased at a faster rate in mining and secondary industrial employment than the estimated increase in the prices of commodities consumed by the African. *Prima facie*, there is some evidence that the real wage for some types of African employment has therefore increased. It will be noted that the major share of this improvement has occurred since 1950.

In view of the further increases in the aggregate wage bill since 1954, it is likely that an improvement in real incomes has continued. Estimates prepared by the Central African Statistical Office indicate that the global African wage bill rose from £34·4 million in 1955 to £47·2 million by 1958. This was accompanied by a rise of about 11 per cent. in the average numbers employed. On this basis, the average money wage (including allowances for rations and accommodation) throughout the economy increased from £62 per annum in 1955 to nearly £78 per annum by 1958.[1]

In Southern Rhodesia since 1950, several adjustments in the character of the African labour market appear to have been under way simultaneously. The employment of indigenous males in the money economy has for the first time exceeded the numbers remaining in indigenous agriculture by a considerable margin. At the same time, the wage labour force in Southern Rhodesia has altered its composition. Indigenous males have

TABLE XII

AVERAGE WAGES (EXCLUDING THE VALUE OF RATIONS) RECEIVED BY AFRICANS EMPLOYED IN MINING AND SECONDARY INDUSTRIES, SOUTHERN RHODESIA, FOR SELECTED YEARS (£S PER ANNUM)

	Mining	Secondary industries
1939	16.0	14.2
1946	19.2	15.2
1948	23.0	23.1
1950	26.8	28.1
1952	43.4	38.5
1954	46.0	—

Notes and Sources: No estimates for secondary industries are available for 1954. Calculations are based on data contained in the sources noted in Table XI.

formed a larger share of the aggregate numbers of males employed in the money economy. Further, the real wage received by the African wage-earner has noticeably improved. The improvement, however, has not been uniform throughout the money economy.

Industries in which the proportion of non-indigenous workers has tended to increase (e.g. European agriculture) have not recorded the same improvement in wages as industries in which the proportion of indigenous workers in the labour force has tended to rise (e.g. mining and manufacturing).

The pattern reflected in this sequence of events would appear consistent with the earlier hypothesis concerning the role of the

[1] *Monthly Digest of Statistics*, vol. vi, no. 3 (Supplement), and vol. vii, no. 3.

indigenous economy in the determination of the real wage rate in the money economy. The Southern Rhodesian economy has, in recent years, apparently reached and indeed begun to pass the quasi-full employment position. This has occurred with the increased employment of indigenous males and their withdrawal from the indigenous economy. In the years 1930 to roughly 1950, the money economy had pressed against this ceiling. But it then continued its expansion through the use of extraterritorial labour. The volume of employment was thus enabled to grow without a rise in real wage rates. As the money economy has turned increasingly to internal sources for its supplies of labour since 1950, there has been an upward pressure on the real wage rate.

Post-War Changes in the Labour Market in Northern Rhodesia

By the mid-1950s, the labour market in Northern Rhodesia reached a position broadly similar to that in Southern Rhodesia. Wage employment opportunities in Northern Rhodesia have always been fewer in number than in Southern Rhodesia —

TABLE XIII

AVERAGE NUMBERS OF AFRICANS IN WAGE EMPLOYMENT IN NORTHERN RHODESIA, SHOWING THE DISTRIBUTION BETWEEN MINING AND EUROPEAN AGRICULTURE, FOR SELECTED POST-WAR YEARS (000S)

	Average numbers employed	Mining	%	European agriculture	%
1946	140.6	31.0	22	26.0	18
1948	158.4	36.5	23	25.0	16
1950	160.2	40.0	25	32.5	20
1953	269.0	46.0	17	44.2	16
1955	255.3	44.7	18	35.7	14
1956	265.9	46.0	17	31.6	12
1957	278.0				
1958	267.0				

Sources: Aggregate estimates for 1957 and 1958 are those of the Central African Statistical Office; data for other years are drawn from the *Annual Reports of the Department of Labour* and the *Annual Reports on African Affairs*.

in the post-war years, aggregate employment in the former has been roughly half the volume of the latter. (Estimates of the average numbers employed for selected post-war years are shown in Table XIII.) Mining and European agriculture have continued to be the primary sources of employment to Africans in Northern

Rhodesia. But the major part of the expansion in the employment aggregate of the territory has occurred outside these
activities. With the considerable increase in public works
expenditures since the war, employment by the government and
by the building industry has grown at the most rapid rate.

In contrast to Southern Rhodesia, Northern Rhodesia has
not imported labour in any quantity in the course of this expansion in its money economy. On the contrary, the territory, on
balance, has continued to be a net exporter of labour, the bulk
of it going to Southern Rhodesia. With the emergence of an
increasing number of favourable employment opportunities
locally, the exodus of males from the territory has fallen.
According to the official estimates, the number of taxpayers at
work outside Northern Rhodesia, which was put at more than
57,000 in 1948, had been reduced to just over 46,000 by 1955.[1]
Some immigrant labour has been attracted into Northern
Rhodesia, primarily from Nyasaland and Portuguese East
Africa. According to the census returns, immigrants accounted
for roughly 14 per cent. of the African wage-earners in 1951
and for approximately 17 per cent. in 1956.[2]

While the increase in local employment for wages has been
accompanied by a slight reduction in the emigration of
Africans indigenous to Northern Rhodesia, the aggregate
number of indigenous males in employment (internally and
externally) has steadily increased. In addition, a larger number
of African males are self-employed in the money economy than
is the case in Southern Rhodesia. Commercial fishing and
trading are the principal activities. In 1950/1, some 40,000
males were believed to be engaged in these pursuits as their
principal activity.[3]

The total drain of adult man-power away from indigenous
agriculture is proportionately comparable to the recent
experience of Southern Rhodesia. A comparison of the numbers
of adult males on the tax registers of Northern Rhodesia with
the estimates of the average numbers in wage employment
(including an allowance for those in independent cash activity)

[1] See *Annual Report on African Affairs, 1948* and *Annual Report of the Department
of Labour, 1955, Northern Rhodesia.*
[2] *Census of Population, Northern Rhodesia, 1951*, and *Census of Population, Federation
of Rhodesia and Nyasaland, 1956.*
[3] *Central African Territories: Comparative Survey of Native Policy*, Cmd. 8235, p. 74.

Q

reveals that more than half of the male taxpayers are absent from indigenous agriculture. In 1954, taxpayers numbered over 456,000. The official estimate of the number of taxpayers at work for wages, both inside and outside Northern Rhodesia, was over 238,000. But the latter estimate does not include the self-employed in the money economy. Their addition would swell the percentage of absentees from indigenous agriculture to well over 50 per cent. of the taxpayers.[1] At first inspection, it would appear that in Northern Rhodesia, as in Southern Rhodesia, the ratio of male absenteeism from indigenous agriculture had passed the stage at which it could be tolerated without a reduction in agricultural output.

In an assessment of the possible effects of this situation, the course of average wage rates may be examined along the lines previously followed for Southern Rhodesia. Computations by the Central African Statistical Office provide estimates of the territorial wage bill paid to Africans. These, however, include the value of income received in kind. The aggregate wage bill may be adjusted by the average numbers in employment to obtain an approximate calculation of the average income received per African employee. The results are shown in Table XIV, compared with similar calculations for Southern Rhodesia, in several post-war years.

These calculations indicate that the average income per African employee was roughly comparable in both Rhodesias until 1951. But in 1953, the average income in Northern Rhodesia advanced considerably beyond the average prevailing in Southern Rhodesia. These results, in their crude form, may be misleading. In each territory, one industry departed markedly in its wage scales from the norm for the remainder of the economy. In Southern Rhodesia, European agriculture depressed the global average. In Northern Rhodesia, on the other hand, the mining industry has pushed up the average for the economy as a whole. The average wage may be recalculated for both territories with these abnormal industries excluded. On this basis, it appears that the average wage in non-mining employments in Northern Rhodesia advanced from roughly

---

[1] Based on data contained in the *Annual Reports on African Affairs, Northern Rhodesia.* By 1957, the register of male taxpayers had risen to nearly 493,000; just under 267,000 were reported as being at work for wages.

£40 per annum in 1951 to nearly £70 in 1953. In Southern Rhodesia, the average wage, apart from European agriculture, moved from approximately £50 per annum in 1951 to slightly over £70 in 1953.[1] It must be restated that these calculations include the value of income received in kind.

TABLE XIV

AGGREGATE AFRICAN WAGE BILL (INCLUDING INCOME RECEIVED IN KIND), NORTHERN RHODESIA AND THE AVERAGE INCOME (INCLUDING KIND) COMPARED WITH SOUTHERN RHODESIA FOR SELECTED POST-WAR YEARS

	Aggregate wage bill (including income in kind), (£000,000s)	Average wage (including income in kind), N. Rhodesia (£s per annum)	Average wage (including income in kind), S. Rhodesia (£s per annum)
1946	3.4	24	26
1948	4.8	30	31
1951	10.6	46	43
1953	20.7	77	58
1955	22.2	85	62
1957	27.9	100	74
1958	26.4	99	78

Notes and Sources: Aggregate wage bill estimates are drawn from the *National Income and Social Accounts of Northern Rhodesia, 1945–1953*, Table XVIII, p. 39; the average wage in these years has been calculated from the estimates of the average numbers of Africans employed. Data from 1955 and after have been drawn from the *Monthly Digests of Statistics*; in some years, the Central African Statistical Office's calculation of the average numbers employed differs slightly from the estimates published by the Northern Rhodesian Department of Labour.

With the exclusion of the 'abnormal' employments in both territories, the general uniformity in the average levels of wages reached by 1953 in the two Rhodesias further suggests that the evolution of the labour market had reached similar stages in both territories. Northern Rhodesia, with a much lower aggregate volume of employment, has relied mainly on its indigenous

[1] These estimates are derived from the National Income Accounts of Southern and Northern Rhodesia, adjusted to exclude the wage bill (including income in kind) for European agriculture in Southern Rhodesia. Data for the latter have been obtained from the *Monthly Digest of Statistics, Federation of Rhodesia and Nyasaland*, November 1956; estimates of the income in cash and kind received by African mine employees in Northern Rhodesia have been published in ibid., April 1955, pp. xiii-xiv.

population to supply the bulk of its wage labour force. As a result, the money economy there has apparently reached quasi-full employment.

But the case of Northern Rhodesia differs from that of its southern neighbour in that the 'abnormal' industry in its wage pattern is one which offers an income, in cash and kind, substantially above the rates prevailing in the rest of the territory. The mining industry there merits consideration as an illustration of the costs to the employer of obtaining a settled and stabilized African labour force.

In the argument thus far, it has been assumed that upward pressure on the real wage rate would arise if the money economy attempted to attract additional male labour into employment when its absence would result in a reduction in agricultural output. At this point, the real income offered to the wage-earner would need to increase sufficiently to offset the loss in income in indigenous agriculture. But it does not follow that the additional labour obtained on these terms would yet be prepared to detach itself completely from its traditional community. For this alternative to be attractive in economic terms, a rise in the real wage sufficient only to compensate for the reduction in agricultural output would not be adequate. In addition, the wage-earner's real income would have to increase further to provide for accommodation for himself and his family, on a permanent basis, in the urban areas. In practice, there may be non-economic barriers to the achievement of stabilization of the labour force by this method. The social ties of his tribal community may slow the transition of the African to an urbanized status. And, particularly in Southern Rhodesia, the possibilities of acquiring tenure in the money economy may also be restricted by the social value system of the governing minority. Permanent de-tribalization may be precluded by the legal disabilities placed on the African in the urban areas.

In the Copperbelt of Northern Rhodesia, the policy of deliberate stabilization of the labour force is being put to the test. The copper-mining groups have attempted to check the high rates of labour turnover characteristic of African employment by providing comfortable facilities for the employee and his family. The implementation of this policy has largely been a post-war phenomenon. The Northern Rhodesian companies were later in introducing these arrangements than were their counterparts in the Belgian Congo. The delay was primarily a reflection of the depression years and the uncertainties which they brought concerning the future of the industry in Northern Rhodesia. The companies were then reluctant to undertake long-term commitments. The post-war boom in copper removed their doubts. In recent years, the Northern Rhodesian mining companies have carried through an ambitious programme of housing and welfare services for African workers and their families.

The results of this policy have generally been satisfactory in reducing the rates of labour turnover and absenteeism. But in achieving them, the copper companies have been obliged to incur costs which few other employers in Central Africa are, at present, in a position to bear. Their magnitude may be measured by the average value of income received in kind by African workers in the Northern Rhodesian mining industry. In 1953, the sum amounted to more than £42 per worker; this represented more than a 50 per cent. increase on the average annual value of income in kind received in 1949.[1] In addition, the mining companies have paid higher cash wage rates than any other employer in Central Africa. The advance in the average levels has been most marked since 1949. By 1954, the average money wage in Northern Rhodesian mining was more than double that paid in the mining industry of Southern Rhodesia.[2]

The introduction of an African trade union into the wage-fixing machinery on the Copperbelt has facilitated the more rapid rate of advance in Northern Rhodesia. But the principal factor responsible is undoubtedly the prosperity which the copper industry has enjoyed. African employees have shared in this through bonuses based on the price of copper. The formation of the African Mine Workers' Union has provided the African employee with a spokesman and an instrument through which strike action could be mounted in support of wage claims. But it would be mistaken to maintain that the

[1] These calculations have been derived from comparisons of the aggregate wage bill of the Northern Rhodesian mining industry, including income received in kind, with the cash wage bill of the industry. Data are obtained from the *Monthly Digest of Statistics*, April 1955, pp. xii–xiii.

[2] Based on data in Ibid., p. xii.

African Mine Workers' Union has been the major influence on the wage determination. Its role is contained within bounds set by the government of the territory. As the events following the disturbances in 1956 demonstrated, the stake of the government of the territory in the revenues earned by the industry is too great to permit a prolonged work stoppage. After a series of sporadic strikes by the African workers, the government declared a state of emergency and suspended all but one of the officials of the union.[1]

The effect of the increases in real income, both through the advances in money wages and in the improvements in the standards of the facilities, has provided to the copper-mining industry of Northern Rhodesia a permanent labour force, largely freed from the barriers to efficiency and productivity presented by the high rates of labour turnover. This industry has afforded sufficient incentives to its African labour force to overcome the advantages of retaining a stake in the indigenous economy. In this respect, the industry is unique in the economic life of Central Africa. The de-tribalization of the African mine worker has brought a host of social problems in its wake. But, in purely economic terms, the experience of the industry provides a striking example of the manner in which wage employment may overcome the competition of indigenous agriculture for male labour, if the real wage rate is allowed to increase sufficiently.

The Labour Market in Nyasaland

The position which has been reached on the Copperbelt in Northern Rhodesia illustrates one of the alternatives facing the money economies of Central Africa if they are to continue their expansion. The circumstances of Nyasaland, in a completely different way, exemplify another. The evidence available on wage and labour trends within Nyasaland is meagre — much more so than for the Rhodesias. Before 1954, no official estimates were published covering the wage bill paid to African workers employed in the Protectorate, nor can their numbers be established with any degree of certainty. The observations of an official report in 1955 suggest, however, that the improvement

[1] For details, see *The Branigan Report*.

in real wages which African workers in the Rhodesias have begun to enjoy has not been matched in Nyasaland. As it noted:

The present minimum wage varies from 30s. in rural areas to 40s. in towns per 30 day ticket, and although it has risen to this figure from about 10s. in 1939, it has done little more than keep pace with the increase in the cost of living.[1]

This finding refers to the official minimum wage, not to the money wage which is actually paid.[2] But the specimen wage rates prepared by the Labour Department do not indicate that employers have paid much more than the minimum for agricultural labourers.[3] When it is recalled that the European plantations employ roughly two-thirds of the local wage labour force,[4] a substantial gap between the wage levels in Nyasaland and those in the Rhodesias is clear. This conclusion is supported by the estimates prepared by the Central African Statistical Office. These indicate that the average earnings of Africans employed in Nyasaland were roughly £46 per annum in 1958 — a rate 40 per cent. below the average then prevailing in Southern Rhodesia and less than half the average rate in Northern Rhodesia.

If the hypothesis concerning the influence of the indigenous economy upon the real wage is to be sustained for Nyasaland, it should follow either that the money economy has not drawn off male labour in sufficient volume to disrupt the production of the indigenous economy or that other forces have been at work to

---

[1] *An Outline of Agrarian Problems and Policy in Nyasaland*, (Government Printer, Zomba, 1955), p. 6.

[2] The circumstances in which minimum wage legislation has been introduced in Nyasaland suggest that the minimum may easily tend to be a maximum. The rationale for a legal minimum has been that, because wages were so low within the Protectorate, it could not compete for its own labour with surrounding territories. This point was stated explicitly in 1943: 'It was generally agreed that higher wages and better living standards might be expected to result in some of the better workmen remaining in this country instead of going south in search of more remunerative employment', *Report of the Committee Appointed by His Excellency the Governor to Consider Existing and Draft Labour Legislation* (Government Printer, Zomba, 1943), p. 5.

[3] *The Annual Report of the Labour Department, Protectorate of Nyasaland, 1955*, p. 41, shows the specimen cash wage in agriculture as 1s. 8d. per day.

[4] Calculated from estimates shown in the *Annual Reports of the Labour Department, 1953 and 1955*. The published figures refer to the numbers employed at the peak period of the year; the relative position of agriculture throughout the year may thus be overstated.

keep the real wage rate from rising. Although it is far from satisfactory, the evidence bearing on the first of these possibilities indicates that absenteeism from the indigenous economy in Nyasaland has probably reached proportions at least as high and quite likely higher than in the other two territories. Wage employment opportunities within the territory have been limited and much of the money economy's demand has been for casual workers in the peak agricultural seasons. The employment figure in the 1956 census shows some 164,000 Africans in European employment on census day.[1] The census, however, was taken in the season of peak activity in European agriculture. Estimates for 1955 indicate that the average employment throughout the year was closer to 100,000.[2] But to this must be added the substantial volume of man-power which Nyasaland supplies to other territories. Precision in these figures is lacking, but the official reckonings have placed the numbers of males working outside the territory in the range of 150,000 since the war.[3] Africans who are self-employed off the land as petty traders and fishermen also take a larger number of males than in the Rhodesias. An estimate covering 1950/1, for example, put their numbers at 48,000.[4]

While these approximations are crude, it would appear that the money economy — in one form or another — has claimed in the range of 300,000 Nyasaland males in recent years. Comparison of this aggregate with the adult male population is a less straightforward exercise than in the Rhodesias. The tax registers of Nyasaland are chaotic for statistical analysis. Technically, Nyasalanders working outside the territory are still subject to tax in their home district. Those working in Southern Rhodesia, for example, can pay their tax there and have it remitted to Nyasaland through the Southern Rhodesian Government. But the treatment of emigrant workers in the provincial tax rolls of the Protectorate is far from uniform. Alternatively, estimates have been prepared by the Provincial Commissioners of the number of 'able-bodied males' in Nyasaland's population. These are also ambiguous and are not con-

---

[1] *Monthly Digests of Statistics, Federation of Rhodesia and Nyasaland.*
[2] *An Outline of Agrarian Problems and Policy*, p. 2.
[3] *Colonial Annual Reports, Protectorate of Nyasaland, 1945–1955.*
[4] *Central African Territories: Comparative Survey of Native Policy*, Cmd. 8235, p. 74.

sistent from year to year. The 1949 estimate was roughly 444,000; an estimate roughly 25,000 lower was returned for 1953 although, according to the same report, the population had meanwhile increased.[1] The treatment of emigrant labourers in these calculations is left obscure. An estimate published for 1950/1, however, specifically took emigrant labourers into account in approximating the distribution of Nyasaland's available labour. The aggregate shown was 487,000, which included 146,000 employed outside the Protectorate.[2]

These calculations, despite their imperfections, indicate that many more adult males from Nyasaland are outside the indigenous economy of the territory than remain within it. This is the situation which would normally give rise to an upward pressure on the real wage rate. But another factor prevents this from happening in Nyasaland — the shortage of land. Population pressure is felt there in acute form. And a situation has arisen in which the indigenous economy can no longer maintain *per capita* output and accommodate an increase in numbers in the traditional fashion — i.e. through bringing more land under cultivation. In these circumstances, the indigenous economy, without a substantial change in its techniques, cannot preserve even the low standard of real income which it has conventionally achieved. As was emphasized in an official report on the problem in 1955, 'Everywhere cultivation is extending more and more into marginal areas less suitable for the purpose by reason of inferior soil and steeper slopes and the process is accelerated by the rapid erosion and wastage of such land'.[3] The report further noted that the African's reaction 'to these pressing problems was to escape from them,' — i.e. by emigrating.

But emigration is hardly a satisfactory solution. The social disruption which it brings has been a long-standing source of concern to the government of the Protectorate. Exodus from the territory has not been checked, but its rate of increase has been retarded. In fact, the official estimates of the numbers of males

[1] Calculated by summing the estimates shown for the provinces individually in the *Reports of the Provincial Commissioners, 1949 and 1953.*
[2] Cmd. 8235, p. 74.
[3] *An Outline of Agrarian Problems and Policy,* p. 2.

working outside the territory showed little change in the aggregate from 1947 to 1955.[1] Formal recruiting from Nyasaland has been brought under control and a ceiling placed on the numbers who can be drawn out of the territory by this means. Further, the migrant labour agreement of 1948 between the three Central African governments has recognized the right of Nyasaland to retain within its borders sufficient adult males to meet its own economic requirements and to maintain its social structure. Restrictions on the exodus of individuals cannot be effectively enforced, but the government of the territory is at least discouraging their movement.

Circumstances within Nyasaland mean that the money economy there can continue to obtain indigenous labour, despite the high percentage of absentees from the indigenous economy, without pushing up the real wage. Because of the shortage of land and the impediments it imposes to the extension of African agriculture, labour is forced out of the indigenous economy. At this stage, monetization of the indigenous economy and improvement in the real income of the indigenous population do not mean the same thing. In this further respect, the position of Nyasaland contrasts with that of the Rhodesian territories.

But the present contrast in the state of the indigenous economies of Nyasaland and the Rhodesias may not be a permanent one. It was noted in Chapter III that one district in particular in Southern Rhodesia had begun to feel land shortage. This phenomenon was not general throughout the native areas. Restrictions on the land area available to the indigenous economy threaten its traditional organization and government has been aroused by the mounting size of its population to introduce reforms. But the margin there is thin. The time may not be far distant when, as in Nyasaland, the customary practices of the indigenous economy may be unable to maintain *per capita* real output.

Conclusions on the Interaction between the Two Economies in the Labour Market

For the moment, at least, the Rhodesian territories appear to have reached a form of quasi-full employment. The supply of

[1] Cf. *Colonial Annual Reports, Protectorate of Nyasaland, 1947–1955.*

indigenous labour is no longer perfectly elastic and the real wage appears to have increased. It is at this point that the conditions necessary to satisfy the second criterion of economic development may begin to be realized. The monetization of the indigenous economy might now proceed progressively through time and increase the *per capita* real income of the indigenous population. Of the two ways for achieving this — the sale of labour or the sale of agricultural surpluses — only the former has been open to all members of the indigenous economy. Agricultural production for the money economy has been localized and restricted to the areas served by the communications system. But wage employment as a means of increasing real income has potentially been available to all the able-bodied males in the indigenous economy. Until recently the money economy confined its demands on the man-power of the indigenous economy to those who could be spared without reducing *per capita* output in indigenous agriculture. In effect, this meant that the increase in wage employment was contained within the limits set by the growth in population. The *per capita* real income of the indigenous economy did not improve through time as a result of its contact with the money economy. Instead the monetization of the indigenous economy only kept pace with the rise in population.

But the quasi-full employment position has altered this situation. The money economy's demand for indigenous labour has exceeded the increment provided by population growth and the real wage rate has begun to rise. With the supply of indigenous labour no longer perfectly elastic at a low real wage rate, the further expansion of the money economy may begin to satisfy the second criterion of economic development as well as the first. Potentially, at least, this may occur. Whether or not it does, in fact, is another matter. For this situation may call forth adaptations and adjustments in the money economy.

CHAPTER X

ADJUSTMENTS WITHIN THE MONEY ECONOMY

FROM the preceding examination of trends in the market for African labour, it would appear that the Rhodesias have recently reached the stage at which the interaction between the indigenous and the money economies has approximated the conditions of quasi-full employment. A new and unfamiliar situation has thus arisen. The supply of labour from the indigenous economy is no longer perfectly elastic and indigenous workers can no longer be drawn into wage employment without an increase in the real wage. Potentially, these circumstances may have sweeping implications for the further expansion of the money economy, the viability of the value system of the governing minority, and the economic improvement of the indigenous peoples. The task now at hand is one of analysing the adjustments of the money economy to quasi-full employment and their possible consequences.

For the money economy, quasi-full employment obviously implies that expansion cannot continue on the traditional terms. Formerly, indigenous labour had been abundant and cheap and it could be obtained at a wage rate which was not directly tied to its productivity in the money economy. Instead the minimum wage rate was established by the alternative real income obtainable from indigenous agriculture. These circumstances also were favourable to the functioning of the value system of the governing minority, for they were compatible with the creation of attractive economic opportunities for European immigrants. African labour could be treated largely as an homogeneous commodity; its price was low and there was little incentive to differentiate it with skills. Meanwhile the more skilled and remunerative posts in the money economy could be reserved for Europeans. But, once the supply of indigenous labour has become less than perfectly elastic, one of the basic economic props to the value system is less secure. These circumstances may be more propitious for the improve-

ment of the real income of the indigenous peoples and for the
fulfilment of the second criterion of economic development.
With quasi-full employment, real income at the disposal of the
indigenous population may rise and the absorption of indigenous labour into the money economy may proceed at a pace
exceeding the growth in the male population of working age.

Quasi-full employment may thus mark a turning point in the
economic development process in the Rhodesian territories.
Whether in fact both criteria of economic development will
then be satisfied is, however, uncertain. The value system of the
governing minority still exercises a formidable influence over
economic affairs and it clings to two objectives: the continued
expansion of the money economy and the attraction of a
larger European population.

Clearly, quasi-full employment calls for adjustments in the
traditional pattern of relationships between the indigenous and
the money economies in the Rhodesian territories if economic
expansion is to be sustained. Consideration of the possible
further courses open to the Rhodesian economic system and
their likely effects is now in order.

Directions of Potential Adaptation at Quasi-full Employment

In its adaptation to quasi-full employment, the money
economy is faced with two broad choices. On the one hand, it
may attempt to achieve a *modus vivendi* with the indigenous
economy which will check the upward pressure on the real
wage. Alternatively, it may accept rising real wages for
indigenous labour and accommodate its operations to them.
Several variations on each of these themes are possible. Each
must now be considered in turn.

If the money economy wishes to check the upward pressure
on the real wage of indigenous labour, one method is to slow its
own expansion. This might be accomplished, without a modification in the techniques employed in the money economy, by
confining the demand for indigenous labour to the increment
in the male labour force made available by the normal growth
in the population. With a deceleration in demand for African
labour, forces within the indigenous economy might in time
upset the balance of quasi-full employment. For it must be
recalled that quasi-full employment is far from being a stable

situation. It rests on terms of contact between the money and the indigenous economies which may be altered. If fresh lands are no longer available within the indigenous economy and alternative techniques for maintaining the productivity of the soil are not economically open to African farmers, population growth will lead to a deterioration in indigenous agriculture. Its *per capita* real income would then fall and the terms on which indigenous labour would be prepared to enter wage employment would change. In these circumstances, it would then be possible for the money economy to obtain indigenous labour without a rise in the real wage. From the earlier analysis of the state of indigenous agriculture, it would appear that this situation has already emerged in Nyasaland and that it may not be far distant in Southern Rhodesia.

Marking time, even temporarily, is not an attractive prospect to the money economy. Slowing its own expansion and waiting for decay in indigenous agriculture can arrest the rise in real wages of indigenous labour. But, in addition to being undesirable in itself, a slower rate of growth would not create an ideal environment for attracting European immigrants. Nor would the second definition of economic development be satisfied in these circumstances. Moreover, a complete breakdown in the indigenous economy would produce a dangerous situation, unleashing political and social unrest which would be difficult and expensive to control.

The burden of adjustment to quasi-full employment might be shifted to the indigenous economy by altering relationships between the two economies in another fashion. Without the risk of a complete collapse in the indigenous agricultural systems, piecemeal reforms might be introduced. Conceivably these could have the effect of detaching male labour from the land. At best, this would be a delicate operation. But it might be possible — through a revision in land tenure arrangements, for example — to increase the availability of male labour for wage employment while simultaneously allowing the conventional level of *per capita* real income from indigenous agriculture to be maintained. If a policy of this sort were successful, the money economy could continue its expansion on the traditional terms, but this effect might not be immediate. A period of waiting would probably be required before the money economy could draw forth labour without a rise in the real wage rate.

A more interesting set of possibilities arises if the money economy attempts to expand without interruption after quasi-full employment has been reached. In so doing, it would be obliged to accept rising real wages for its indigenous labour force and to adjust its operations to them. Fundamentally, this situation would require that the value productivity of African labour should be increased. Much depends on the manner in which this might be accomplished. Several possibilities are open, each with differing consequences for the economic circumstances of the indigenous population.

One method of increasing the value productivity of African labour would be consistent with both definitions of economic development. If the value productivity of African labour were to be increased by equipping it with more training and more skill, the money economy could grow while higher real incomes flowed to the indigenous population. This would imply that the former homogeneity of the African labour force would be broken up. Part of the cleavage between the two economies within the Central African economic system would be removed and the colour barrier might be scrapped. This solution might be the ideal reconciliation of the two definitions of economic development. Before quasi-full employment was reached, no economic pressure towards this type of adjustment existed. But whether the value system of the Rhodesias (which has been permitted to thrive under a different set of conditions), will be receptive to this solution may be questioned. The opening of skilled posts to Africans would challenge one of the time-honoured devices for attracting European immigrants. And it would also threaten the political and social premises around which Rhodesian society has traditionally been organized. If the African is to be admitted as a more productive performer in the money economy, efficiency demands that his tenure in the European areas should be more permanent. He must be allowed to grow roots in the urban areas and cast loose his ties with the indigenous economy. These are adjustments which Rhodesian society has traditionally tended to resist. They are obviously incompatible with the policies of geographical separation of the races and with the premises of 'indirect rule'.

The amendments called for are thus not entirely economic in character — instead they affect the entire institutional fabric of Rhodesian society.

Two other methods for increasing the value of the African worker's product are potentially available. One involves a change in techniques. By adopting more capital-intensive methods of production, the money economy might be capable of keeping the value product of the African labourer ahead of his rising wages, even without advancing him in skill. Potentially, this shift might also create additional skilled positions which could continue to be filled by European immigrants. This approach might have a further effect. To the extent that the introduction of higher techniques economizes on the use of unskilled labour, African workers might be displaced and released for other employments. Part of the upward pressure on the real wage could thereby be relieved. These adjustments might permit the money economy to expand without a sharp break with the precedents of the value system. But expansion could be continued without a deepening of capital if the restrictions of the value system were relaxed. If the artificial props to the European wage scale were removed and if Africans were trained to enter skilled positions, the deepening of capital might be unnecessary.

There is a further direction in which the money economy may move while attempting to absorb higher wages for African employees. In some lines of production, it can increase the value of their product by shifting its production to higher value forms of output. To achieve this effect, additional capital may not be necessary. The technical possibilities for this adaptation are not uniform throughout the economy. In some industries, output is specific and cannot be shifted. This is largely the case in mining.[1] But in other lines of activity greater flexibility may be possible.

Direction of Adjustments in the Money Economy of the Rhodesias

It is now necessary to examine the response which the money economies have made to quasi-full employment. An empirical

---

[1] The value of the output of the mining industries can, of course, be increased by additional refining and processing operations. This adjustment would require the application of more capital.

discussion, however, can best take the form of illustrations of trends. It will be recalled that the money economies of the Rhodesias apparently reached the quasi-full employment position only about 1950. Their experience since that date is too recent and too brief to support definitive conclusions about the further directions of the Rhodesian economic system. But the adjustments which have occurred in the money economy do permit a few tentative observations.

To employers of African labour, quasi-full employment may not be perceived as a sudden departure from the previous pattern. For two reasons, the rise in the money costs of African labour and an improvement in real wages as seen by the African employee need not coincide in their timing. The prices of sub-sistence goods, which the employer has been obliged to provide, may rise and in fact have risen considerably in the post-war years. The money wage bill has thus been forced up even to maintain the same real wage. Further, to the extent that employers have recruited labour extraterritorially, their wage costs have been inflated through time. The expenses of recruiting and transporting immigrant workers add to the total wage costs of the employer without any corresponding improvement in the real wage of the African employee. Both of these factors may blunt the sharpness with which the quasi-full employment situation is observed by the employer in the money economy. From his vantage point, quasi-full employment may appear as a climax to a longer-term process of rising money costs of African labour. The pressure for further and more substantial increases in his money wage bill will be felt most forcefully when quasi-full employment is reached. But, in part, his adaptation to this situation may have begun at an earlier point in time.

A preliminary survey of the responses of the money economy to quasi-full employment may be conducted in two phases. In the first, the general pattern of adjustment may be noted for the period since 1950. The second (because of the longer-term forces contributing to an increase in the costs of African labour), may turn to the employment pattern in particular industries over a longer period. These methods of analysis, in combina-tion, may yield some insight into the most likely channels of further adjustment. To illustrate the forces at work, the Southern Rhodesian economy may be used. Its money economy

R

has the heaviest volume of African employment and the activities of the money economy are there most diversified.

From a first glance at post-1950 developments in the Southern Rhodesian economic system, it would not appear that any single line of adaptation has been made. Aspects of each of the possible courses discussed above have appeared. On the first point — that of slowing the rate of expansion in the employment of indigenous labour — it is clear that a deceleration has occurred. For example, the aggregate employment of African labour in Southern Rhodesia, which expanded by roughly 40 per cent. between 1946 and 1951, grew by less than 10 per cent. between 1951 and 1956.[1] A complex combination of forces has contributed to this result. The reduction in the rate of growth in African employment follows naturally from the advance in money wages. This in itself has led to some normal economies in the use of African labour. The engagement of African employees for the prestige which their numbers might lend to the employers' firm or household has been discouraged and a fresh incentive to improve the supervision of African labour has been provided. Some of the waste in the use of man-power has thus been eliminated. The expansion in African employment has been further dampened by the displacement of unskilled labour through the introduction of labour-saving techniques.

The Southern Rhodesian Government has also intervened directly in the indigenous economy in a manner which may have the effect of increasing the availability of male labour for wage employment. This has begun with the implementation of the Native Land Husbandry Act of 1951. The Act requires that the communal form of land tenure and shifting cultivation traditionally practised should give way to a system of freehold ownership with settled cultivation. It is still too early to judge the results of these innovations. But, like the enclosure movement in England, the effects of this measure may be two-edged. On the one hand, the supply of male labour for wage employment may, in the long term, be increased by forcing it off the land. But implementation of the Act is also intended to improve the efficiency of African agriculture, to increase its *per capita* output, and to make surplus production available for sale to the money economy. The success of this part of the plan is

[1] See discussion of these points in chapter IX.

not insured by an improvement in the physical productivity in African agriculture. It depends also upon the provision of a transport network adequate to give African producers access to the markets of the money economy. Whether the Southern Rhodesian Government will be prepared to finance these requirements is not yet clear. All that can be said is that the transition to freehold tenure and the prevention of fragmentation will mean that little of the natural increment to the population can find room in indigenous agriculture. It may be pushed into wage employment for the lack of an alternative. This result would tend to depress the real wage for indigenous labour, although its effects would not be felt immediately. If the improvement in agricultural practice is combined with the provision of facilities enabling African producers to sell surpluses in the money economy, the opposite effect on the real wage rate might be produced. For, in that the opportunities for acquiring money income from agricultural production would be increased, the real wage necessary to attract labour (beyond that made available as a result of population pressure on the land) would be pushed upwards.

There is also some evidence to suggest that the money economy of the Rhodesian territories is making at least a partial adaptation to quasi-full employment by allowing a few Africans to increase their value productivity with greater skills. The most dramatic illustration is supplied by the 1955 agreement on African advancement in the Copperbelt. Although the number of Africans affected by this break in the colour barrier has been limited in the first stages of its implementation, the longer-term effects may be substantial. Southern Rhodesia has also adopted a more flexible attitude towards the position of the African worker with the passage of a new Industrial Conciliation Act in 1959. Action on this legislation followed five years of discussion and study. The report of the original select committee recommended that Africans be permitted to join European trade unions, to hold jobs formerly reserved for Europeans, and to receive European rates of pay.[1] The bill which was finally enacted is less revolutionary. While it endorses the principles of multi-racialism in trade unions, it authorizes the

---

[1] See *Report of the Select Committee on Subject of Native Industrial Workers' Unions Bill, 1954* (presented to the Legislative Assembly, March 1956).

formation of 'branches' on racial lines. What this will mean in practice has yet to be spelled out.

A loosening of restrictions has also emerged in minor modifications to the Land Apportionment Acts in Southern Rhodesia. A step in the direction of encouraging greater stability in the African labour force has been taken by the Southern Rhodesian Government with the inauguration of the home ownership scheme for Africans in urban areas. Only a handful of the African labour force, however, is likely to be affected by these arrangements for some time. Even small beginnings could foreshadow larger events. But the further prospects of settling Africans in the urban areas of the colony may founder on the same rock which threatens the sale of cash surpluses by indigenous agriculturalists. Extensive capital outlays are required for an adequate housing programme for the African peoples and — at least in the early stages — public funds will probably be called upon to provide them. The real wage of the African employee, even though it is rising, is not yet sufficient to enable a significant number to accumulate the resources to finance their own dwellings. In the original plan, the government was to bear the initial construction costs and to negotiate the sale of houses to African families through long-term mortgages. It is on the question of finance that the future of urbanization for African families may hang. The historical record of the public finances of the territory lends little support to the view that African housing will receive more than a low priority in the allocation of public funds. Local private as well as external lenders have advanced some funds to the government for this purpose.

It is now necessary to consider how far the Southern Rhodesian economy has attempted to adjust to quasi-full employment through changing its methods and its types of output. For this purpose, an inspection of major industries in the money economy since 1930 may be made. It must be remembered that rising money costs of African labour may have stimulated adjustments even before quasi-full employment was reached.

The mining industries, which originally formed the basis of the money economy, may be examined first. Their structure is obviously conditioned by the physical endowments of the area. These are the gifts of nature and resources invested in their exploitation are largely specific and cannot be shifted to higher value forms of output. But there is the alternative of changes in the techniques of production through a deepening of capital as the costs of African labour increase.

To gain an impression of the alterations in techniques within the mining industry of Southern Rhodesia, an inspection of changes in the average output per African worker is worth while. This is not a completely satisfactory measure of changes in the capital intensity of the industry over time. Some increases in the average output of the African worker might, for example, be achieved through improvements in management and supervision without a change in techniques. But this approach is the best available in the circumstances and it may offer some clues to the long-period trends in the structure of the industry. A crude approximation of average output can be derived from the returns on the average numbers of Africans employed by the several types of mines and the data on annual mineral production. These estimates are not ideal for the present purpose. Production per worker, when measured in terms of the volume of final output of the industry, obscures variations in the quality of ore. A more satisfactory basis of assessment would be the tonnage of ore raised. This adjustment can be made for the gold industry of the colony; for the other two major mining activities — asbestos and chrome — only data on final output are obtainable. The form in which data on African employment are collected is also defective. Compilations prepared by the Chief Government Mining Engineer measure the volume of African employment in each category of mining. But no attempt is made to differentiate those engaged in current production from those employed for the development of new workings. Qualitative observations will therefore be necessary in interpreting the results of these calculations.

The gold-mining industry of Southern Rhodesia presents the most straightforward case. In this industry, allowance can be made for variations in ore quality by basing the computation on the tonnage of ore milled rather than on the volume of final output. These calculations may be observed in Table I. The pattern they reveal is striking and consistent with the view that rising money costs of African labour have encouraged a shift to higher techniques. It will be noted that the tonnage milled per African worker declined in the early 1930s, that it has generally risen since the war, and that the sharpest rise has occurred from 1949 onwards. These trends coincide with the changes in the composition of the industry. The drop in average output in the 1930s was associated with the heavy influx of small workers

TABLE I

SHORT TONS OF ORE MILLED AND AFRICAN EMPLOYMENT IN
GOLD MINING, SOUTHERN RHODESIA, 1929–56

	Short tons of ore milled (ooos)	African labour force (average numbers employed)	Short tons milled per African worker
1929	1,636	22,647	72
1930	1,389	21,898	63
1931	1,390	23,930	58
1932	1,750	30,031	58
1933	2,381	42,452	56
1934	3,050	54,767	56
1935	3,734	66,765	56
1936	4,350	71,431	61
1937	4,397	71,680	61
1938	4,382	67,095	65
1939	4,507	64,546	70
1940	4,660	65,912	76
1941	4,683	62,674	75
1942	4,393	57,127	77
1943	3,964	50,148	79
1944	3,645	46,184	79
1945	3,601	45,369	80
1946	3,394	46,929	72
1947	3,074	45,991	67
1948	2,881	38,850	74
1949	3,082	34,121	90
1950	3,023	32,387	94
1951	2,740	28,873	95
1952	2,639	25,000	105
1953	2,515	22,024	114
1954	2,533	21,402	118
1955	2,392	20,110	119
1956	2,401	20,004	120

Sources: *Annual Reports of the Chief Government Mining Engineer, Southern Rhodesia.*

attracted into the industry following the 1931 rise in the gold price. Most of these operations were small-scale and used labour-intensive methods. Since the war, and particularly since 1950, the industry has tended to resume its pre-1931 pattern with a concentration of production in the larger mines. The small workers of the 1930s are passing from the scene. But while the distribution of the industry's output between the larger and the smaller mines was roughly the same in 1956 as it had been in 1929, the tonnage milled per African employee was substantially higher at the end of this period than in the beginning.

These comparisons can serve only as rough indicators of the changes in techniques in the industry. But they do suggest that the industry as a whole has tended towards more capital-intensive operations in recent years. Two effects have been combined in this performance. The gold mines which relied on labour-intensive techniques have gone out of production; meanwhile the larger properties have apparently introduced methods more capital-intensive than those they had found it profitable to employ when African labour was cheaper. It would thus appear that the alterations in the composition of Southern Rhodesian gold industry during this period cannot be accounted for entirely in terms of the deterioration in ore quality, the rising costs of mine stores, or the fixed price of its product. The relationship between the industry and its African labour force has also been a factor in this transition. While a large number of producers could prosper when the supply of African labour was perfectly elastic at a low wage, only the larger propositions and those capable of introducing higher techniques have survived comfortably as quasi-full employment has been approached.

Trends in the methods of production of asbestos and chrome cannot be established with the same degree of clarity. Calculations of output per African worker must be based on the volume of the final product and not on the amounts of ore processed. Moreover, the complications introduced by the statistical treatment of African employment are more pronounced. This difficulty was not serious in the case of gold mining. The new mines brought into production in the 1930s were small and shallow in depth; the time lag between the development stage and actual production was then short. Subsequently, the story of the gold industry has been one of the abandonment of old properties, not the development of new ones. Employment returns on the asbestos and chrome industries, however, are substantially inflated by the inclusion of workers engaged in the development of several new and fairly large properties, particularly during the Korean War. Another factor has made the calculations of output per African worker more uneven in these two industries than in gold. Prices of asbestos and chrome have fluctuated widely over these years and have brought with them sharp variations in the volume of output.

When allowance has been made for these special factors affecting asbestos and chrome mining, it would nevertheless appear that they also have tended to shift towards more capital-intensive methods of production. The crude calculations of output per African employee, based on the tonnage of final output, are shown in Table II. It will be noted that figures on average output were far from stable during the depression years. In both industries, a rise in average output was associated with a reduction in employment and cutbacks in production. Prices broke sharply. Only the larger and stronger producers remained in operation and development works were suspended. But when prices began to rise in the war years, smaller propositions were again brought back into production. Output per African worker again fell. Since the war, the average output per African employee has tended to move upwards. In some years, however, this trend has been interrupted by the entry of new firms developing fresh properties. As the labour force employed for development work has been included in the aggregate, the figures for output per African worker have been drawn down for the industry as a whole. Another special factor has influenced the performance of the chrome industry. It will be recalled that transport bottlenecks have held back the industry since the war. As a result of this situation, actual output per African worker has probably been higher in the post-war years than shown in Table II. These calculations are based on the official statements of the ore tonnages shipped during each year. Quantities actually raised have often been greater — but current production which is held in stockpiles is not included in the official computations.

The statistical coverage of asbestos and chrome mining does not permit all of the relevant variables to be isolated. When account is taken of the special circumstances of these industries, these results suggest that they have tended to repeat the pattern observed in the gold industry. With the costs of the African labourer rising, his output has apparently been increased through a deepening of the capital employed by the mines.

European agriculture, the major employer of African labour in Southern Rhodesia, has been able to absorb rising money wages in quite a different fashion. The technical possibilities of substituting capital for labour in the agricultural production of the colony are limited. But in the operations suited to mechani-

TABLE II

AFRICAN EMPLOYMENT AND OUTPUT PER AFRICAN WORKER, ASBESTOS AND CHROME MINING, SOUTHERN RHODESIA, 1929–56

| | Asbestos | | Chrome | |
	African employees (average numbers)	Short tons per African employee	African employees (average numbers)	Short tons per African employee
1929	13,032	3·3	4,275	68
1930	11,937	3·2	5,148	44
1931	5,500	4·4	2,209	41
1932	3,297	4·9	668	25
1933	3,103	9·6	753	52
1934	3,955	8·1	965	82
1935	5,248	8·1	879	133
1936	6,401	8·7	2,258	89
1937	7,100	8·0	6,142	50
1938	8,494	7·0	5,483	37
1939	8,987	6·5	3,267	47
1940	8,857	6·3	3,989	70
1941	9,126	4·8	5,380	66
1942	9,084	6·2	7,861	49
1943	9,335	6·2	8,238	39
1944	9,863	5·9	6,684	46
1945	9,740	5·7	5,241	39
1946	8,911	6·3	4,315	39
1947	9,171	5·9	4,234	40
1948	9,509	7·3	4,671	54
1949	9,116	8·8	5,866	46
1950	12,204	5·9	5,421	59
1951	14,206	5·5	5,923	56
1952	14,590	5·8	7,211	49
1953	13,993	6·4	9,198	49
1954	11,707	6·8	9,191	48
1955	11,660	9·0	9,002	50
1956	11,353	10·5	8,612	52

Sources: *Annual Reports of the Chief Government Mining Engineer, Southern Rhodesia.*

zation, labour-saving innovations have been made. The growth in the use of the tractor in Southern Rhodesian farm work has expanded rapidly since the war (see Table III). In the 1930s, the tractor was an unusual sight on the European farms of the colony. Records were not kept of the numbers of tractors employed before 1947, but it is apparent that almost the entire tractor complement of the European farming community has been acquired since the war. Meanwhile the number of acres cultivated per tractor in European agriculture has steadily fallen.

A calculation of African employees per cultivated acre indicates what might, at first sight, appear to be a contradictory phenomenon. The average has not fallen and, compared with pre-war years, has actually risen (see Table IV). The explanation lies in the changing composition of the industry's output. Tobacco growing has demanded more labour-intensive operations than had been employed when maize was the major crop.

TABLE III

TRACTORS EMPLOYED BY EUROPEAN FARMERS IN SOUTHERN RHODESIA, 1947–57, AND ACREAGE CULTIVATED PER TRACTOR

	Number of tractors	Acreage cultivated per tractor
1947	1,155	566
1948	2,116	318
1949	3,448	214
1950	4,484	175
1951	5,184	162
1952	5,905	143
1953	6,610	126
1954	7,318	113
1955	8,151	102
1956	9,053	94
1957	9,745	85

Sources: *Annual Reports on Agricultural and Pastoral Production, Southern Rhodesia.*

But with revenues per acre from tobacco in the range of four to five times greater than from maize, the heavier labour requirement — despite the increased cost of African workers — has been economic. Tobacco has obviously been more profitable than maize and the natural endowments of the colony, combined with special circumstances in international markets, have permitted European farmers to produce it. But the shift to tobacco cultivation has also permitted the European agricultural industry to adjust easily to the higher wage costs associated with quasi-full employment.

The recent emergence of secondary industries illustrates

another aspect of the process of increasing the value product of the African worker. The problem in this setting is different in character. It is not one of shifting the composition of output in an established activity, but rather one of altering the productive structure of the money economy as a whole. Manufacturing activities obviously offer scope for increasing the value product of the African worker and keeping it ahead of increases in the money wage — more scope than such industries as mining, for example. While some firms in the mining industries have not been able to adapt to the approach of quasi-full employment and the relative position of mining has declined, the money economy has not unnaturally sought new activities to sustain

TABLE IV

EUROPEAN AGRICULTURE IN SOUTHERN RHODESIA:
ACREAGE UNDER CROPS AND THE NUMBER OF
AFRICANS EMPLOYED PER ACRE FOR SELECTED YEARS

	Total acreage under crops (000s)	African male employees	Acreage per African employee
1930	403	67,837	6.0
1939	450	93,636	4.8
1943	518	114,305	4.5
1947	654	147,412	4.4
1951	840	181,366	4.6
1954	825	194,327	4.2
1957	826	204,275	4.0

Sources: *Annual Reports of the Department of Agriculture, Southern Rhodesia.*

its expansion. Not only does the growth of secondary industries provide a means for accommodating higher wages for Africans to economic expansion, but it is also compatible with the attraction and absorption of European immigrants.

These several illustrations of the responses of the money economy to quasi-full employment indicate that no single choice has been made. Elements of each of the possible courses leading out from quasi-full employment have emerged in recent experience. It is clear that quasi-full employment presents new problems and offers new opportunities. Potentially, a re-orientation of the traditional patterns of the Rhodesian economic system may result. While no one course has been taken, it can be said that a shift to more capital-intensive methods of production in the established industries and the initiation of new activities using techniques of higher capital intensity would require the fewest compromises in the traditional system. This is not to suggest that an upward shift in the capital-intensity of the money economy has been undertaken for this reason. Part of the adjustment is a natural result

TABLE V

COMPARISONS OF EUROPEAN AND AFRICAN EMPLOY-
MENT IN THE MINING INDUSTRIES OF SOUTHERN
RHODESIA, 1929–56

	African employment (average numbers)	European employment (average numbers)	Number of Africans employed per European
1929	46,981	1,853	25.2
1930	45,342	1,631	27.2
1931	35,202	1,432	24.6
1932	36,050	1,693	21.3
1933	48,269	2,177	22.2
1934	62,339	2,595	24.0
1935	76,226	2,899	26.3
1936	84,092	3,092	27.2
1937	90,600	3,102	29.2
1938	87,847	3,120	28.2
1939	83,759	3,023	27.6
1940	85,760	2,875	29.8
1941	84,015	2,544	33.0
1942	81,862	2,412	33.9
1943	78,497	2,293	35.2
1944	75,155	2,235	33.8
1945	71,699	2,202	32.5
1946	70,648	2,429	29.1
1947	69,873	2,438	28.7
1948	63,391	2,345	27.0
1949	58,602	2,280	25.7
1950	59,548	2,396	24.9
1951	60,688	2,530	25.0
1952	61,030	2,644	23.1
1953	59,557	2,679	22.3
1954	56,482	2,647	21.3
1955	56,026	2,818	19.9
1956	55,813	2,902	19.3

Sources: *Annual Reports of the Chief Government Mining Engineer, Southern Rhodesia.*

of increases in the relative costs of African labour. Moreover, industrial expansion has merit in its own right. One of the side effects of this type of adaptation may be the creation of more berths which, under the traditional arrangements of Rhodesian society, can only be filled by Europeans. In mining, for example, the European share of the total work force has risen, although the absolute volume of employment in the industry is still below the peaks established in the 1930s (see Table V). Secondary industries have absorbed a large share of the post-war influx of Europeans into the Southern Rhodesian labour market. Unlike the case of mining, African employment has expanded in secondary industries at the same time. In the early post-war years, it appeared that the ratio of European to African employees was also rising in this sector, but this may have been only temporary. The post-Federal censuses of manufacturing have not isolated the patterns of employment by territories.

Skills are urgently needed for the further growth of the money economy and they have always been in short supply. The traditional Rhodesian solution to this problem has been to import them, although not all of the European work force can be regarded as skilled. This technique has had the advantage of speed. Without the skills brought by European immigrants, the rate of growth in the money economy would certainly have been lower. Skills can also be produced at home. This process may be slower but it is less expensive. Over the long run, it may also lend greater stability to the social structure.

There is another dimension to this problem which is too much a part of the present reality of Central Africa to be ignored, although one can speculate only hesitantly about its significance. Despite the economic inducements offered to European immigrants, it may be that the Rhodesias will be unable to attract them in the desired volume. The influx of immigrants in the past few years has fallen sharply from the levels of the mid-1950s. In part, this phenomenon has been affected by political uncertainties. If the recent experience of Kenya is any guide, reductions in the supply of European immigrants might, paradoxically, lessen some of the traditional resistance of the settler community to the removal of restrictions on economic opportunities for Africans. Reserved privileges for Europeans lose much of their function if immigrants cannot be induced to take them up.

Types of Industrialization and their Implications

At this stage in Central Africa's economic evolution, industrial expansion is clearly desirable. Without it, prospects for maintaining improvement in *per capita* real income for the indigenous population and for building a stable society are far from bright. At the same time, much depends on the form which industrial growth is given. Different approaches are available and their consequences for economic development (in the two senses considered in this study) are not identical.

Like many underdeveloped economies, the Rhodesias now entertain ambitions for impressive industrialization. The hesitations which earlier characterized the official attitude towards the stimulation of secondary industries have passed. Protection for infant industries — which found few supporters in the 1930s and even in the immediate post-war years — has been introduced by the Federal Government. But the most important commitment to the pursuit of large-scale industrialization has been the construction of the Kariba hydro-electric project. A smaller and less expensive scheme which would have supplied anticipated power requirements for a considerable time was shunned in favour of the ambitious Kariba undertaking.[1]

It is the apparent faith of the Federal Government that the provision of hydro-electric power will overcome one of the obstacles in the path of intensified industrialization. Once power is available, it is frequently argued, external investment will flow in to make use of it. Whether this confidence is well-grounded is not abundantly certain. While cheap power is a necessary condition for large-scale industrial expansion, it is not a sufficient condition. The pattern of income distribution which the Rhodesian system has produced does not provide the most hospitable environment for the production of consumer goods to serve local effective demand. From the experience of the money economy to date, there is little basis for a confident prediction that home-produced manufactured goods will find a welcome market among European consumers. Production to serve the consumption requirements of the African population may be more promising. But no large strides in this direction can be expected unless both money and real incomes of the African population expand at a much faster pace.

A policy of large-scale industrialization may be supported in the interests of promoting a high rate of growth in the money

[1] The alternative plan — the construction of a smaller hydro-electric project on the Kafue River in Northern Rhodesia — could probably have been built for less than a third the cost of Kariba. For technical details, see the *Report of Kariba Gorge and Kafue River Hydroelectric Projects, 1951*, Inter-territorial Electric Power Commission of the Central African Council.

economy. But it does not necessarily follow that the requirements of the second criterion of economic development will
simultaneously be satisfied. Indirectly, the pursuit of rapid
industrial growth may conflict with sustained improvement in
the real income of the indigenous peoples. The public overhead
investments called for by an industrial society are heavy.
Requirements, not only for power but also for further improvement in the transport and communications system, would add
to the already heavy financial strains of Central African
governments. Outlays on these facilities could easily absorb
nearly all of the capital resources which governments could
mobilize both at home and abroad. Little might remain for the
construction of roads in the reserves or for the housing of
Africans in urban areas. Quasi-full employment might thus
pass by default. With time and further increases in the indigenous population, the agricultural situation in the African areas
may worsen to the point that the supply of indigenous labour
for wage employment again becomes perfectly elastic.

Industrialization, however, may be of two types. The type
to which emphasis has been given in recent Rhodesian policy
seeks a rapid and a large-scale expansion of industry. If
methods are sufficiently capital-intensive, the higher money
wage of the African worker may be absorbed without substantial amendment in the traditional pattern of income
distribution. Industrialization in this form has heavier capital
requirements than would be necessary if restrictions on the
labour market were removed. On the other hand, the growth of
industry, without these restrictions, is desirable for the fulfilment
of the second criterion of economic development. Clearly, the
creation of employment opportunities outside the native areas is
essential to a future rise in *per capita* real income for the
indigenous peoples. But industrial growth, forced at a pace
which requires the bulk of the capital obtainable by government,
may conflict with this end. A less ambitious expansion, with the
more modest capital requirements permitted by a removal of
restrictions in the labour market, is more likely to promote long-
term improvement in real income for the indigenous population.
The capital resources available to governments need not then be
earmarked almost exclusively to the overhead facilities
demanded by an industrial economy. More resources might

then be available to overcome the obstacles which have restricted the entry of the indigenous peoples into the money economy. And the prospects for implementing reforms in African agriculture and a housing programme for stabilizing the indigenous labour force in urban areas might be improved.

That it is even worth while to discuss these possibilities suggests that the economic scene in the Rhodesias has undergone substantial amendment in the period covered by this survey. Since 1930, the terms of contact between the indigenous and the money economies have altered. At the beginning of this period, conditions in the indigenous economy permitted the money economy to order its relationships with the indigenous population on the terms established by an uncompromising version of settler supremacy. African labour could be drawn forth in abundant supply at a low real wage. In these circumstances, the value system of the governing minority could flourish and the money economy could be directed without challenge towards the goals set by the governing minority. In the intervening years, the money economy has grown and economic development, as interpreted by the governing minority, has been achieved. When the expansion of the money economy created a demand for African labour which might have led to quasi-full employment, the importation of extraterritorial workers forestalled the rise in real wages which would otherwise have been forthcoming. Economic development, as defined in the second sense, was blocked. For only a small fraction of the indigenous population could effectively enter the money economy through the marketing of agricultural surpluses. To the bulk of the indigenous population, only wage employment was open as a means for acquiring money income. Even these opportunities were restricted by the employment of extraterritorial labour in the money economy. The supply of African labour was thus kept perfectly elastic and the participation of the indigenous peoples in the money economy could proceed no faster than population grew.

But time and the growth of the money economy have changed these relationships. No longer is the supply of indigenous labour perfectly elastic. A further withdrawal of indigenous man-power cannot be accomplished without disturbance in the productive relationships of indigenous agriculture. Meanwhile the expedient which formerly postponed the emergence of quasi-full employment — the importation of unskilled workers from other territories — has failed to supply the increment to the African labour force demanded by European employers. A higher proportion of the African wage employees has been drawn from the indigenous economy. Improved real wages have been necessary to induce indigenous workers to enter wage employment. The money economy of the Rhodesias is thus no longer able to sustain its expansion on the traditional terms. Moreover, one of the economic factors which initially supported the value system of the settler minority has passed from the scene.

The Rhodesian territories, as a result, have recently entered a fresh phase in their economic experience. Adjustment in the familiar patterns of Rhodesian society is called for. New circumstances have created, at least temporarily, an environment more favourable to the improvement in the real income of the indigenous population and the fulfilment of the second criterion of economic development. Economic forces have also created a pressure for reform in the institutional framework which earlier preserved the dualism of Rhodesian society. Conceivably, the pressure on its established institutions could be relieved through adaptations in the productive structure of the money economy — adaptations which could allow the money economy to continue its growth but at a cost higher than would be necessary if the handicaps imposed on the contact of Africans with the money economy were scrapped. Whether present policies can succeed in transforming the Central African economic systems into an industrial society is far from certain. But measures aimed in this direction may not be compatible with growth in *per capita* real income of the indigenous population. Delays in improving the productivity and the access to markets of indigenous agriculture may result in restoring perfect elasticity to the supply of indigenous labour. The more promising conditions for economic development in the second sense brought by quasi-full employment may thus evaporate.

Whatever the path ultimately travelled by Central African society, it must certainly differ in some respects from the old. The forces at work are complex. Economic analysis alone cannot

S

penetrate into their ultimate resolution. But the study of the interaction between the money and the indigenous economies in the context of economic development illuminates some of the basic issues at stake in the present transitional phase of Central African society.

SELECT BIBLIOGRAPHY

Sources used in this book have been noted in the footnotes accompanying the text. A brief list of documents, books, and articles on matters relevant to economic development in Central Africa may be useful in further studies.

I. Documents (apart from the recurrent reports of Central African officials, government departments and statutory bodies)

A. Reports of Commissions and Committees appointed by Central African governments

1. Southern Rhodesia

Report of the Native Affairs Committee of Enquiry, 1910–11

Report of the Commission Appointed to Enquire into the Matter of Native Education in All Its Bearings in the Colony of Southern Rhodesia, C.S.R. 20, 1925

Report of the Lands Commission (the 'Morris Carter Commission'), C.S.R. 3, 1926

Report on Industrial Relations in Southern Rhodesia, by Henry Clay, C.S.R. 3, 1930

Report of the Maize Enquiry Committee, C.S.R. 2, 1931

Report of the Committee of Inquiry into the Economic Position of the Agricultural Industry of Southern Rhodesia, C.S.R. 16, 1934

Report of the Commission of Enquiry into Certain Sales of Native Cattle in Areas Occupied by Natives, C.S.R. 24, 1939

Report of the Commission Appointed to Inquire into the Control and Co-ordination of Transportation in Southern Rhodesia, C.S.R. 27, 1940

Report of the Committee to Investigate Economic, Social, and Health Conditions of Africans Employed in Urban Areas, 1944

Commission of Enquiry into the Rhodesia Railways, 1945

Report of the Commission of Enquiry into the Mining Industry of Southern Rhodesia, 1945

Report of the Committee of Enquiry into the Protection of Secondary Industries in Southern Rhodesia (the 'Margolis Report'), 1946

First, Second, and Third Interim Reports of the Development Co-ordinating Commission, 1948–49.

Report to the Minister of Agriculture and Lands on Agricultural Development of Southern Rhodesia, by Professor Sir Frank Engledow, C.S.R. 23, 1950

Report of the Commission Appointed to Inquire into the Iron and Steel Industry of Southern Rhodesia, C.S.R. 29, 1954

Report of the Urban African Affairs Commission (the 'Plewman Report'), 1958

2. Northern Rhodesia

Report of the Finance Commission, 1932

Report on the Present Position of Agricultural Industry and the Necessity or Otherwise of Encouraging Further European Settlement in Agricultural Areas, by S. Milligan, 1934

Report of the Commission Appointed to Enquire into Disturbances in the Copperbelt, Northern Rhodesia (the 'Forster Commission'), 1940

Report of the Commission on the Administration and Finances of Native Locations in Urban Areas of Northern Rhodesia, 1944

Report on the Development of Secondary Industries in Northern Rhodesia, by W. J. Busschau, 1945

Report of the Committee Appointed to Enquire into the European Farming Industry, Northern Rhodesia, 1946

Report of the Land Commission, 1947

Report of the Committee Appointed to Investigate European Education in Northern Rhodesia, 1948

Report of the Commission Appointed to Enquire into Advancement of Africans in Industry, Northern Rhodesia (the 'Dalgleish Report'), 1948

Final Report of the Commission of Inquiry into the Cost of Living in Northern Rhodesia, 1950

Report on the Kafue Hydro-electric Project, 1953

Report of a Commission of Inquiry into the Future of the European Farming Industry of Northern Rhodesia (the 'Troup Report'), 1954

Report of the Commission Appointed to Inquire into Unrest in the Mining Industry in Northern Rhodesia in Recent Months (the 'Branigan Report'), 1956

3. Nyasaland

Report of the Committee Appointed to Enquire into Emigrant Labour in Nyasaland, 1935

Report on the Direct Taxation of Natives in the Nyasaland Protectorate and Other Cognate Matters, by Eric Smith, 1937

Report of the Commission Appointed to Enquire into the Tobacco Industry of Nyasaland, 1939

Report of the Post-war Development Committee, 1945

Report of the Land Commission for Nyasaland, 1946

Fiscal Survey of Nyasaland, 1947

An Outline of Agrarian Problems and Policy in Nyasaland, 1955

Report on an Economic Survey of Nyasaland, 1958–59 (the 'Jack Report'), C. Fed. 132, 1959

B. Reports of Commissions Appointed by the United Kingdom Government

Report of the Commission on Closer Union of the Dependencics in Eastern and Central Africa (the 'Hilton Young Report'), Cmd. 3234, 1929

Report of the Commission Appointed to Inquire into Disturbances in the Copperbelt, Northern Rhodesia (the 'Alison Russell Report'), Cmd. 5009, 1935

Report of the Commission Appointed to Enquire into the Financial and Economic Position of Northern Rhodesia (the 'Pim Report'), Col. No. 145, 1938

Report of the Commission Appointed to Enquire into the Financial Position and Further Development of Nyasaland, (the 'Bell Report'), Col. No. 152, 1938

Rhodesia-Nyasaland Royal Commission Report (the 'Bledisloe Report'), Cmd. 5949, 1939

Report of the Advisory Commission on the Review of the Constitution of Rhodesia and Nyasaland (the 'Monckton Report'), Cmnd. 1148, 1960 and appendices

C. Reports of Special Interest Prepared by the Central African Statistical Office

Balance of Payments, Southern Rhodesia, 1946–1952

National Income of Southern Rhodesia, 1946–1952

National Income and Social Accounts of Northern Rhodesia, 1945–1953

Report of the Sample Census of African Agriculture of Southern Rhodesia, 1948–1949

Report on the Census of Agriculture of Northern Rhodesia, 1949–1950

Report of the Demographic Sample Survey of the African Population of Southern Rhodesia, 1948

Report of the Demographic Sample Survey of the African Population of Northern Rhodesia, 1950

Preliminary Report on the Second Demographic Survey of the Indigenous African Population of Southern Rhodesia, 1953

Censuses of Industrial Production, Southern Rhodesia, 1938–1953

Census of Industrial Production, Northern Rhodesia, 1947

Monthly Index of Industrial Production, Federation of Rhodesia and Nyasaland

Northern Rhodesia Family Expenditure Survey, 1951

Southern Rhodesia Family Expenditure Survey, 1950–1951

II. Brief List of Books and Articles Pertaining to Central African Economic Affairs

ALLAN, WILLIAM. 'African Land Usage', *Rhodes-Livingstone Journal*, vol. iii (1945), pp. 13–20
—— *Studies in African Land Usage in Northern Rhodesia*. Rhodes-Livingstone Institute Papers, no. 15, 1949

ANDERSON, DUNCAN L. 'Hydro-Electric Power for the Federation', *Optima*, vol. vi (1956), pp. 37–43

Board of Trade, United Kingdom. *The African Native Market in the Federation of Rhodesia and Nyasaland: a Report on the Central African Native as a Consumer*. H.M.S.O. London, 1954

BRELSFORD, W. V. *Copperbelt Markets: a Social and Economic Study*. Government Printer, Lusaka, 1947

COLSON, E. *Life among the Cattle-owning Tonga: the Material Culture of a Northern Rhodesia Native Tribe*. Rhodes-Livingstone Institute Occasional Papers, no. 6, 1949

COLSON, E. and GLUCKMAN, MAX (eds.). *Seven Tribes of British Central Africa*. O.U.P., 1951

DEANE, PHYLLIS. *Colonial Social Accounting*. C.U.P., 1953
—— *The Measurement of Colonial National Incomes: and Experiment*. N.I.E.S.R. Occasional Papers XII, C.U.P., 1948

FRANKEL, S. H. *Capital Investment in Africa*. O.U.P., 1938

GANN, L. H. *The Birth of a Plural Society: the Development of Northern Rhodesia under the British South Africa Company, 1894–1914*. Manchester U.P., 1958

GLUCKMAN, MAX. *The Economy of the Central Barotse Plain*. Rhodes-Livingstone Institute Papers, no. 7, 1941

GRAFFTEY-SMITH, A. P. 'A Central Bank for the Federation', *Optima*, vol. vi (1956), pp. 83–87

GRAY, R. *The Two Nations: Aspects of the Development of Race Relations in the Rhodesias and Nyasaland*. O.U.P., 1960

IRVINE, A. G. *The Balance of Payments of Rhodesia and Nyasaland, 1945–1954*. O.U.P., 1959

LEYS, COLIN. *European Politics in Southern Rhodesia*. O.U.P., 1959

MASON, PHILIP. *The Birth of a Dilemma: the Conquest and Settlement of Rhodesia*. O.U.P., 1958
—— *Year of Decision: Rhodesia and Nyasaland in 1960*. O.U.P., 1960

MITCHELL, J. CLYDE. 'Distribution of Labour by Area of Origin on the Copper Mines of Northern Rhodesia', *Rhodes-Livingstone Journal*, vol xiv (1954), pp. 30–36
—— 'A Note on the Urbanization of Africans in the Copperbelt', *Rhodes-Livingstone Journal*, vol. xii (1951), pp. 20–27

NEWLYN, W. T. and ROWAN, D. C. *Money and Banking in British Colonial Africa*. O.U.P., 1954

ORDE-BROWNE, G. St. J. *Labour Conditions in Northern Rhodesia*. H.M.S.O., London, 1938

PRAIN, R. L. 'The Problem of African Advancement in the Copperbelt of Northern Rhodesia', *African Affairs*, vol. liii (1954), pp. 91–103

RICHARDS, A. I. *Land, Labour and Diet in Northern Rhodesia: and Economic Study of the Bemba Tribe*. O.U.P., 1939

THOMPSON, C. H. and WOODRUFF, H. W. *Economic Development in Rhodesia and Nyasaland*. Dobson, London, 1955

WATSON, W. *Tribal Cohesion in a Money Economy: a Study of the Mambwe People in Northern Rhodesia*. Manchester U.P., 1958

WILSON, GODFREY. *The Economics of Detribalization in Northern Rhodesia*. Rhodes-Livingstone Institute Papers, nos. 5 and 6, 1942

WILSON, G. and M. *An Analysis of Social Change: Based on Observations in Central Africa*. C.U.P., 1945

WOODRUFF, H. W. *The Federation of Rhodesia and Nyasaland* (Overseas Economic Survey Series). H.M.S.O., London, 1954

INDEX

PRINTED IN GREAT BRITAIN IN THE CITY OF OXFORD
AT THE ALDEN PRESS
AND BOUND AT THE KEMP HALL BINDERY, OXFORD